bird

MUSIC IN AMERICAN LIFE

A list of books in the series appears at the end of this book.

THE LIFE AND MUSIC OF CHARLIE PARKER

bird

CHUCK HADDIX

UNIVERSITY OF ILLINOIS PRESS

Urbana, Chicago, and Springfield

Frontispiece: Charlie at Billy Berg's, 1946.
(Used by permission of the University
of Missouri–Kansas City Libraries,
Dr. Kenneth J. LaBudde Department
of Special Collections.)

Library of Congress Cataloging-in-Publication Data
Haddix, Chuck.
Bird : the life and music of Charlie Parker /
Chuck Haddix.
Pages cm. — (Music in American life)
Includes bibliographical references and index.
ISBN 978-0-252-03791-7 (hardcover : alk. paper) —
ISBN 978-0-252-09517-7 (e-book)
1. Parker, Charlie, 1920–1955.
2. Jazz musicians—United States—Biography.
I. Title.
ML419.P4H34   2013
788.7'3165092—dc23   2013003509
[B]

For Bill Tuttle, a scholar, bon vivant,
and always an inspiration.

"Come, fill the Cup, and in the fire of Spring,
Your Winter garment of Repentance fling;
The Bird of time has but a little way
To flutter—and the Bird is on the Wing."

—Rubaiyat of Omar Khayyam

Contents

Acknowledgments

I would like to thank a number of individuals and institutions: above all, Richard Wentworth, Willis G. Reiger, and the staff at the University of Illinois Press for their outstanding stewardship of this biography.

Kudos to Teddy Dibble for introducing me to Bird's music, for his friendship and his help with this manuscript. Thanks to Norman Saks and Carl Woideck, who gave so much to this biography. Arigato to Yoko Takemura for her enthusiastic support of this project and Kansas City jazz. A special thanks to Kelley Martin, Stuart Hinds, Kelly McEniry, Bonnie Postlewaite, and the rest of the staff in the Miller Nichols Library at the University of Missouri–Kansas City for their friendship and their support of this project.

Thanks to Donna Ranieri for providing images from the Frank Driggs collection. Thanks also to Bruce Bettinger and John Hans for their help with the photos in this book. A special thanks to Frederick R. Swischer for his help with the musical analysis. I am grateful to Victoria Menninger for her help with the final edit of the manuscript.

As always, thanks and much love to my ever-lovin' wife, Terri Mac, and our children: Sam, Mimi, Will, Phoebe, and Bex.

bird

Introduction

A clap of thunder heralded the passing of Charlie "Bird" Parker. Baroness Pannonica de Koenigswarter, who gave Charlie refuge and comfort during his final days in her suite at the Hotel Stanhope on Fifth Avenue, recalled, "At the moment of his going, there was a tremendous clap of thunder. I didn't think about it at the time, but I've thought about it often since; how strange it was." One musician speculated that Charlie disintegrated into "pure sound."

Charlie Parker had lived life to its fullest. Robert Reisner, a friend of Charlie's and author of *Bird: The Legend of Charlie Parker*, observed, "Charlie Parker, in the brief span of his life, crowded more living into it than any other human being. He was a man of tremendous physical appetites. He ate like a horse, drank like a fish, was as sexy as a rabbit. He was complete in the world, was interested in everything. He composed, painted; he loved machines, cars; he was a loving father. He liked to joke and laugh. He never slept, subsisting on little catnaps. Everyone was his friend—delivery boys, taxicab drivers. . . . No one had such a love of life, and no one tried harder to kill himself." Dr. Richard Freymann, the attendant physician during Charlie's final days at the Stanhope Hotel, judged him to be fifty-three years old. He was thirty-four at the time of his death.

Charlie's early death came as no surprise to those who knew him well. After becoming hooked on heroin at age sixteen, Charlie struggled with drug addiction and alcohol abuse for the rest of his life. Over the years, his massive consumption of alcohol and drugs ravaged his already fragile physical and mental health. Bandleader Jay McShann observed, "I knew it was going to happen sooner or later. The way he was goin' with that dope and all. He could only last so long."

Nevertheless, during his short life, Charlie changed the course of music. Like Louis Armstrong, Duke Ellington, Miles Davis, and John Coltrane, he was a transitional composer and improviser who ushered in a new era of jazz and influenced subsequent generations of musicians.

Originally from Kansas City, Charlie moved to New York where he pioneered bebop—a revolution in jazz. Bursting with fresh ideas and virtuosity, his solos and compositions have inspired musicians and composers across a broad spectrum of music, ranging from Moondog, a contemporary composer and street musician, to the rock group the Red Hot Chili Peppers. Jazz historian Martin Williams judged that Charlie influenced "everyone." In 1965, jazz pianist Lennie Tristano observed, "If Charlie Parker wanted to invoke plagiarism laws, he could sue almost everybody who's made a record in the last ten years."

Charlie's brilliance and charisma also inspired dancers, poets, writers, filmmakers, and visual artists. Jack Kerouac emulated Charlie's improvisational style in his poem "Mexico City Blues," writing, "I want to be considered a jazz poet blowing a long blues in an afternoon jazz jam session on Sunday. I take 242 choruses; my ideas vary and sometimes roll from chorus to chorus or from halfway through a chorus to halfway into the next." Kerouac's novel *The Subterraneans* features a cameo appearance by Charlie. Waring Cuney, Robert Pinsky, Robert Creely, and numerous other poets have also sung Charlie's praises in verse. Clint Eastwood paid homage to Charlie's tortured genius with his film *Bird*. In 1984, the Alvin Ailey Dance Company celebrated Charlie with *For "Bird" With Love*. Artist Jean-Michel Basquiat honored Charlie with many artworks, including *Charles the First*.

Surprisingly, considering Charlie's broad influence on music and arts, details of his personal life have remained largely enigmatic. Because of his erratic lifestyle and addictions, few documents or artifacts from his life survived. His saxophones usually ended up in pawnshops, and the music he hastily scribbled on the back of envelopes on the way to recording sessions disappeared afterward. He rarely committed his thoughts to paper and was not forthcoming about his personal life during interviews.

His chameleon-like ability to empathize with those he met socially and professionally left vivid but vastly differing impressions. Frances Davis in *Bebop and Nothingness* explained that "among fellow musicians, Charlie was in the eye of the beholder: what he was like as a person depends on whom you ask." This is evident in the remembrances of Charlie published in Robert Reisner's book *Bird: The Legend of Charlie Parker*. It is almost as if those interviewed recall eighty-two different Charlie Parkers.

These differing accounts are understandable, considering Charlie's numerous self-contradictions. He was alternately generous to a fault and then miserly. A loving husband and father at home, he was an obsessive philanderer while on the road. An addict, he lectured younger musicians about the dangers of drugs, advising them to "do as I say, not as I do." He rarely showed up on time for engagements, if at all, but once on stage he took charge. A high school dropout, he was well read and well spoken. The ultimate hipster, he used his considerable charm to con friends and strangers alike. He was known for his many acts of kindness and cruelty. A musical genius who struggled with mental health problems, he yearned for normalcy. A man of few words, he let his horn do the talking.

While biographical details of Charlie's life have remained sketchy, his music has been well documented. Charlie recorded prolifically for a number of record labels, and fans obsessively recorded him on the bandstand and at jam sessions. As a result, most biographies have focused on his music and recordings rather than how his addictions, his relationships, and the events in his personal life influenced his career and music. What has been written about his life has focused on his infamous public exploits like the time he rode a horse into a Manhattan tavern or when he showed up naked in the lobby of the Civic Hotel in Los Angeles looking for change to make a phone call. Charlie's legend has been embellished with each retelling until it reached mythic proportions. Separating the man from the myth has proved to be an elusive effort for those who have written about Charlie—until now. This is the story of the life and music of Charlie "Bird" Parker.

CHAPTER 1

Kansas City Blues

harlie "Bird" Parker grew up in Kansas City, a community divided against itself by the Kansas-Missouri state line. Born in Kansas City, Kansas, Charlie came of age musically while hanging around the alleyways behind the nightclubs that lined Twelfth Street in Kansas City, Missouri. The two Kansas Cities were, culturally and politically, worlds apart. Kansas City, Kansas, established by the Wyandotte Indians, faced its larger counterpart Kansas City, Missouri, across the Kaw Valley at the confluence of the Missouri and Kansas Rivers. Bassist Gene Ramey summed up the difference between the two Kansas Cities during the 1920s and 1930s. "Kansas was a dry state in the days I'm talking of, but Missouri was wide open," Ramey explained. "People who lived in Kansas went over to Missouri and raised hell. It was like some people say of New York—a place to go and have fun in, and then you get on out."[1]

Democratic political boss Tom Pendergast lorded over Kansas City, Missouri, which was known as the "Paris of the Plains."[2] Gambling, drugs, and prostitution thrived as local authorities looked the other way. During Prohibition, liquor flowed freely in the hundreds of clubs dotting Kansas City south from the Missouri River to beyond the city limits, known as "out in the county." Musicians from across the southwestern territories flocked to Kansas City, where jobs were plentiful. Pianist Mary Lou Williams found Kansas City to be a "heavenly" place, with "music everywhere in the Negro section of town, and fifty or more cabarets rocking on 12th and 18th Streets. . . . Now at this time, which was still Prohibition, Kansas City was under Tom Pendergast's control. Most of the night spots were run by politicians and hoodlums, and the town was wide open for drinking, gambling and pretty much every form of vice. Naturally, work was plentiful for musicians."[3] "Tom's Town" served as a business and entertainment center for the Midwest.[4]

Kansas City, Kansas, grew at a slower pace than Kansas City, Missouri. At every turn, Kansas City, Missouri, out-hustled its smaller counterpart on the Kansas side. Being located in Kansas further inhibited the junior Kansas City's growth. Kansas, an agricultural state with vast wheat fields, cultivated few major cities. The state legislature, dominated by farmers from small towns, voted for rural interests at the expense of Kansas City, Kansas, and other metropolitan areas.

Missouri joined the union as a slave state in 1820 as part of the Missouri Compromise. Kansas, settled by abolitionists from the East Coast, entered the union as a free state in 1861. The town of Quindaro, located in the river bottom below Kansas City, Kansas, served as a stop on the Underground Railroad, offering refuge for slaves fleeing Missouri. During the Civil War, murder and mayhem swirled across the state line as local militias—Jayhawkers from Kansas and Bushwhackers from Missouri—traded raids on towns and farmhouses. After the war, bitterness smoldered across the state line.

Kansas, a state of reformers and crusaders in the spirit of abolitionist John Brown, took the lead in the temperance movement. In 1880, Kansas became the nation's first state to amend its constitution to prohibit the sale and possession of alcoholic beverages. A decade later, Carrie Nation, a large, stern woman clad in black, embarked on temperance crusades across Kansas, smashing up saloons with a hatchet.

In April 1901, Nation arrived to a chilly reception in Kansas City, Missouri. After staging an impromptu temperance rally in front of the saloons on Twelfth Street, she landed in jail, charged with blocking the road. Judge Thomas McAuley fined her five hundred dollars and ordered her out of town by six o'clock that evening, with the stipulation that the fine would be suspended if she never returned to Kansas City. When handing down Nation's sentence, the judge advised her that "Missouri is not a good place for short-haired women, long-haired men and whistling girls." The judge then added, "You may smash saloons in Kansas and raise all kinds of trouble there, but you must observe the law here. Kansas City is a law-abiding city." To that irony, Nation retorted, "Kansas City ships all this hell-broth into Kansas."[5] Nation's campaign, as well as widening support for prohibition through the First World War and pressure from groups like the Anti-Saloon League, led to the enactment of the Volstead Act in 1919, banning the production, sale, and transportation of alcohol nationally. While Kansas held the dry moral high ground, Kansas City prospered handsomely from Prohibition brought about by the influence of Nation and other temperance crusaders.

The completion of the Hannibal Bridge in 1869, the first bridge across the Missouri River, brought the railroad to Kansas City and transformed it from a trading outpost on the frontier into a railroad hub and center of commerce. In 1917, at the peak of rail traffic, 271 trains passed daily through Union Station, the massive stone Beaux Arts train station located on the southern edge of downtown. The Irish and other immigrants flooded Kansas City to work on the railroad and meatpacking plants. African Americans migrated in droves to Kansas City, the first stop outside the Deep South. New arrivals settled in African American communities in the Steptoe community of Westport, the Eighteenth and Vine area in Missouri, or across the river in Kansas City, Kansas. Like other migrants, Charlie's parents, Addie and Charles, gained a foothold in Kansas City, Kansas, and then stepped up across the state line.

Addie Brower Boxley was the youngest daughter of five children born to Alfred and Myriah Boxley. Petite with long, straight hair and high cheekbones, Addie grew up in Pittsburg County, located in the rolling hills of southeastern Oklahoma.[6] As a teenager, she worked as a maid for a household of six headed by Mary H. Morris on Main Street in McAlester, the county seat.[7] Seeking to improve her life, Addie caught the Missouri-Kansas-Texas Railroad, affectionately known as the "Katy," to Kansas City, where she met Charlie's father.

Like Addie, Charles came to Kansas City from the South. He was born in 1886, the first of six children, to Ella and Reverend Peter C. Parker, an evangelical preacher. The family traveled widely across the South, living at various times in Mississippi, Tennessee, and Alabama. As a youth, Charles strayed from the straight-and-narrow path traveled by the rest of his family. A dancer and entertainer, he toured on circus and vaudeville circuits. After Reverend Parker died around 1909, Ella, Charles, and other family members moved to the Kansas City area. They lived briefly with Ella's mother Jane Goodloe and her sister in a rooming house at 311 West Sixth Street in the heart of a crowded slum on the northern rim of downtown Kansas City, Missouri, before moving to Kansas City, Kansas.[8] Charles and his younger brother John Francis Parker helped support the family by working as waiters on the railroad. Charles, who fancied himself a man about town, freelanced as an entertainer on the side.

A few years later, Ella bought a brick duplex at 844 Washington Boulevard, three blocks north of Minnesota Avenue, the main business thoroughfare in Kansas City, Kansas. The family, including Charles and John, moved in with Ella. Charles and John spent long stretches away from home working on the railroad. During layovers in Chicago, Charles romanced a young woman of Italian descent. In 1914, she bore a son named John Anthony Parker. Shortly afterward, Charles moved John Anthony and his mother from Chicago to Ella's duplex. Ella lavished affection on her new grandson, whom the family nicknamed Ike. A year later, Ike's mother decided to return to Chicago. She wanted to take the light-skinned Ike with her and pass him off as white, but Ella and Charles vigorously objected. Recognizing Ike's strong bond with Ella, his mother left him in his grandmother's care and returned to Chicago.[9]

Soon after, Charles met Addie, and they married in 1916. The newlyweds moved in with Ella and the extended family. When Addie became pregnant, they moved into a two-room apartment at 852 Freeman Avenue, above the Kesterson and Richardson Grocery Store, a two-story brick building located in the heart of the African American community scattered across the steep hill bordering the northeastern edge of Kansas City, Kansas. Streets paved with bricks terraced the incline that ended abruptly at limestone bluffs overlooking the city of Quindaro nestled in the Kaw River Valley.

On August 29, 1920, Doctor J. R. Thompson delivered Charlie Parker in the family's apartment.[10] Addie, a doting mother, spoiled Charlie, a pudgy precocious child with a cherubic smile. She dressed him in the finest clothes and fussed over his long hair. Charlie walked at eleven months and began speaking complete sentences at age two. "He was the most affectionate child you ever saw," Addie declared years later. "When he was two he'd come to the door and say, 'Mama are you there?' And I'd say, 'Yes I'm here,' and he'd go on playing. Since he could talk he'd say 'Mama I love you.'"[11]

Addie paid less attention to Charlie's older half brother Ike, who lived up the hill with his grandmother. Ike was well aware that Charlie received more affection from Addie and Charles. Nevertheless, he adored his younger brother. Ike often ambled down the hill to play with Charlie, who affectionately called his older brother Ikey.[12]

Working as a waiter on the Chicago, Rock Island, and Pacific Railroad, Charles traveled widely, staying away from home for long periods. During his short stints at home, Charles spent more time in the nightclubs on the Missouri side than at home, much to Addie's concern. His drinking and long absences alienated Addie. Years later she explained, "He was a drunkard. I tried so many times to get him to stop but all he would say was 'Ten years from today I will stop drinking.'"[13] The couple separated in 1924. Charles moved to his mother's duplex up the hill. Addie stayed at the apartment on Freeman and found work as a cook.[14]

In September 1925, Addie enrolled Charlie in Douglass School, located at Ninth Street and Washington Boulevard, a block west of Ella's duplex. Kindergarten through seventh-grade students attended the twenty-room brick schoolhouse named for abolitionist Frederick Douglass. After graduating from Douglass, students moved next door to Sumner High School. Charlie, an enthusiastic student, missed only one day of school his first year. Schoolmate and future bandleader Oliver Todd remembered Charlie as a feisty scrapper. "It was about 1925 or '26. I was on the school playground when this little guy [Charlie] would come from out of nowhere and started beating on me. The guys on the school ground would say, 'Hey Ollie here comes your boy.' He was a little bitty guy. Small for his age then."[15] Charlie attended Douglass through the second grade.

During the summer of 1927, Addie and Charles reconciled and moved to Kansas City, Missouri. As before, Ike stayed behind with his grandmother. Charles quit the railroad and settled down to work as a janitor for a brick six-apartment building on the northeast corner of Thirty-Sixth and Wyandotte in a middle-class white neighborhood, known as Uptown. Two-story shirtwaist houses, duplexes, and apartment buildings lined the broad streets of the Uptown area, which was bordered by Main Street on the east and Broadway to the west, Kansas City's two main north-south commercial strips. The Pla-Mor entertainment complex, located a few blocks north, boasted the glittering "million dollar ballroom," a regular stop on the national band circuit.

The family moved into a spacious upstairs apartment in a brick fourplex at 3527 Wyandotte Avenue, just north of the apartment building where Charles Sr. worked. Tall, white, fluted Ionic columns framed the unit's broad, gray, wood front porches. Charlie played on the sidewalk in front of the apartments beneath elm trees arching over the street.[16] He attended Penn School in Westport, a historic area located a mile south of the family's apartment.

Settled in the 1830s, Westport prospered by outfitting wagon trains embarking on the trails west. In October 1864, Westport was at the center of the largest Civil War battle west of the Mississippi River, ending with the rout of the Confederate forces led by General Sterling Price. Union sentiments prevailed, and Westport became a mixed-race community. Arthur Saunders, a classmate of Charlie's at Penn School, recalled, "There was not much prejudice in Westport. There were three main groups—white, black, and mixed. At a club in an area known as The Valley, mixed-race couples gathered to socialize. No one bothered them."[17]

Penn School, located at 4237 Pennsylvania Avenue, was the first school established west of the Mississippi River devoted to educating African American children. The red-brick three-room schoolhouse, named after Quaker William Penn, stood on a limestone outcropping just west of Broadway. Parents of students who attended Penn worked as janitors, domestics, and laborers in the area. Art Saunders's mother, the school's janitor, fired up the potbellied stove on chilly mornings. Students shared a cup for drinking water. The ring of an old-fashioned bell marked the day's schedule. During recess, students played on the grassy knoll down the hill south of the school. After school, Charlie and his friends flocked to Manor Bakery, located a few blocks north, to pick up day-old cakes and cookies.[18]

Fellow student Jeremiah Cameron fondly recalled his days at Penn School and his friendship with Charlie. "There was much warmth everywhere in that room in the Great Depression days of the early 1930s, from Miss Brownlee Baird, the teacher who taught me (us) what the English sentence was all about, to us poor students, who I think realized in those days of Jim Crow, that though we had little of this world's goods, we had each other." Cameron recalled Charlie as "no great light as a student," but "someone who was soft-spoken and gentle; though like me, he was not a Westporter, living in janitor quarters, like me, down near 36th and Broadway, he had all that kindness and sense of inclusion that marked the old Westport area, a little black village, surrounded by an uncaring and separate white community."[19] Traveling between the two communities, Charlie learned early on how to navigate the white world.

Charlie walked to school up Broadway, past the art deco Uptown Theater, drug stores, grocery stores, hotels, and apartments. Arthur Saunders met Charlie the first day of school, and they became fast friends. Saunders described Parker as "pleasant and intelligent—a nice guy, who was popular at Penn. I wanted to be an artist and he wanted to be a musician."[20] Saunders distinctly recalled Charlie's picking up the alto saxophone during the fifth grade, when the school district introduced a music program at Penn. In an interview with Marshall Stearns in 1950, Charlie remembered not being ready for his first saxophone. "Well, my mother bought me a horn . . . but I wasn't ready for it then. I didn't get interested in a horn until I got interested in the baritone horn when I was at High School. But I'd had that saxophone for a few years."[21]

In 1931, Penn students donned wings for a pageant, "Birdland," held at the local Baptist church. Decked out in winged costumes, they lined up in rows in front of the school for a photograph commemorating the event. According to Frank Douglas, whose father, Dale F. Douglas Sr., attended Penn, "They had this pageant and the students were playing birds in costume. When the music teacher caught the boys goofin' off he told them 'you yardbirds get here in the school.'"[22] Charlie picked up on the colloquialism and began referring to his favorite food, chicken, as yardbird, foreshadowing his future nickname.

In the summer of 1932, Addie left Charles Sr. for good. She found work as a custodian in the offices of Western Union in Union Station and rented a spacious two-story house at 1516 Olive Street located northeast of Eighteenth and Vine, the business and spiritual center for the African American community.[23] To help make ends meet, Addie took in boarders. Charlie completed seventh grade at Sumner School, located at 2121 Charlotte Street, one of four grade schools for African Americans in the Kansas City, Missouri, school district.[24]

Soon after moving to Olive Street, Charlie became friends with Sterling Bryant, who lived around the corner. Bryant, a Boy Scout and drum major, had moved to the area with his family after his mother died. Charlie spent considerable time hanging around Bryant's house, the center of activity for neighborhood kids. He taught Bryant how to play "Pinetop's Boogie Woogie" on the piano. Charlie, Bryant, and Charlie Vincent, another friend from the neighborhood, spent their days playing checkers and horseshoes, shooting marbles, and foraging for pop bottles in alleys to redeem for money. Evenings they roamed widely, flirting with girls. One night, near Twenty-Second and Brooklyn, a group of boys jumped Bryant in a dispute over a girl, knocking out one of his teeth with brass knuckles. Charlie came to Bryant's rescue and fought off the gang. The two remained friends through high school.[25]

In September 1933, Charlie enrolled in Lincoln High School. The freshman class included 766 students.[26] Lincoln, the only secondary school for African Americans in Kansas City, got its start in 1880 when African American civic leaders petitioned the school board to establish a high school for African American students. The board granted the request, and after the Christmas holiday a high school department with eighteen students was established within Lincoln Ward School at Eleventh and Campbell Streets. The enrollment increased to thirty-four the next year. In 1890, a separate two-story, four-room high school building was erected next to Lincoln Grade School. The student population quickly outgrew that building, and in 1906 a new Lincoln High School opened at Nineteenth Street and Tracy Avenue. Lincoln offered the standard high school curriculum along with music, arts, shoe repair, auto mechanics, sewing, carpentry, and other vocational skills.[27]

Charlie gravitated to Lincoln's acclaimed music program, which included a band, an orchestra, and glee clubs. Bandmaster Alonzo Lewis carried on the tradition of excellence established during the 1920s by Major N. Clark Smith, widely known as "America's greatest Negro bandleader," and classical composer William Dawson. The band's repertoire included classical works and spirituals along with compositions by Samuel Coleridge-Taylor and other African American composers.

Charlie, having loaned his alto saxophone to a friend, picked up the school's baritone horn. He later recalled, "When I first went to High School, I was interested in music, you know. So they gave me one of these, um, alto horns, you know? 'Coop, coop! Coop, coop! Coop, coop! Coop, coop!' so then I liked the baritone horn. When my successor graduated I got right in, you know? When what's-her-name graduated, the baritone player. . . ."[28] Charlie played the baritone horn in the band and orchestra.

Addie disliked the way the baritone horn dwarfed her son, so she bought him another alto saxophone. Pianist Lawrence Keyes, an upper classman at Lincoln, recalled Charlie's horn being "ragged as a pet monkey, rusty and patched up with rubber bands."[29] Charlie proudly carried his new horn as he made his way through the school day, stashing it on adjacent desks during classes.

Charlie found kindred souls in Keyes and trombonist Robert Simpson. The three became friends while hanging out after school practicing and talking about music. Keyes, a large youth with a ready smile, taught Charlie chords on the piano. Charlie practiced diligently, improvising changes on chords. He later joked that "the neighbors threatened to ask my mother to move once when we were living out West. They said I was driving them crazy with the horn. I used to put in at least 11 to 15 hours a day. . . . I did that for a period of 3 to 4 years."[30]

After hours, Charlie continued his musical studies in the brick alleyways behind the clubs on Twelfth Street. Addie worked nights, leaving Charlie at home by himself. After she left for work, Charlie made the rounds of clubs. During one of his nightly sojourns, Charlie met Ernest Daniels, an experienced drummer. Originally from Little Rock, Arkansas, Daniels moved to Kansas City with his family in 1925. After graduating from Lincoln High School, Daniels played in Dan Blackburn's Municipal band and Harry Dillard's WPA Orchestra. Charlie and Daniels became close friends and jammed together. "When we first got to know each other," Daniels recalled, "he [Charlie] used to come by my window at twelve or one in the morning, throw a pebble against the window, and we'd go to jam sessions and play."[31] Daniels, who was nine years older than Charlie, guided his young protégé through the neon riot of Kansas City's bright nightlife.

Music reverberated from the hundreds of clubs scattered throughout Kansas City. Bassist Gene Ramey, who came to Kansas City in 1932, marveled at the vibrant music scene:

> We heard Joe Turner at the Hawaiian Gardens, and then we'd go down to the Sunset Club. That was really something—about twelve feet wide and sixty feet long. It was just like going down a hallway. They hired a piano player and a drummer to come on at midnight, but we'd get over there before that and sometimes there'd maybe be ten musicians up on the stand. That was where I first met Prez [Lester Young] and Ben Webster. They took a liking to me, so they had me going over there every night. They'd fight it out till daylight, sometimes to ten o'clock in the morning. . . . The Lone Star, where Pete Johnson was playing, was directly across from the Sunset. It was a nightclub, a little like Ryan's in New York, a little less crowded than the Sunset. . . . Another place where we had after-hours jam sessions was the Subway, over on 18th Street. Piney Brown ran it and he was a big man in that all black neighborhood, although Felix Payne was actually the boss. Piney was a friend to the musicians and in with the politicians, because he could get you out of jail. Felix Payne had an open lottery right on the street, with a roulette wheel and everything. You could go in there and gamble, and there was always peace, although that was the area where you found the hustlers and good restaurants. [32]

In the mornings, drunken patrons staggered out into daylight as bartenders swept out the clubs and prepared for the arrival of a stream of laborers stopping by to pick up buckets of beer on their way to work. The clubs never closed and the music never stopped.

Charlie's late night carousing caused him to be frequently absent from school. Addie, an indulgent mother, more often than not let her sleepy son stay home. Lawrence Keyes observed, "If he [Charlie] had been as conscientious about his school work as he was about music, he would have become a professor, but he was a terrible truant. It was a surprise if he came a whole week."[33] Blessed with a brilliant mind and instant recall, Charlie got by with little effort. Mrs. Brownlee Baird, a teacher who had transferred to Lincoln from Penn, tried her best to keep Charlie focused on school—to little avail.

In the spring of 1934, love arrived on Charlie's doorstep. On April 10, Fannie Ruffin and her six children, neighbors from a few blocks away, moved in to the second floor. Charlie stood at the bottom of the stairs at Addie's side and watched the family carry their things upstairs without offering to help. Rebecca, the middle child, felt Charlie's eyes following her as she helped tote the family's bags upstairs.[34]

The two families settled in together. Charlie found companionship with the Ruffin children, particularly Rebecca, who was two years his senior. A pert beauty with lively eyes and a broad smile, she wore her straight hair parted down the middle with short bangs and a girlish flip in the back. She thought it odd that Charlie still wore knickers, but she nevertheless found him attractive. Fannie disapproved of her daughter's budding friendship with Charlie, whom she referred to as an "alley rat" for his fondness of playing marbles at the side of the house with Sterling Bryant.[35]

Charlie withdrew from school after completing his freshman year. In the depths of the Great Depression, 352 freshmen left Lincoln at the end of the school year to help support their families. Not Charlie. He was not required or inclined to work. Addie would have none of Charlie working. She tended to his every need. Rebecca declared: "You want to know about Charlie Parker? I'll tell you about Charlie Parker—he was lazy! . . . He didn't have to do anything because Parky [Addie] took care of him."[36] Spoiled by Addie, Charlie became accustomed to getting what he wanted by manipulating others with his considerable charm.

Charlie and Rebecca spent the summer strolling hand in hand around the Eighteenth and Vine neighborhood. Charlie loved movies, particularly westerns. He and Rebecca regularly attended matinees at the Lincoln and Gem Theaters on Eighteenth Street. The Lincoln, the largest theater in the area, featured first-run films and stage shows. The Gem showed westerns and B movies. Afterward, Charlie and Rebecca lingered over cherry sodas before meandering back home at twilight.

That fall, in 1934, Charlie returned to Lincoln High School to be close to Rebecca. He relished walking Rebecca and her sister back and forth to school. When Rebecca took a job in the library, Charlie stopped by punctually at 5:00 every night to walk her home. Later, after Rebecca and the others in the house were asleep, Charlie made his rounds of clubs, pursuing his dream of becoming a jazz musician.

Armed with more enthusiasm than ability, Charlie started playing with kid bands in nightclubs, Lincoln Hall, and other non-union venues. Initially, he showed little promise. Gene Ramey, who crossed paths with Charlie at jam sessions, remembered. "He had a thin, sweet tone that was pretty bad. I would see him from time to time and each time there was some improvement but not enough to show much chance of him ever becoming more than an adequate musician."[37]

Charlie's dubious musical reputation preceded him to the bandstand. That winter, Oliver Todd reluctantly let Charlie join his band, the Hottentots. "I tried to take him under my wing," explained Todd. "He was very green. If you had told me then that he would be famous I wouldn't have believed it. He had a lot to learn." Todd added, "He was very determined. . . . He worked hard."[38]

The Hottentots played at Frankie and Johnnie's, a dive located downtown. The bandstand situated in the front window of the club was so drafty that band members performed in overcoats to stay warm. The club owner, who was unimpressed with Charlie, insisted that Todd fire him. Robert Simpson came to Charlie's rescue. Simpson, who suffered from ill health that ended his life prematurely, rode a streetcar across town and implored Todd not to fire Charlie.[39] In the end, Todd fired Charlie anyway.

Nightclubs in Kansas City served up prostitution, gambling, and narcotics along with liquor. Marijuana, morphine, and benzedrine were readily available. Milton Morris, the owner of the Hey-Hay Club at Fourth and Cherry, posted a sign on the bar advertising marijuana joints for twenty-five cents each. Surrounded by drug use, Charlie began smoking marijuana. His fondness of the herb caused a rift with Arthur Saunders. "Charlie was playing with a small band in a night club owned by Felix Payne," Saunders explained. "My second cousin was married to Payne's son, so I was able to get in the club. Charlie was smoking reefers at the time and we had heated words."[40] The clean-cut Saunders and Charlie drifted apart. The fallout between Saunders and Charlie over drugs established a pattern of behavior that alienated Charlie from straight society for the rest of his life.

Despite Charlie's increasing indifference to school, he managed to complete tenth grade. When Rebecca graduated on June 7, 1935, Charlie performed with the orchestra for the graduation program. The orchestra played "Pomp and Circumstance" by Elgar, and "Theme No. 1" from "An Imaginary Belle" by Coleridge-Taylor. At the dance afterward, Charlie swept Rebecca off her feet with his nimble footwork. The quote accompanying her senior photo in the Lincoln yearbook, *The Lincolnite*, tellingly queried, "Have you seen Charles?"[41]

A month later, Charlie joined Lawrence Keyes's Ten Chords of Rhythm, launching his musical career at age fourteen. In midsummer, Keyes formed the Ten Chords of Rhythm, drawing from Lincoln High School students and older, experienced musicians. A small advertisement in the *Kansas City Call*, Kansas City's African American weekly, announced the band's debut on Sunday, August 4, at Lincoln Hall, a modestly decorated dance hall that catered to the younger set. Lincoln Hall spanned the top floor of the Lincoln Building, a three-story red-brick building located on the southeast corner of Eighteenth and Vine. Matlaw's, a popular clothing store, anchored the first floor. Medical, legal, and other professional offices lined the hallways of the second floor.

The advertisement touted the Chords as "Kansas City's Newest Dance Orchestra featuring Elmer Brown, K.C.'s own Little Cab and those four boys of Syncopated Harmony, The Solid Senders." Young dance fans paid fifteen cents to listen and dance to the latest big band hits faithfully rendered by the Chords of Rhythm from "9 until ?"[42] At the end of the evening, band members split the money collected at the door. The Chords played a regular Sunday engagement at Lincoln Hall. Band members were non-union, but these Sunday night affairs were so popular they made more than their union counterparts.[43]

In mid-September, the band added Friday nights at Lincoln Hall to its schedule. With steady work lined up for the foreseeable future, Keyes expanded the band to twelve pieces. Keyes, a talented arranger, crafted new arrangements of standards for the band, which featured Vernon Walker, Charlie Parker, and Milton Chapman on saxophones; Wendell Oliver, Ed McDowell, and William Smith, trumpets; Robert Simpson, trombone; Ernest Daniels, drums; Wilfred Berry, guitar; Charles Forrester, bass; Elmer Brown, conductor; and Bernard Jackson, business manager. Seeking to round out the band's schedule with private parties, Keyes informed the *Kansas City Call* that he was "especially interested in engagements for club parties and other affairs" and promised "the best in entertainment."[44]

Band members made good money playing at Lincoln Hall, but in order to move up to larger venues they had to join the African American Musicians Protective Union, Local 627. The union supplied bands for Paseo Hall, Lincoln Theater, Labor Temple, and other major halls and clubs in the Eighteenth and Vine area, along with white venues, including the Pla-Mor and El Torreon ballrooms, theaters, and amusement parks. Members of Local 627, affiliated with the national American Federation of Musicians, worked both sides of Kansas City's color line, playing more jobs than their white counterparts who belonged to Local 34.

Established in 1917 by music educators and part-time musicians, Local 627 grew to include eighty-seven members by 1927. The next year, members elected William Shaw president. Flutist Shaw, a barber by trade, put the union's house in order. He instilled discipline in the ranks, tracked down errant members, and unionized non-union halls and clubs. By 1930, the union's ranks had increased to three hundred members.[45]

The union quickly outgrew its headquarters in the Rialto Building on the corner of Eighteenth Street and Highland Avenue. On December 2, 1929, the union staged a battle of the bands at Paseo Hall to fund a new union headquarters. The battle featured George E. Lee's Recording Orchestra, Andy Kirk's Twelve Clouds of Joy, Bennie Moten's Recording Orchestra, Paul Banks's Ten Rhythm Kings, Walter Page's Blue Devils, and George Wilkerson's Musical Magnets. Paseo Hall, a spacious dance hall at Fifteenth Street and Paseo Boulevard, sported stages at either side of the hall. The bands traded sets until early the next morning, when the audience judged the winner by whooping, stomping, and clapping. The battle's resounding financial success enabled the local to purchase a two-story, red-brick apartment building at 1823 Highland Avenue. Members remodeled the building, creating a rehearsal space upstairs and offices on the ground floor. Union members dedicated their new hall on May 4, 1930.

On Halloween 1935, George E. Lee brought the Chords of Rhythm into the ranks of Local 627. Lee had recently disbanded what remained of his orchestra after a nine-month tour of the Midwest and South. An overbearing bandleader, Lee drove his band great distances between engagements. His band members, tired of traveling for little pay, deserted, one by one, until only a handful remained. Returning to Kansas City, Lee lined up a Halloween engagement at Paseo Hall. Unable to build a full-size band in time for the Halloween dance, Lee engaged the Chords of Rhythm. The afternoon of the dance, Lee escorted Charlie and other band members to Local 627. Lee invested in the band, paying a portion of their two-dollar initiation fee. William Shaw signed up the new members. Shaw issued Charlie card number 76, making him a professional musician at age fifteen.

Lee billed the band as his "Original Brunswick Orchestra," evoking the salad days of his career when he recorded for the Brunswick label in 1929. The Chords of Rhythm, glad to play Paseo Hall, went along with the ruse. Lee fronted the band through a request program featuring "Accent on Youth," "Isn't This a Lovely Day," "Lulu's Back in Town," "Sweet and Slow," St. Louis Blues," "Twelfth Street Rag," and "Avalon." After the dance, Lee and the band went their separate ways.

Charlie and other band members maintained their union affiliation, ending the Chords' regular engagements at the non-union Lincoln Hall. The Chords played occasional dates at Paseo Hall along with a series of dances at Charwood Hall in St. Joseph. The Chords, forced to compete for top jobs against Andy Kirk and His Twelve Clouds of Joy, Harlan Leonard and His Rockets, and other more established bands, received short shrift on jobs allocated by the union. Band members soon discovered that they were making less money than when they were non-union. They disbanded after a final engagement at Paseo Hall on Christmas night, 1935.

Earlier that month, Charlie had dropped out of Lincoln High School for good to pursue his musical career. In retrospect, Parker's cousin Myra Brown felt that he wanted to get on with his career because "he knew his time was short."[46] Charlie joined the band at the Green Leaf Gardens on Twelfth Street near Charlotte Street. Gene Ramey, who was working nearby at the Bar-Lu-Duc, befriended Charlie. "He [Charlie] played a whole year at the Green Leaf Gardens. . . . I got to know him real well and could see him start to develop as a musician and a person."[47]

After work, Charlie and Ramey faithfully visited the late-night jam session at the Reno Club featuring William "Count" Basie and his Barons of

Rhythm. Basie had just come into his own as a bandleader after scuffling around the southwestern territories and Kansas City as a member of the Blue Devils and the Bennie Moten band.

Originally from Red Bank, New Jersey, Basie arrived in Kansas City on July 4, 1927, with the Gonzelle White Revue for a show at the Lincoln Theater. A year later, he joined the legendary Blue Devils, one of the leading territorial bands. The bands that ranged across the southwest and western United States during the 1920s and 1930s were referred to as territorial bands after the immense territories they toured. Bandleaders, based in small towns spread across Texas and Oklahoma, carved up the western United States into territories. Bandleaders had to obtain permission to play in territories controlled by other bandleaders. Bennie Moten, George E. Lee, and other bandleaders based in Kansas City swapped territories and band members with the Blue Devils and other territorial bands.

In 1929, Basie joined the Bennie Moten Orchestra, Kansas City's top band. He learned to be a bandleader while apprenticing with Moten. After Moten's untimely death from a botched tonsillectomy in April 1935, Basie filled in for the regular pianist at the Reno Club at Twelfth and Cherry. In short order, he stole the pianist job and took over leadership of the house band. Basie totally revamped the band by adding top soloists from the Moten band and former Blue Devils. Musicians lined up in the alley behind the club waiting their turn to challenge saxophonists Buster Smith and Lester Young, trumpeter Oran "Lips" Page, along with other star soloists with the nine-piece Basie band.

Charlie and Gene Ramey learned their craft, apprenticing with the veteran musicians they met in the alleyway behind the Reno. Buster Smith took an interest in Charlie, showing him how to play double time and other tricks of the trade. Guitarist Efferge Ware tutored the young Ramey and Charlie in progressions, chords, and changes. The young musicians put their lessons to good use by practicing all night long in the vast expanse of grass in the median of Paseo Boulevard.[48]

The Basie band hosted a weekly Spook Breakfast at the Reno that commenced Monday morning at 4:00 A.M. and continued all day long. He modeled the widely popular Spook Breakfasts after the breakfast dances he attended years earlier in Harlem. "Spook was an in jive word among entertainers. It really didn't have anything to do with color. It was something that entertainers used to call themselves. I don't really know where it came from. Maybe it had something to do with being mostly nighttime people. So we kept late hours, spooky hours. The hours when spooks came out."[49] Maids, chauffeurs, and other service industry workers, who had Mondays off, packed the Spook Breakfasts, where the jam sessions became a right of passage for young musicians, a test of their manhood.

In late spring 1936, Charlie, overconfident and eager to prove himself, sat in at the Reno Club Spook Breakfast. When Charlie faltered while playing "Honeysuckle Rose," drummer Jo Jones threw a cymbal at his feet. The audience echoed Jones's gesture of displeasure with a chorus of caterwauls. As Gene Ramey described the incident, "I remember one night in particular when we were to jam with Basie, and Charlie made no answer. Jo Jones waited until Bird started to play and, suddenly, in order to show how he felt about Bird, he threw a cymbal across the dance floor. It fell with a deafening sound, and Bird, in humiliation, packed up his instrument and left. Major Bowes was popular then, and Jo Jones had given the contestant Parker the gong, like *The Amateur Hour* maestro used to do." Ramey added, "However, this gave Bird a big determination to play. 'I'll fix these cats,' he used to say. 'Everybody is laughing at me now, but just wait and see.'"[50]

Publicly humiliated, Charlie retreated from Twelfth Street to the comfort of his mother's home. With time on his hands, Charlie practiced his saxophone and ardently wooed Rebecca. A few months earlier, Fannie Ruffin had moved her family out of Addie's house after one of the Ruffin sisters found Rebecca alone with Charlie in his room. She forbade Rebecca from seeing Charlie, but the two continued their romance on the sly.

In mid-June, Charlie proposed to Rebecca. "Charlie proposed to me on the steps of Crispus Attucks School," Rebecca related. "He said, 'Rebeck,'—he called me Rebeck—'will you marry me?' I said I would have to ask my mother, and [then] he took me home. I asked her and she said, 'Well Rebecca, you've graduated, so I guess so.' That's how it started."[51] She accepted Charlie's proposal and moved back to Addie's house.

Since Charlie was only fifteen years old, Addie had to consent to the marriage. She shrugged off the age difference between Charlie and Rebecca and welcomed the marriage.[52] Whatever made Charlie happy made Addie happy. Addie helped Rebecca fashion a wedding dress, then escorted her downtown and bought her a wide-brim hat and a new pair of shoes.

On July 25, 1936, Charlie and Rebecca married at the Jackson County Courthouse, located a block west of the Reno Club. Just before the ceremony, Charlie confessed that he had forgotten to buy a ring for Rebecca. Addie slipped off her wedding ring for his use at the ceremony. Afterwards, Addie hosted a reception at her house with cake and punch. Charlie's father, his uncle John, Ike, and other family members along with Addie's boarders gathered to wish the young couple well. Cash-strapped, Charlie and Rebecca spent their honeymoon night at Addie's house.

For the first time, Charlie felt like the man of the house. Rebecca speculated, "If he [Charlie] was married, his mother couldn't tell him what to do anymore. Even though she didn't do that, he wanted to show the world he lived in that he was a grown man with a wife . . . and he chose me."[53] Charlie went back to work to support Rebecca. Shying away from the joints on Twelfth Street, he played in union-sponsored bands at resorts dotting the Lake of the Ozarks, nestled in a mountainous area 150 miles southeast of Kansas City. Charlie came of age musically during an extended engagement in the Ozarks in the summer of 1937. Alone in the hills, Charlie diligently practiced on his saxophone, preparing for his return to Twelfth Street.

CHAPTER 2

Buster's Tune

The Ozark Mountains cover fifty thousand square miles of southern Missouri, northern Arkansas, and eastern Oklahoma. Caves and cold springs riddle the hollows of the rocky hills, thickly forested by hawthorn, oak, hickory, maple, and basswood trees. Rugged individuals of Scots-Irish descent settled the isolated area during the early nineteenth century. Extended families scratched out a living on remote farms, raising livestock and cultivating fruit and pecan orchards. They rounded out their food supply by hunting, fishing, and foraging for wild berries and meaty morel mushrooms. Referred to as "hillbillies" by their city cousins, they kept to themselves and cast a suspicious eye on outsiders.

Beginning in the mid-nineteenth century, mining companies from St. Louis, Kansas City, and St. Joseph extracted the area's rich deposits of lead, zinc, and other minerals. Sportsmen and vacationers followed with the construction of roads and railways. The creation of the Lake of the Ozarks during the late 1920s turned Eldon and other small settlements nestled in the hills into boomtowns. When it was completed in the spring of 1931, the

129-mile-long, dragon-shaped Lake of the Ozarks was the largest manmade lake in the world, with a shoreline longer than the coastline of California. The Saturday after the grand opening of the lake, 2,914 cars passed over Bagnell Dam. Local hotels, unable to accommodate the flood of tourists, called on residents to take the overflow into their homes.[1]

Bruce's Ozark Inn, Lakeside Casino, Pla-Port Resort, Ozark Tavern Hotel, and a host of other resorts, lodges, roadhouses, and fishing camps sprang up around the lake. Vacationers, mainly from St. Louis and Kansas City, demanded the style of jazz they enjoyed back home. Kansas City's Local 627 supplied resort owners with bands for the summer-long engagement. Most of the towns in the region, skirting the southern edge of an area known as Little Dixie, were sundown communities, where African Americans ventured out at their own risk after dark. Musicians from Kansas City faced with a long journey back and forth over winding roads through racially hostile towns maintained low profiles and stayed onsite for long stretches at the resorts where they worked.[2]

On Thanksgiving Day 1936, Charlie traveled to the Ozarks with a union band for the grand opening of Musser's Ozark Tavern, located three miles south of Eldon, Missouri, at the junction of Highways 52 and 54. Clarence Musser, a hotheaded stump of a man who usually packed a handgun, operated the Musser Tavern Company based in Kansas City. Having grown up in a rough, racially mixed neighborhood, Musser was colorblind. All he cared about was the color of a person's money or a person's talent. He delighted in flouting local racial conventions by booking African American bands in his tavern.[3]

Band members traveled to the engagement caravan style in two sedans. Musser, guitarist Lon Tolbert, trumpeter Clarence Davis, and pianist Carrie Powell led the way in the first car. Ernest Daniels, Charlie, and bassist George Wilkerson brought up the rear in the second car. Eight miles north of the resort, the car carrying Charlie skidded on a wet patch, veered off the road, and turned over five or six times. Musser and the musicians in the first sedan raced back to rescue the three injured musicians. The force of the accident hurled Daniels sixty feet into a freshly plowed field, puncturing his lung and lacerating one of his legs. Charlie broke three ribs and fractured his spine. George Wilkerson suffered a fatal head wound.

Daniels vaguely recalled the aftermath of the crash. "I've been told it was at night and so they took us to a cabin, Charlie Parker and I, and we stayed there all night. . . . We had a doctor in. I remember one of the first things the doctor did was give me a shot of whiskey. . . . Anyway, the next day they brought us back to Kansas City, Charlie Parker and I, and I guess the bass player. . . . He's the one that got killed. And they brought us back to Kansas City, and Charlie Parker rode in—he rode back in the ambulance with the driver, he sat up there with the driver and the piano player, which was a lady."[4] Back in Kansas City, the ambulance delivered Charlie and Daniels to Wheatley-Provident Hospital.

Initially, doctors feared Charlie would never walk again. Charlie recuperated at home, under the care of Addie and the family doctor, J. R. Thompson. With few options available, Doctor Thompson prescribed heroin to relieve Charlie's excruciating pain. Rebecca recalled that "the heroin eased the pain a lot, but the doctor warned Charlie and his mother how bad it was for him. The doctor told me that if Charlie kept using heroin, he wouldn't live but 18 to 20 years more. There was the possibility of overdosing on the stuff."[5] Charlie developed a taste for heroin while gradually healing over the next few months. He soon became addicted. For the rest of his life, he struggled with his heroin habit.

The wreck destroyed band members' instruments. Mr. Musser generously bought Ernest Daniels a set of drums and Charlie a brand new alto. For years, Charlie had wrestled with his mouthpiece and instrument, which was in a perpetual state of disrepair. The new horn gave him a lift.

In the summer of 1937, Charlie returned to the Ozarks with George E. Lee for an engagement at Musser's Ozark Tavern that stretched from June to September. Musser had steadily developed the tavern into a resort over the course of the year. The complex grew to include a fourteen-room hotel, eight English-style brick cottages, a swimming pool, tennis courts, and the spacious Crystal Ballroom that featured music nightly.[6] Charlie and other band members stayed at the resort. Free from distractions, Charlie mastered chord changes, substitutions, voicing, and inversions. He came of age musically that summer in the flinty, rolling Ozark Mountains.

At the end of the season, Charlie confidently returned to the clubs on Twelfth Street. His musical transformation astounded musicians who knew him prior to his Ozarks sojourn. Gene Ramey explained, "In the summer of 1937 Bird took a job with George E. Lee in the Ozarks region of Missouri. When he came back, the difference was unbelievable." Ramey added, "Basie's 'Jones-Smith' record had come out and Bird startled everybody by playing Lester Young's solo on *Lady Be Good* note for note. 'Here comes this guy,' the cats used to say. 'He's a drag!' They couldn't believe it, because six months before he had been like a cryin' saxophone player."[7] Equipped with his new alto, seventeen-year-old Charlie became an in-demand soloist on Twelfth Street.

Just as Charlie's career began to flourish, his relationship with his wife Rebecca withered from his infidelity and use of narcotics. "I remember coming home from my job where I worked part time doing housework for a family out south [Kansas City]," Rebecca related. "I was getting some coffee and as I looked out the kitchen window, I saw a cab pull up. Well, Charlie didn't know I was home because usually when he was asleep, I was at work. Well, that day I wasn't feeling well—I was pregnant—and came home early. Charlie was in a cab with a light-skinned girl. He pulled her to him and kissed her. Then he got out. I was mad and hurt."[8]

Worse yet, Charlie naively stashed love letters from his girlfriend under his pillow. Rebecca suspected that Addie passed the letters on to Charlie. "His mother would get the letters and give them to him. I thought he was awfully dumb for leaving them under the pillow in OUR bed . . . like a wife doesn't fluff up the pillows when she goes to sleep. It goes to show just how young he was."[9]

Around the same time, Rebecca became aware of Charlie's drug habit. Doctor Thompson's worst fears became realized when Charlie continued using narcotics after his recovery. Heroin and other drugs were readily available in the clubs on Twelfth Street and in the North End, an Italian neighborhood north of downtown. Hundreds of pushers worked the city, supplied by a syndicate that sold over a million dollars of narcotics annually.[10]

Drummer Bud Calvert recalled driving Charlie to the North End to score narcotics: "I'd haul Bird around to the North End, I forget, around 7th or 8th and Holmes and Cherry for a dope fix, you know your heroin or something other. I'd wait in the car while he went in and got a fix. He never tried to egg me on or entice me to go in and make it with him. I'd sit there and he made it. The curious thing about Charlie, I never seen him out of hand when he was high or after he got a hit he could always play. He handled it very well. . . . He never got logey or looked like he was out on it or anything else."[11]

Rebecca tolerated Charlie's marijuana smoking but disdained his use of the needle. "I remember they all smoked pot; but this stuff [heroin] was different, and Charlie would do some before gigs after that. Being on his feet for so much all night, he felt he needed it. It was strange to see him shoot himself in the arm. I didn't like that."[12] Rebecca dug Charlie's syringe and spoon out of the dresser drawer and showed it to Addie. Confronted by evidence of her son's drug use, Addie admonished Charlie, telling him "I'd rather see you dead than using that stuff." Charlie gave Rebecca a dirty look and disappeared for several weeks.[13]

Despite his personal problems, Charlie found steady work with the Tommy Douglas band at Amos 'n' Andy's Club, located right across the street from the Reno Club. Douglas, an overbearing bandleader who resembled boxer Joe Louis, could quickly assemble bands but had trouble keeping them together. A steady stream of young players, attracted by Douglas's modern approach to clarinet and saxophone, passed through the ranks of his bands. Guided by Douglas, Charlie honed his solo execution.

Douglas disdained Charlie's drug use but admired his virtuosity. "I cut the band down to seven pieces after Basie left [the Reno Club], and Charlie Parker was with me then. He was around 16 or so then, and high. I told him he was in for trouble, and had to give a taxi driver ten and fifteen dollars because he'd hock his horn for some stuff. Finally he lost his horn, and I got mad and wouldn't get it for him. The taxi driver soaked [sic] it somewhere and wouldn't tell. When I was blowing, he'd be sitting there smiling and tapping his foot. I figured this was because he was high off that jive, but he was digging. I took a Boehm system clarinet over to him one day to teach him how to play it, and he came back the next day playing all the parts, he was brilliant. It wasn't any time at all before he was playing all that execution, and it was that clarinet that started him soloing."[14] Charlie soon left the Douglas band and returned to freelancing.

On January 10, 1938, Rebecca gave birth to a baby boy. Charlie was working out of town when Rebecca delivered. Before leaving, he made her promise not to name the baby until he returned. Rebecca recalled, "He [Charlie] wasn't there when Leon was born and for the first four months, our child was called 'Baby Parker.' On his next visit home he named him [Leon Francis]. He wanted to name him, so I waited."[15]

Leon's birth and the opportunity to work with alto saxophonist Buster Smith brought Charlie temporarily back in line. Charlie seized the opportunity to join Smith's band at Lucille's Paradise, a smart cabaret located at 1711½ East Eighteenth Street, next to *The Kansas City Call*, Kansas City's African American newspaper. Charlie idolized Smith. In turn, Smith musically adopted his young admirer. "I'd seen him [Charlie] running around in 1932 or 1933 when he was just a kid," Smith explained. "Charlie would come in where we were playing and hang around the stand, with his alto under his arm. He had his horn in a paper sack—always carried it in that paper sack. . . . Well he used to tell me he wanted to play like me. He'd say, 'Buster, you're the king.' And I'd say 'No, you're the king,' and he'd say, 'No man, you're the king.'"[16]

Originally from Texas, Smith came to Kansas City with the Blue Devils, one of the leading territorial bands from the southwest. When the Blue Devils disbanded in 1933, Smith joined the Bennie Moten band. Over the years, Moten, a shrewd businessman and generous leader, picked off members of the Blue Devils, one by one. Smith followed Count Basie, Eddie Durham, Lips Page, Lester Young, and Walter Page into the Moten organization. After Moten's death, Smith joined Count Basie's Barons of Rhythm at the Reno Club. Smith was co-leader and created arrangements for the nine-piece band. He left the band before it departed for New York and national fame in the fall of 1936.

After leaving Basie, Smith freelanced as an arranger for Claude Hopkins in Chicago and the Nat Towles band in Omaha before returning to Kansas City to join the Dee "Prince" Stewart band at the Club Continental. A large, well-appointed nightspot located downtown near Twelfth and Wyandotte Streets, the Club Continental catered to the young dance set. Stewart, who was hotheaded and combative, proved to be ill suited to lead the band, so Smith stepped in as the de facto leader and arranger.

In the spring of 1938, Smith formed his own big band by raiding the Stewart band and recruiting young players. Charlie elbowed his way up to the front of the line to join the band. Although Smith had to pare the band down to six pieces for an engagement at Lucille's Paradise, Charlie made the cut. The band included Smith and Charlie on alto, Odell West tenor saxophone, Billy Hadnott bass, Emile Williams piano, Willie McWashington drums, and Charles "Crooke" Goodwin vocals. Charlie and other young band members rose to the occasion, making Smith's Paradise Orchestra one of the top local bands, rivaling the Tommy Douglas band and Harlan Leonard's Rockets. Out of respect for Smith, Charlie put on his best public behavior and stayed straight on the bandstand. Smith recalled, "When he was with me [he] didn't ever drink or smoke anything."[17]

The Smith band made its debut at Lucille's in early March 1938. Operated by S. D. and Lucille Webb, Lucille's had opened in 1935 with two booths, a table, and a novelty bar. Comely and gregarious, Lucille worked the front of the house greeting patrons, while S. D. ran the kitchen, which served barbecue and sandwiches. The business prospered, and in the spring of 1937 they remodeled Lucille's, expanding into a second storefront. The newly remodeled club, which sported green booths with red trimmings, could accommodate one hundred patrons. KXBY-AM 1530, an experimental high-fidelity station formerly known as W9XBY, broadcast nightly from Lucille's from 11:30 P.M. to midnight, bringing the band to a broader audience.

Charlie apprenticed with Smith on the bandstand at Lucille's. "In my band we'd split solos," Smith explained. "If I took two, he'd take two, if I took three, he'd take three, and so forth. He always wanted me to take the first solo. I guess he thought he'd learn something that way. He did play like me quite a bit I guess. But after a while, anything I could make on my horn he could make too—and make something better out of it. We used to do that double time stuff all the time. Only we called it double tongue. . . . I used to do a lot of that on clarinet. Then I started doing it on alto and Charlie heard me and he started playing it."[18] Buster showed his young protégé how to add cork to the keypad, shortening the distance between the key and the pad, making the horn's action faster.

Charlie soon matched Smith's virtuosity. Jay McShann mistook Charlie for Smith while listening to the band's broadcast over KXBY. "I listened at 'em [the Smith band] broadcast one night," McShann recalled. "I saw Buster the next mornin.' 'Buster, man, I heard the broadcast last night. Sure did sound good.' Prof says, 'No, no. That was Charlie Parker. That wasn't me.

Charlie played the broadcast.' They sure sounded alike. I thought sure it was Prof [Smith]."[19]

Charlie put the lessons he learned from Smith to good use at jam sessions. Charlie took on all comers, regardless of race. Interracial jam sessions were discouraged by both the white and African American unions. Charlie flouted that convention by regularly jamming with saxophonist Charlie White, drummer Bud Calvert, and other young white musicians. Buster Smith explained, "But mostly he [Charlie] jammed with the . . . [w]hite boys when they'd come around town there, and go find some highway place—they'd be over there jammin' . . . jammin' until daylight. He used to go in some of them good-time houses, with a piano player. . . . Where they can play all them tough numbers like 'Body and Soul' and stuff like that, and 'Cherokee.' . . . That's really how you learn how to play the horn, change all them chords and keys, and playing on key and moving a half-tone up and all that kind of stuff."[20]

While leading the small ensemble at Lucille's, Smith maintained his twelve-piece band for special occasions. Charlie played in both bands. That April, Smith's big band opened for Count Basie's triumphant homecoming. After leaving Kansas City, the Basie band rose to top ranking nationally on the strength of a series of hit recordings for the Decca label. Smith had co-authored one of the band's biggest hits, "One O'Clock Jump," with Basie and Eddie Durham while they were members of the Bennie Moten band. When registering "One O'Clock Jump" with ASCAP, Basie neglected to include Smith and Durham as co-composers, cutting them out of royalties. Despite the slight, Smith came to regret leaving the band and tried to reconcile with Basie. Band members, who were still mad at Smith for leaving the band at the Reno Club, vetoed the idea of his rejoining the band.[21]

The Basie band returned to Kansas City for a date at the whites-only Pla-Mor Ballroom on April 9, 1938, with a follow-up dance for an integrated audience at the cavernous Municipal Auditorium on April 11. Since the Musicians Relief Association of Local 627 sponsored the dance, union rules came into play requiring a local band to open the show. Union president William Shaw, anticipating a packed house at the Municipal Auditorium, chose Tommy Douglas's Aristocrats of Rhythm and Buster Smith's Paradise Orchestra to open for the Basie band that evening.

Thirty-one hundred dancers turned out to welcome Basie back home. The Douglas and Smith bands traded sets from 8:00 to 10:00, and then the Basie band hit the stage to thunderous applause. The *Kansas City Call* reported the "Count played 'solid senders' until 2 o'clock Tuesday morning and the dancers at this time were still reluctant about leaving and gave the Count a tremendous ovation for his night's work."[22] Charlie and Smith mingled backstage with Basie band members, renewing old acquaintances. For Charlie, sharing the bill with his hero, Lester Young, and Jo Jones, the source of his humiliation at the Reno Club two years earlier, amounted to sweet vindication. To Smith, the evening served as a reminder of his missed opportunity with the Basie band. He began contemplating following Basie's footsteps to success in New York.

The next month, the Smith big band played at the premiere of the Vine Street Varieties, an African American revue broadcast from the Lincoln Theater over WHB Saturday afternoon from 3 to 4 o'clock. The Varieties, the first local broadcast of an all African American variety show, created a sensation in the community. The program featured top local bands accompanying visiting musicians, comedians, dancers, gospel singers, blues shouters, whistlers, and entertainers of all stripes. Patrons lined up around the block to pay a dime to cheer on local entertainers performing on the broad stage of the Lincoln, a grand theater seating fifteen hundred patrons.

The band's radio broadcasts and increasingly prestigious engagements made Charlie a local celebrity. Charming and charismatic, Charlie attracted an entourage of young musicians and fans who followed him around town. Jazz journalist Dave E. Dexter Jr. observed that Charlie "could charm the leaves from the trees. When he wanted something, he got it."[23]

Charlie used his charisma to scam favors and small amounts of money from his fans. He regularly conned his friend Sylvester "Snooky" Calloway, a Monarch Cab driver, into squiring him around town, then ducked the fare. "I used to take him to 3rd and Cherry at Mom's where we could get two joints for .25, dynamite" Calloway recalled. "That was for about 3 months, then we came a bit south to Eighth and Campbell in the alley where I would sit there for hours, waiting for him. I would never go and leave him stranded. He would say, 'Snooky I will take care of the fare after I get off my gig Jim.' I would see him early the next day after a jam in the Subway Club at 18th and

Vine. Then we would go through the same routine again, the pat for me, the heavy for him, then I would take him home."[24] Calloway and the others who were hustled by Charlie shook their heads and forgave him, considering it part of his charm.

At the end of June, the Smith band closed out at Lucille's and moved to the Antler's Club, a rough-and-tumble tavern located near the meatpacking plants in the West Bottoms. Once again, Smith was forced to abandon his dream of a big band for a small ensemble to suit the size of the club. After a few weeks at the Antlers, Smith decided to go to New York and find work for his big band. "I said I'm gonna go somewhere . . . where I can use the big band," Smith remembered. "I'm going all the way to New York. I went on the train back to New York. Got up there and got to arranging for Basie, two or three others around there, and that's where I lost that band."[25]

Before leaving Kansas City, Smith promised to send for band members when he found work in New York. Smith left Charlie in charge of the band. Without Buster's fatherly influence, Charlie resumed abusing drugs and alcohol. The band quickly fell apart and Charlie returned to freelancing.

In November 1938, Charlie joined the Jay McShann band at Clair Martin's Plaza Tavern. Jay Columbus McShann, trim with an engaging grin, hailed from Muskogee, Oklahoma. A masterful pianist who ranged effortlessly from barrelhouse to modern styles, McShann began his career in Oklahoma and the southwestern territories. As a youth he cut his musical teeth with Al Denny's band and Eddie Hill's Bostonians, two leading territorial bands.

During the Great Depression, when jobs dried up in the southwest, musicians from the territorial bands migrated to Kansas City, where jobs were plentiful. Unlike most veterans of the territorial tradition, McShann came to Kansas City by serendipity rather than design. During a layover in Kansas City on a trip to Omaha in the fall of 1936, he stopped by the Reno Club to check out the Basie band. "I took a bus trip in the last of 1936, like November or December. I was on my way to see my Uncle Odie McShann in Omaha. Stopped in Kansas City for a rest stop. I thought I'd go down to the Club Reno to see Count Basie. But Basie had gone east. Bus Moten had the band there. That's Bennie's nephew. There were some guys I knew that were playin' with Bus. They called out to me from the bandstand: 'Hey, Mac!' they said. 'Stay here with us.' I said, 'Man, I ain't got no bread. I can't live in Kansas City. Besides, I'm goin' up to see my uncle. I'm just on a rest stop.' So [Billy] Hadnott give me his keys. He said, 'You stay at my apartment as long as you want. I'll stay out at my gal friend's.' Well . . . I couldn't turn that down. I said, 'Okay.'"[26]

McShann quickly found steady work with drummer Elmer Hopkins at the Monroe Inn, a neighborhood tavern on Independence Avenue located in an Irish and Italian neighborhood in the northeast section of town. Journalist Dave E. Dexter Jr., who lived in the area, gave McShann his first national press coverage. Dexter, who was the first to write about Kansas City jazz and Count Basie in national publications, touted his latest find in his monthly column in *Metronome* covering the Kansas City scene. "McShann is undeniably the greatest pianist in Kaycee, and consistently shows solid, swing style as good as Count Basie ever got off while playing the Reno Club here a few months back. He's due to go up."[27] For the time being, McShann was content to stay at the Monroe Inn, where he got off work early enough to check out the action on Twelfth Street.

McShann first met Charlie Parker during a late-night jaunt on Twelfth Street. "We'd always get through about 1:00 or 1:30, so that would give us a chance to go in and catch what was happening in town," McShann recalled. "That's how I happened to hear Bird one night. He was in the Bar-Lu-Duc Night Club on 12th and Charlotte. Music was piped out in the street. So we stopped to see who was blowing. Bird was sitting up there blowing. I said, 'Man, where you been.' He said, 'I'm from Kansas City.' I said, 'I thought I'd met all the musicians in town.' He said, 'I been working with George Lee down in the Ozarks. It's hard to get musicians to go to the Ozarks and I wanted to do a little woodsheddin'.' So I went to the Ozarks with George Lee.' He said, 'But I'm from Kansas City,' [and] I said, 'man you sure sound different.' He said, 'Maybe we will get a chance to work together.' I said, 'Always hopin'.' Later on we did get a chance to work together."[28]

In the spring of 1937, McShann left the Monroe Inn to fill in for the pianist in the ten-piece Prince Stewart band at the Club Continental. When the regular pianist returned to the band in the fall, McShann struck out on his own as a leader, opening with drummer Harold Gadson at Wolf's Buffet located on the northwest corner of Eighteenth and Vine. Wolf's served up a stage show featuring shake dancers, female impersonators, and comedians along with a well-stocked buffet. A stream of patrons circulated between Wolf's, Lucille's Paradise, and other clubs dotting the Eighteenth and Vine area.

With the help of Walter Bales, a wealthy white patron, McShann moved uptown to Clair Martin's Plaza Tavern located on the Country Club Plaza, a fashionable shopping district, located west of Main Street on Forty-Seventh Street. The Plaza, which was modeled after the architecture of Kansas City's sister city, Seville, Spain, catered to the wealthy country club set. Bales, a business executive with Travelers Insurance and an amateur musician, liked to play duets with other pianists. He often got together with Count Basie for an afternoon of four-handed piano at Jenkins Music, a large downtown music store. They became close friends, and Bales helped fund the Basie band's departure from Kansas City.

Left without a musical partner, Bales contacted William Shaw about a replacement for Basie. Shaw sent Jay McShann over to Bales's house. Initially, Bales was a little skeptical of McShann, but the two hit it off, and they often got together for piano duets. Bales, a socially connected bon vivant, hired McShann for a party at a local country club. "This guy Walter Bales, he belonged to the Indian Hills country club and he asked me if I wanted to do a date out there at the country club," McShann recalled. "So I told him yeah, so I got a guy to work in my place at Wolf's and I went out there and did that date. I went out there and did that date and boy oh boy I got a lot of tips. I had my pockets full [of] money. When I got through playing the guy said I got this bushel basket full of booze and I said I'll take it. So he said how much I owe you for tonight and I said I don't know. He said well make up your mind and I'll be back in a minute and make out a check for you. So he went on up front and came back and said you remember how much you want for the night. I said no I haven't quite got it together yet and he said will $25.00 be alright. I said oh yes, yes. I wanted to holler. I wanted to jump up and down and holler. I made so much in tips I didn't think I would be paid. I came in that night through 18th Street and started giving away bottles."[29]

In May 1938, McShann opened at Clair Martin's. McShann assembled a small combo for the engagement. "I stayed at Wolf's for another two weeks and then I went to work at Martin's 210 on the Plaza," McShann remembered. "Walter Bales got the gig for me. He and Martin went to school together. He told me a friend of mine might be needing a band. This was on the Plaza and they did not have any black bands there. So we were the first black band to go in there."[30]

The McShann band alternated between Martin's and the Club Continental. In mid-October 1938, McShann hired Charlie to replace Edward "Popeye" Hale as one of the band's leading soloists. The *Kansas City Journal-Post* noted the band's new lineup. "The Jay McShann and George E. Lee dance bands are attracting comment at the Plaza tavern and the Brookside tavern, respectively, both operated by Clair Martin. McShann, a pianist, features the singing of Selma Long, Jesse Price and Bob Mabane. Billy Smith's trumpet, William Scott's tenor and Charlie Parker's alto sax also are prominent. Gene Ramey is the hard-working bass fiddle slapper."[31]

On Friday, November 11, Charlie and the McShann band shared the bill with Harlan Leonard's Kansas City Rockets at the newly refurbished Gold Crown Tap Room at Twelfth and Highland. The Gold Crown, a popular tavern, delivered liquor with a fleet of brand new 1938 motorcycles. The floor show featured blues shouter Walter Brown, balladeer Earl Coleman, and Rubye Rachelle, a devotee of Ella Fitzgerald. Charlie became close friends with Brown and Coleman.

That evening Leonard closely watched Charlie on the bandstand. Leonard, an alto saxophonist who rarely soloed, needed a strong soloist to lead the Rockets' saxophone section. At first glance, Charlie seemed to fit the bill.

Leonard had taken over a young, undisciplined band from Tommy Douglas in February 1937. Over the next year, he polished the band, preparing for its national debut—with mixed results. The band came together but lacked the orchestral polish, strong soloists, and originality needed to succeed nationally. With the help of Benny Goodman, John Hammond, and Dave Dexter, Leonard won an audition with Willard Alexander, an agent for the Music Corporation of America (MCA). Alexander arrived in Kansas City on October 13, 1938, to check out the Rockets. Leonard's high hopes for the band were dashed when Alexander judged the band not ready. *Kansas City Call* columnist E. LeRoy Brown Jr. reported that, after the audition, Alexander criticized the band for a lack of "variety," adding that "changes would have to be made before the boys could step into the big time racket," and he was not "satisfied with certain instruments in the band." Alexander promised a follow-up audition in December, before catching the last flight to New York that evening.[32]

In response to Alexander's suggestions, Leonard adjusted the band's lineup. He ordered Edward Phillips to take drum lessons and hired Winston Williams, a strong bass player, to anchor the rhythm section. Watching Charlie solo at the Gold Crown Tap Room, Leonard thought he had found the soloist needed to lead the reed section, freeing him to concentrate on developing a new book and polishing the band for Willard Alexander's return visit. Unaware of Charlie's drug use and unreliability, Leonard wooed him away from the Jay McShann band.

In late November, Charlie joined the Leonard band. McShann, a genial bandleader, wished Charlie well. Charlie found kindred spirits in the band. Pianist Rozelle Claxton, bassist Winston Williams, tenor saxophonist Odell West, Jesse Price (known as the "Mad Drummer"), and other band members favored the modern style of jazz Charlie was pioneering on the bandstand and at late-night jam sessions. The switch to the Leonard band marked a professional step up for Charlie, but a financial setback as well. Leonard was a tight-fisted bandleader who paid band members scale and closely monitored the repayment of advances. Charlie cashed his first check from Leonard for seventy-five cents at Matlaw's, a clothing store in the Lincoln Building at Eighteenth and Vine.

The band showed immediate improvement. In his weekly column, E. Leroy Brown Jr. judged that Winston Williams, trumpeter William Smith, and Charley Barry [Charlie Parker] have "greatly improved the band and with a few minor changes in arrangements, there is certain to be more heard from this fine Kansas City aggregation."[33] Willard Alexander passed on the scheduled December audition, but John Hammond and Dave E. Dexter Jr. promised to continue advocating on Leonard's behalf with MCA.

In mid-December, Charlie appeared on the Vine Street Varieties with an all-star orchestra drawn from the Leonard band led by Jesse Price. The band featured Rozell Claxton piano, Winston Williams bass, Odell West tenor, and "Sleepy" Tomlin, a former member of the Lunceford band, on trumpet. The band performed "Old Man Mose," "Lady Be Good," and "Honeysuckle Rose."[34] Leonard, who was concerned about losing Charlie and the others to Price, appeared with his full band on the Vine Street Varieties the following week. Leonard groomed Charlie for stardom with the band, billing him as the 'Saxaphonist [*sic*] Supreme" for a Christmas night dance at Dreamland Hall, located at Cottage and Vine.

Just as Charlie's star rose with the band, he began missing practices and engagements. His frequent absences threw the band off. Leonard, who was determined to lead the Rockets to national fame, had little patience for Charlie's transgressions, and let Charlie go in late January 1939. Years later, Leonard observed, "We could never count on him showing up."[35] On February 11, 1940, Leonard returned Charlie's union card to Local 627.

Charlie's drug use and unreliability also caused strife at home. He argued with Addie and fought with Rebecca. Addie, fed up with the domestic turmoil, ordered Charlie to leave. "We had some terrible quarrels, and I said, 'One house isn't built for two nasty people. You know mother loves you, but you've got to obey mother or else you got to leave here. . . . Rebecca was four [two] years older than he was and wanted to be his mother," Addie explained. "He wouldn't stand for that and started beating up on her, you know. I told him that wasn't right and it would only cause a lot of trouble and the best thing to do was leave, and he went to Chicago."[36] Stung by his mother's rebuke and unable to work locally, Charlie hopped a freight train for Chicago, the first stop on his journey to New York, where he hoped to reunite with Buster Smith, his musical father.

CHAPTER 3

Hootie Blues

Arriving in Chicago early the next morning after his abrupt departure from home and family in Kansas City, Charlie headed straight for a jam session at the 65 Club, hoping to hustle up a few gigs and a place to stay. He worked his way through the crowd, borrowed a saxophone, stepped up to the microphone, and stopped the show with his quicksilver execution and ideas. Vocalist Billy Eckstine, saxophonist Budd Johnson, and other musicians gathered at the bar took note of the brilliant young stranger. Eckstine recounted how Charlie dazzled the crowd that morning:

> The vogue then was to have a Breakfast Dance on one day of the week. Every club in Chicago at some time or another would have a Breakfast Dance with the show going on at 6:30 in the morning. One spot there, the 65 Club had a Breakfast Dance one morning and they had a little combo with King Kolax on trumpet, a kid named Goon Gardner, who could swing like mad, on alto, John Simmons on bass and Kansas Fields, drums.
>
> It was more or less a jam show, for after the show all the musicians would blow in there. We were standing around one morning when a guy comes up that looks like he just got off a freight car: the raggedest guy you'd want to

see at this moment. And he asks Goon: "Say man can I come up and blow your horn?" Now Goon was always a kind of lazy cat. Anybody that wanted to get on the stand and blow, just as long as Goon could go to the bar and talk with the chicks, it was all right with him. So he said: "Yes, man, go ahead."

And this cat gets up there, and I'm telling you he blew the bell off that thing! It was Charlie Parker, just come in from Kansas City on a freight train. I guess Bird was no more than about 18 then, but playing like you never heard—wailing alto. . . . He blew so much until he upset everybody in the joint, and Goon took him home, gave him some clothes to put on and got him a few gigs. Bird didn't have a horn, naturally, so Goon lent him a clarinet to go and make gigs on. According to what Goon told me, one day he looked for Bird, and Bird, the clarinet and all was gone—back somewhere.[1]

Charlie left as abruptly as he arrived. Without saying goodbye, he pawned Gardner's clarinet and caught a freight train to New York, where he turned up unannounced on Buster Smith's doorstep.

Smith took Charlie in over his wife's objections. "Charlie got downhearted when it looked like I wasn't going to send for them [the band], so he just caught a train and hoboed up there [New York]. . . . He sure did look awful when he got in," Smith observed. "He'd worn his shoes so long that his legs were all swollen up. He stayed up there with me for a good while at my apartment."[2] With little money to spare and out of respect to Smith, Charlie stayed straight.

Charlie's arrival coincided with the opening of the 1939 World's Fair. The fair, held at Flushing Meadows Park in Queens, celebrated the future with displays of tear-shaped automobiles, robots, dishwashers, and nylon stockings. Forty-five million visitors streamed through the fair's Futurama, the League of Nations, and Perisphere. The fair's excitement and promise of a bright future reverberated throughout New York, still struggling to recover its footing from the blow of the Great Depression.

A long-established entertainment Mecca, Harlem rolled out the red carpet for visitors to the World's Fair. Located in Upper Manhattan, Harlem ranged from 110th Street on its south edge (which was the northern boundary of Central Park) to the East River, west to Morningside Park, east to Fifth Avenue, and north to 155th Street. The Apollo Theater, along with the Savoy, Renaissance, and State Palace ballrooms, featured Jimmy Lunceford, Lucky

Millinder, and other top bands. Small's Paradise and other nightclubs dotting Harlem showcased all-star combos. Charlie joined the throngs making the rounds in Harlem. He paused awestruck in front of the Savoy Ballroom, where in a few years he would make his national debut.

Like all newly arrived musicians, Charlie had to wait to join union local 802. Meanwhile, he worked busing tables at Jimmy's Chicken Shack where Art Tatum played solo piano. Charlie absorbed Tatum's technique of interpolating melodies at breakneck tempos. After work, he frequented jam sessions at the Uptown House, a popular gathering spot for modernists, where he put to good use the lessons he learned from Tatum.

Clark Monroe operated the Uptown House, a smoky basement club in a brownstone located at 198 West 134th Street in the heart of Harlem's entertainment district. Monroe, a gregarious, dapper, handsome ladies' man, was known as the "dark Gable," because of his resemblance to matinee idol Clark Gable. Originally a speakeasy, the Uptown House operated as an after-hours club. The music started late and continued well past the 4:00 A.M. curfew for clubs. Pianist Allen Tinney fronted the band and ran the jam session. Charlie and other young musicians, hoping for a break, lined up to take the stage and challenge more experienced players.

Most older musicians failed to appreciate Charlie's ideas and tone, but they grudgingly admired his masterful technique. Charlie found a friend and musical foil in guitarist William Biddy Fleet, ten years his senior. Like Charlie, Fleet had been experimenting with alternate chords, melodies, and progressions. "Bird liked my playing, and it wasn't because I played that much. Lot of guitar players was playing more guitar than I," Fleet confessed. "But the voicings of my chords had a theme within themselves. You could call a tune, and I'd voice my chords in such a way that I'd play the original chord to the tune, and I'd invert 'em every one, two, three or four beats so that the top notes of my inversions would be another tune. It would not be the melody to the tune I'm playing, yet the chords, foundation-wise, is the chords to the tune. And Bird had a big ear, and he listened. He say, 'Biddy! Do that again.'"[3]

Fleet and Charlie began working together in clubs scattered around Harlem. Charlie often stopped by to jam at Fleet's regular engagement at Don Wall's Chili House, located on Seventh Avenue between 139th and 140th

Streets. One night while sitting in with Fleet at the Chili House, Charlie made the musical breakthrough he had been searching for since his summer spent in the Ozarks. In a paraphrased interview he explained, "I remember one night before Monroe's I was jamming in a chili house on Seventh Avenue between 139th and 140th. Now I'd been getting bored with the stereotyped changes that were being used all the time at the time, and I kept thinking there's bound to be something else. I could hear it sometimes but I couldn't play it. Well that night, I was working over "Cherokee," and, as I did, I found that by using the higher intervals of a chord as a melody line and backing them with appropriately related changes, I could play the thing I'd been hearing. I came alive."[4]

During the day, Charlie stayed in the Smiths' apartment while Buster crafted arrangements for bandleaders and his wife worked at Mary Kirk's newly opened Kansas City Barbecue restaurant. Charlie irritated Smith's wife by sleeping in their bed with his clothes and shoes on. The two frequently argued. "And so he [Charlie] and my wife got to arguing and she and I got into an argument," Smith explained. "She said, 'Charlie's gonna have to get him a room, he's laying in bed with his shoes on.' . . . Well, I talked to Charlie about [it] and he said, 'Well it's nothing, I'm sorry, it's alright.'"[5] Smith reluctantly asked Charlie to move out.

Charlie and Fleet joined Banjo Burney Robinson's band at Dickie Well's Club on Seventh Avenue. That fall, while playing with Robinson's band at a hotel engagement in Annapolis, Maryland, Charlie received news that his father had been murdered by a girlfriend in Memphis. Charlie returned to Kansas City to be with Addie. Charlie hardly recognized his father's body, which was shriveled from blood loss. He asked Addie, "Mama, what made him do it?" She replied, "He liked the lady, I guess."[6] Charlie moved back in with Addie, who warmly welcomed him home.

Charlie returned to freelancing around Kansas City with occasional tours of the territories. In early winter, he joined the Deans of Swing, a young band led by Lawrence Keyes. A group of students at R. T. Coles High School had formed the Deans of Swing in early October 1938. Later that month Keyes took over leadership of the group when he returned from Chicago. As before with the Chords of Rhythm, Keyes professionalized the group, whipping his young charges into shape. The fifteen-piece band played the Blue

Room in the Street Hotel, Roseland Ballroom, and the Century Room at 3605 Broadway, a recently opened ballroom operated by John Tumino. Lanky and gregarious, Tumino also booked groups for Fairyland Park, Kansas City's leading amusement park, and managed Harlan Leonard's Rockets and the Jay McShann band.[7]

McShann had recently brought his band up to full size by raiding the Nat Towles band in Omaha. Walter Bales funded McShann's trip to Nebraska. McShann arrived on a Monday night and recruited local players at a jam session. "All the musicians were coming in, so every time I heard a cat I liked I'd send him a drink and have him come over," McShann divulged. "They all could leave town, but they owed Towles money, so I said 'OK, I'll see you at 7 o'clock in the morning to get you the money you need to pay your debts before you leave town.' One band member told Nat, 'There's a guy in town trying to get your musicians.' Nat said, 'I'm not worried because they all owe me money.' He didn't know I had plenty of money from Walter Bales, who told me to call or go down to the Traveler's Insurance office if I needed more. I told all the musicians I'd meet them at 7 o'clock in the morning. I went down to Travelers, and I knew the clerk was caught off guard, because here's a black musician coming in asking for a couple of hundred dollars, and this must be a heist." Fortunately, Bales called just in time to vouch for McShann.[8] McShann returned to Kansas City with guitarist Leonard "Lucky" Enois and other musicians he needed to expand his band to full size.

On Easter Sunday, March 24, 1940, the twelve-piece Jay McShann band battled Charlie and the Deans of Swing at Roseland Hall, a spacious ballroom for African Americans located at Fifteenth Street and Troost Avenue. Twenty-five hundred dancers jammed the hall for the battle of the bands. The McShann band and the Deans of Swing traded sets until 2:00 A.M. The Keyes band performed "Memories of You," "Tuxedo Junction," and other swing standards. The McShann band favored the Kansas City style, playing Count Basie's "One O'Clock Jump" and Pete Johnson's "Roll 'Em" featuring alto saxophonist Earl Jackson on vocals.[9]

After the battle, Charlie approached McShann about switching to his band. Although Charlie had abruptly abandoned McShann's small band at Martin's years earlier, McShann hired him on the spot. Charlie's offer gave McShann an excuse to get rid of Earl Jackson, who had been complaining about his pay. Step Buddy Anderson recounted, "It was a big band and we were gettin' some fairly nice dough. And that very thing was the cause of Bird subsequently joining the band, because one of the cats was squawking about the dough—Earl Jackson. . . . Earl was first saxophone player, and he . . . could play just as well as Bird—every bit. But Earl screamed on [about] the money and Jay let him go. That's how Bird came to be a member of the band."[10]

Charlie joined the band right before the start of an extended engagement at a walk-a-thon in the ice hockey arena behind the Pla-Mor entertainment complex. Spectators packed the bleachers lining the arena to view the swirling spectacle unfolding across the broad, wood floor. Contestants, who were mostly entertainers looking for a break, put on a show, tripping up and otherwise undermining each other's efforts to hang in the competition. The crowd cheered on the contestants staggering around the rink, while the band played nonstop.

The walk-a-thon gave McShann the opportunity to tighten the sections and develop a book of arrangements. "After opening at the walk-a-thon in the arena at the Pla-Mor we got the band together by using the loft as a rehearsal space," McShann explained. "I sent Scotty [William Scott] and the reed section up there to rehearse. I kept the brass and the rhythm section on the stage. When the brass went upstairs to rehearse, the reeds would come down with the band. At the walk-a-thon they had these games they would pull to eliminate so many people a night. After four or five months about everybody would be eliminated except for two or three people. By the time everybody was eliminated we had a book of 250 or 300 tunes and about 150 head tunes. I often wondered how in the world those guys could remember those head tunes, but they would remember 'em."[11]

After wrapping up the walk-a-thon in early June 1940, the McShann band played a summer engagement at Fairyland Park, an amusement park located at the end of the Prospect streetcar line at Seventy-Fifth Street and Prospect Avenue. During the summer, Kansas Citians flocked to Fairyland Park to cool off in the gigantic Crystal Swimming Pool, enjoy the amusement rides, stroll down the arcade, and dance in the open-air pavilion that featured top local and national bands.

Four hundred dancers showed up for the McShann band's opening the last week of June, breaking the record for season openers. Bob Locke praised the band's progress in his column covering the Kansas City scene for *Down Beat*. "The 14-piece outfit has improved beyond the imagination of any one who hasn't heard it, and should be 1941's sepia sensation. . . . Every man has his heart in his job."[12]

That week, Charlie first met Dizzy Gillespie, in town for an engagement with the Cab Calloway band at Fairyland. Cab Calloway and his Cotton Club Orchestra featuring Gillespie, tenor saxophonist Chu Berry, drummer Cozy Cole, and trumpeter Mario Bauza played Fairyland on Sunday, June 23. Although Fairyland denied admittance to African Americans, John Tumino allowed McShann band members to visit the ballroom on their night off. During the intermission, Step Buddy Anderson, Orville "Piggy" Minor, and McShann invited Gillespie and other Calloway band members to an after-hours session at Kentucky Bar B Q located on the northwest corner of Nineteenth and Vine Streets. Anderson wanted to introduce Gillespie to Charlie, but Charlie failed to show that night.

Anderson made arrangements for the three to meet the next day in front of Kentucky Bar B Q. They walked around the corner to Local 627, where Gillespie accompanied Charlie and Anderson on piano. Anderson distinctly recalled the first encounter between Charlie and Gillespie. "Dizzy listened carefully as Charlie and myself took turns at improvising on the tunes we agreed on. Dizzy played no trumpet, he was there to see what we could do—especially Charlie, because I had placed some pretty strong superlatives around his talent. However, when that little session ended, Dizzy just was not very impressed. He passed out some nice compliments in both our directions; but he was just saying something. Charlie and myself realized, without ever saying so, who Dizzy was really thinking about as being the greatest jazzer he had ever heard. It certainly wasn't me. And it wasn't Charlie Parker either. But it was one of the three of us in that room."[13]

Anderson misjudged Gillespie's reaction to Charlie. Actually, Gillespie was quite impressed by Charlie. "I was astounded by what the guy could do," Gillespie later exclaimed. "These other guys that I had been playing with weren't my colleagues, really. But the moment I heard Charlie Parker, I said, there is my colleague. . . . I had never heard anything like that before. The way that he assembled notes together. That was one of the greatest thrills because I had been a Roy Eldridge fan up until then, but I was definitely moving on into myself. Charlie Parker and I were moving in practically the same direction too, but neither of us knew it."[14] The brief encounter set the stage for a musical partnership that would later change the course of jazz.

The McShann band's run at Fairyland continued until mid-August, when Musicians Local 34 pressured Tumino to hire the Red Blackburn band, a white dance band, to finish out the season. Tumino and McShann, not wanting to cause a fuss, appeased the white local and pursued other opportunities. The McShann band toured the Midwest under the management of Tumino's Consolidated Orchestras of America, playing a string of college dances, amusement parks, and ballrooms with held-over performances at Trocadero Club in Wichita, Riverview Park in Des Moines, and the Turnpike Casino in Lincoln, Nebraska. The band broke the color barrier at the University of Missouri at Columbia, becoming the first African American band to play student dances.

Charlie received his nickname Yardbird during a trip to Nebraska. "We used to go up to the University of Nebraska and play dates up there—you know, 'Big Red' [the University of Nebraska football team], the games, after the games, and so forth," McShann explained.

> We were on our way up there this particular time, and you know how it is traveling on the highway, you run into, you be traveling along and these chickens all run out on the highway. So some of the chickens run out on the highway. So this guy ran over a chicken. So Bird told him, he says, "Hey Pat, back this car up and pick up that yardbird there. You just ran over a yardbird." So sure enough Pat backed the car up, and Charlie got out and he got the chicken—took the chicken into Lincoln with him. During those times we would find private homes where we would stay. . . . he went in and asked this lady, he told her, "Miss, we ran over the yardbird on our way here, just a little ways out of here, and he's still warm, and I wonder if you could cook him for me?" She said, "Yes." So she did. And from then on we started calling him "Yardbird." Some called him Bird; some called him Yardbird. And he did like chicken. . . . Bird's word was "a chicken ain't nothing but a yardbird."[15]

Band members, amused by Charlie's fondness for chicken and his use of the colloquialism he had picked up years earlier while at Penn School, began referring to him as Yardbird.

Charlie's reliability and leadership pleasantly surprised McShann. "What really helped was having Bird in that big band," McShann explained. "When we got to the point when we had five saxophones. When Bird was in the section, you would see him turn, especially on those head tunes he would be giving this cat his note. He'd give him the note he wanted him to make. He might tell 'em and if he didn't tell 'em he'd play it for 'em. And if you see him turning this way he'd be giving this cat his note. Sometimes they'd get off on the wrong notes. Then after while they would all come together."[16] Charlie helped develop the band's book, co-composing with McShann "Hootie Blues," a lazy orchestral expression of the blues.

During a Thanksgiving 1940 weekend engagement at the Trocadero Club in Wichita, Kansas, Fred Higginson, a young jazz fan who worked at radio KFBI, recorded the band to instantaneous cut discs during two late-night sessions. The first session featured an octet from the big band in the wee hours of Saturday, November 30, 1940. The band recorded "I Found a New Baby" and "Body and Soul." Returning to the studio, on Monday, December 2, the band recorded an improvised "Blues," "Honeysuckle Rose," "Lady Be Good," "Coquette," "So You Won't Jump," and "Moten's Swing."[17] Charlie's solo flights on "Body and Soul" and "Moten's Swing" showcase his advanced techniques and ideas. On "Body and Soul," Charlie runs in and out of key while maintaining the ballad tempo. Following Charlie's lead, Buddy Anderson and other band members shift to double time, before resuming the ballad tempo in the out chorus. McShann's bright piano introduces the theme of "Moten's Swing," leading to riffs by the band in the Kansas City style. Charlie then jumps in with an assured solo distinguished by triplets in the second eight-bar section and triplet flourishes at the end of the bridge. The recordings were the first to capture these two signatures of his style.[18]

That winter, the band traveled widely across the Midwest. While on the road, McShann prepared the band for an upcoming recording session for the Decca label. McShann had originally signed a contract with Decca while playing at Martin's on the Plaza. In November 1938, he took the small band to Chicago to record for Decca, but the local union stopped the session. "E. Mayo Williams came through Kansas City and heard the small group at Martin's and offered us a contract with Decca," McShann recalled. "So I signed it and sent it to Decca, and they made arrangements for us to record in Chicago. We went up to Chicago, but I didn't know I was supposed to turn in a contract to the local union. Well, the Chicago union found out about the session when we were getting ready to record and they stopped the session. So we didn't get a chance to record. We had to come on back to Kansas City."[19] McShann put off scheduling a follow-up recording date while he built the big band and developed an original book.

In late January 1941, John Tumino bought a disc-cutting machine to make reference recordings of the band. On February 6, he recorded the band performing "Margie" and "I'm Getting Sentimental Over You." These spontaneous recordings capture the band in transition and feature two solos by Charlie. On "Margie," after a brief introduction, the reed and brass sections state the melody accented by riffs followed by Joe Coleman's mid-range vocal. Following a band chorus, Orville "Piggy" Minor delivers a fiery upper register trumpet solo. In the out chorus, McShann takes a solo highlighted by chord substitutions followed by an understated, bluesy, eight-bar solo by Charlie.

Jay McShann and the rhythm section kick off "I'm Getting Sentimental Over You" with an eight-bar introduction. Joe Coleman follows with a thirty-two-bar vocal rendered in the popular style of the day. Charlie then steps in with a brilliant, lyrical, thirty-two-bar solo capped off with a four-bar codetta. Charlie peppers the opening bars of his solo with thirty-second-note flourishes. His lilting solo then glides along propelled by fleet runs of sixteenth notes. Charlie's strikingly original solo reveals his formidable technique and maturity as a soloist.

By spring 1941, McShann felt that the band was ready to record for Decca. Just before the session, McShann replaced vocalist Joe Coleman, a popular song crooner, with Walter Brown, a blues stylist with a nasal conversational style. Originally from Texas, Brown came to Kansas City in the summer of 1937. Stocky, with a rough complexion, Brown followed Big Joe Turner into the Sunset Club, where he worked as a singing waiter. Local fans crowned Brown the "New King of the Blues," after Turner's departure for the East Coast. McShann recruited Brown for the band during a jam session at the

Kentucky Bar B Q. Brown brought along a catchy new song he had recently composed, "Confessin' the Blues."

On April 30, 1941, McShann's band recorded for the Decca label in Dallas, Texas. The band left Kansas City after a Saturday night date at the Casa Fiesta Ballroom on Thirty-Ninth Street near Main and drove straight through to Dallas. The president of Decca, Jack Kapp, sent his brother Dave to supervise the session. McShann wanted to record the band's modern compositions, but Kapp was more interested in recording blues and boogie-woogie for Decca's Sepia Series, which was marketed to African Americans. After listening to the band's modern numbers, Kapp requested blues and boogie-woogie tunes and then recorded those takes without McShann's knowledge. McShann remembered, "We got down there [Dallas] and Dave Kapp said play the tunes you want to record. We played three or four tunes, so he came out and said, 'Can you guys do any kind of boogie woogie? Play me a boogie woogie.' He smiled because it was a take but we didn't know it was a take. Then he said, 'Play a blues' and we played a blues. He smiled again. He said, 'That's what I want.' He said, 'Do one more blues tune and I'll take what you want to pick out.' So then we picked out "Swingmatism." Then he finally said, 'Personally, I like all this stuff you got, but truthfully I can't sell it.'"[20]

In addition to "Swingmatism," the band recorded "Hootie Blues," "Dexter Blues," "Vine Street Boogie," "Confessin' the Blues," and "Hold 'Em Hootie." Charlie soloed on "Swingmatism," "Dexter Blues," and "Hootie Blues." William Scott based the arrangement of "Hootie Blues" on "Donkey Serenade." McShann and Ramey set the tone of "Hootie Blues" with a staid four-bar introduction. The brass and reed sections follow, playing behind the beat with held notes, leading to an inventive twelve-bar solo by Charlie, which switches to double time in the ninth and tenth bars. Charlie's solo introduces Walter Brown's lazy vocal, which accents the pensive mood of the lyrics, "Hello little girl, don't you remember me. . . . Time ain't been so long, but I had a break you see, well I'm doing all right found me a kewepie doll. . . . She lives two flights up and she sends me with a smile." The full band restates the theme in the out chorus. Kapp, realizing he had just recorded a hit, rushed the masters for "Hootie Blues" and "Confessin' the Blues" into production.[21]

The release of "Confessin' the Blues" backed by "Hootie Blues" caught McShann by surprise. "We went out on the road for a couple of months,"

McShann remembered. "We came into Tulsa, Oklahoma, and ran into a guy who told us he just heard our record at Jenkins, so we went down to Jenkins and listened to it. We didn't know the records had been released."[22] "Confessin' the Blues" took the nation by storm, receiving strong play on jukeboxes. Musicians who flipped the disc over and listened to "Hootie Blues" were astounded by Charlie's groundbreaking solo.

As "Confessin' the Blues" took off, giving the band the lift it needed to rise nationally, McShann stayed in Kansas City for a summer engagement at Fairyland Park, making good on a promise to John Tumino. While leading the house band, McShann rubbed shoulders with Ted Weems, Art Kassel, Lawrence Welk, Larry Clinton, and other leading white bandleaders. McShann's fraternizing with whites at Fairyland Park was the exception to the rule. African Americans were barred from the park except for special occasions. The whites-only park opened its gates to African Americans for Emancipation Day on August 4, 1941. Despite the *Kansas City Call*'s editorial urging a boycott of the park for its Jim Crow policies, African American families packed the park to enjoy the rides and hear the band perform "Confessin' the Blues." By the fall, "Confessin' the Blues" had sold over one hundred thousand copies.

After wrapping up the season at Fairyland, McShann moved the band's headquarters to New York City, following in the footsteps of Count Basie and Andy Kirk. The band freelanced around Kansas City while John Tumino lined up enough dates to carry it to the East Coast. Charlie eagerly grabbed the ticket out of town.

As Charlie's career flourished, his personal life remained in turmoil. A civic cleanup targeting vice and corruption had put a damper on Kansas City's bright nightlife. Missouri Governor Lloyd Stark, who was elected with the help of Tom Pendergast in 1936, aspired to become a United States Senator. Once elected governor, he turned against the Pendergast machine, declaring war on drugs, gambling, prostitution, and corruption in Kansas City. Convicted of income tax evasion in 1939, Pendergast served fifteen months in the federal penitentiary in Leavenworth, Kansas. Lacking strong leadership, the Pendergast machine collapsed under the pressure of a state and local cleanup effort, squeezing jobs for musicians and sources of narcotics.

At home, Addie, now officially widowed, was romantically involved with a suitor named Augustus Daniels. Charlie shared little in common with

Rebecca and was ill equipped to be a father to Leon. Before leaving town, Charlie asked Rebecca for a divorce, telling her, "If I were free, Rebeck, I think I could become a great musician." Addie volunteered to file the necessary paperwork for the divorce but failed to follow through. Charlie left Rebecca and Leon behind with Addie.[23]

The McShann band played a farewell concert at Lincoln Hall on September 28 and then headed out into the southwestern territories. The band attracted fifty-five hundred dancers at the Houston Civic Auditorium, breaking all attendance records.[24] While in Houston, Charlie settled all scores during a cutting contest between members of the McShann and Milton Larkin bands. McShann described the event:

> The first time we went out on the road with the big band we played Houston. And at that time Milton Larkin had a band that sounded like Lunceford. He had [Eddie] Cleanhead [Vinson], Arnett Cobb and Illinois Jacquet and some good trumpet players. He had a hell of a band. I had a guy with me, Moe Ferguson, and he went to their rehearsal. Moe went over there and started blowin' off, so quite naturally they were laying to get him. He wasn't in the class of Jacquet and Arnett. I had slept late that morning and Walter Brown had been down to the session. Moe was blowin' with Jacquet on one side and Cobb on the other. Walter Brown came by the hotel and said, "Hootie, you'd better go down and get Moe he's getting frustrated down there. I just walked out of there and Moe had a big glass of whiskey in front of him. When those guys got through blowin' Moe picked up the glass of whiskey and drank the whiskey and broke the glass in two." I went down there to see what was happening. Bird said, "Wait a minute I'm going down there with you." We went on down there and Bird had his horn. We walked in and these cats really upset Moe because he wasn't expecting nothing like that in Texas. As soon as Bird got a chance he said "wait right here" and he started blowing right from the door. When Bird started blowing from the door everybody listened up and Bird kept blowing down to where the cats were. When Bird got down there, everybody sat down.[25]

The Larkin and McShann bands continued their rivalry with a battle of the bands staged at the Louisiana Fair in Shreveport during early November. Charlie and Eddie "Cleanhead" Vinson hit it off. They disappeared after the show, drinking and carousing until early morning.

On the way east, the band stopped off in Chicago to record for Decca. Seeking to duplicate the success of "Confessin' the Blues," Dave Kapp exclusively recorded Walter Brown and the rhythm section. Charlie and the rest of the band sat out the session. The rhythm section recorded a jump tune, "So You Won't Jump," reminiscent of Count Basie's "One O'Clock Jump," a boogie-woogie number, "Hootie's Ignorant Oil," and six blues, including "New Confessin' the Blues," an updated version of the band's big hit. By recording Walter Brown and the rhythm section instead of the big band, Kapp gave fans who bought the records the false impression that the band was primarily a small ensemble specializing in blues and boogie-woogie. In reality, the big band boasted a modern book and a hard-swinging style accented by the interplay of riffs and solos in the Kansas City tradition. After wrapping up the session, the band embarked on a string of one-nighters leading to New York.

During the band's trip east, the Japanese attacked Pearl Harbor and the Philippines. The spread of war cast an immediate pall across the music industry. Blackouts shuttered nightclubs. Ballroom operators canceled dances at the last minute, leaving bands stranded. Radio stations preempted band broadcasts and signed off early. The draft eroded the ranks of bands. Faced with uncertainty, dance fans stayed home, reducing the demand for bands. The hardships triggered by the war devastated African American bands. While white bands enjoyed extended engagements at hotels and ballrooms, African American bands played mostly one-night stands, traveling great distances between engagements.

The McShann band reached New York ahead of the repercussions of war with the help of the Moe Gale Agency, one of the nation's leading management firms. Moe Gale, known as the "Great White Father of Harlem," also managed the Savoy Ballroom. Bandleaders who wanted to play the Savoy had to sign with the Gale agency. In between stretches at the Savoy, bands managed by Gale toured nationally on a patchwork circuit of theaters, ballrooms, and clubs.

Gale's brother Tim signed the McShann band to a seven-year contract during a Christmas Eve dance in Gary, Indiana. As part of the agreement, John Tumino stayed on to tend to the band's day-to-day operations, and Gale rushed the band to New York for a battle of the bands against the Lucky Millinder orchestra at the Savoy. Millinder, who had only heard the

McShann's small group recordings, sent McShann a postcard, confidently proclaiming, "We're gonna send you hicks back to the sticks."[26]

The McShann band took the wrong route to New York and arrived late at the Savoy, considerably the worse for wear. Nevertheless, that evening they bested the wildly popular Millinder band on its own turf. Gene Ramey recalled the band's triumphant debut at the Savoy. "McShann had one of those big old long Buicks, and I was driving, with about five or six guys in it. I took what I thought was the shortest route to New York, up and over the mountains, instead of taking the Pennsylvania Turnpike. We struggled and struggled, but we finally got to New York, raggedy and tired. When we got up on the bandstand, where the Savoy Sultans used to play, the people were looking at us like we were nothing. Lucky Millinder was on the main bandstand."

"Everything we had was shabby-looking, including our cardboard stands, and we only had one uniform—a blue coat and brown pants. But from the time we hit that first note until the time we got off the bandstand, we didn't let up. We heated it so hot for Lucky Millinder that during his set he got up on top of the piano and directed his band from there. Then he jumped off and almost broke his leg. Well that opening was on Friday, the thirteenth of February, 1942."[27]

The broadcasts from the Savoy introduced Charlie to listeners across the country. Charlie's genius caught the attention of musicians who heard the broadcasts. "That Sunday we had to do a matinee at four o'clock. In fifteen minutes we played only two tunes, 'Moten's Swing' and 'Cherokee,'" Ramey explained. "Bird started blowing on 'Cherokee' at that extremely fast tempo. It was way up there. The program was going out on the radio and somebody in the studio called the man with the ear set and said, 'Let them go ahead. Don't stop them!' We played about forty-five minutes more, just the rhythm section and Bird, with the horns setting riffs from time to time. That night you couldn't get near the bandstand for musicians who had heard the broadcast. 'Who was that saxophone player?' they all wanted to know."[28]

Parker's solos astonished trumpeter Howard McGhee and the rest of the Charlie Barnet band. "Oh, I heard Bird, it was in '42," McGhee recounted. "I was with Charlie Barnet. We were playing at the Adams Theater in Newark. We came off the show, and I turned on the radio, just like I did, and all of a sudden I heard this horn jump through there. Bird, playing 'Cherokee,' with McShann broadcasting—from the Savoy; when I heard this cat play I said, 'Who the hell is that? I ain't heard nobody play like that.' Of all the alto players I knew—I knew everybody—I didn't know anybody who played like what was coming through the radio. So everybody shut up, everybody sittin' there. We just listened till it was over with, then we heard the guy say it was at the Savoy, so that night, the whole band, we all went to the Savoy to hear this horn player, what this cat was playin.'" McGhee and other members of the Barnet band were quite familiar with the changes of "Cherokee," the band's theme song. Chubby Jackson, the bassist for the Barnet band, became so enthralled with Charlie's solo on "Cherokee" that he failed to recognize the melody—a song he judged to have played "nine thousand times a week."[29]

Dizzy Gillespie, who was in between jobs and hoping to work with Charlie, frequently sat in with the McShann band at the Savoy. He stopped by so often that McShann reserved a chair for him. After a few weeks, Gillespie asked to join the band. McShann, already struggling to make the payroll, declined Gillespie's offer. In the end, Gillespie considered his brief association with the band time well spent, affording him the opportunity to work with Charlie.

Charlie and Gillespie became fast friends and musical rivals. They jammed regularly at Minton's Playhouse with drummer Kenny Clarke, pianist Thelonious Monk, and other young modernists. Henry Minton, a tenor saxophonist and union official with Local 82, opened Minton's in 1938. An upscale restaurant with a cabaret in the back room, Minton's was located next to the Cecil Hotel at 210 West 118th Street. Known as the "Showplace of Harlem," Minton's offered "Dining Dancing Entertainment."[30] Rows of small tables with linen tablecloths and vases of flowers lined the music room. The walls on either side of the bandstand were covered with paintings depicting musicians jamming or flirting with women. Minton catered to musicians by laying out a free buffet for those who stopped by to jam at the Monday "Swing Session Night." In late 1940, Minton hired popular bandleader Teddy Hill to manage the club. Hill recruited drummer Kenny Clarke to lead the band. Originally from Pittsburgh, Clarke was a rhythmically progressive drummer who broke with tradition by shifting the rhythmic emphasis from the bass drum to the ride cymbal to break up time. He assembled a band of like-minded modernists, including pianist and composer Thelonious Monk, who was known for his dissonant harmonies and unexpected melodic turns.

Minton's back room served as a laboratory for the development of bebop. Charlie and Gillespie joined Monk, Clarke, and other young progressive musicians at Minton's who were experimenting with new harmonic expressions and phrasing that led to the development of bebop, a new movement in jazz. Mary Lou Williams, who lived in the Cecil Hotel, explained, "Bop is the phrasing and accenting of the notes, as well as the harmonies used. Every other note is accented. Never in the history of jazz has the phrasing been like it is in bop." Williams judged that "Thelonious Monk, Charlie Christian, Kenny Clarke, Art Blakey and Idrees Sulieman were the first to play bop. Next were Parker, Gillespie, and Clyde Hart, now dead, who was sensational on piano. After them came J. J. Johnson, Bud Powell, Al Haig, Milt Jackson, Tadd Dameron, Leo Parker, Babs Gonzales, Max Roach, Kenny Dorham and Oscar Pettiford."[31] Charlie and Dizzy soon emerged as leaders of the burgeoning bop movement, becoming the first to bring the new mode of expression to a broader audience.

In March, Gillespie joined the Les Hite band for a tour of the East Coast. Charlie stayed on with McShann but became irregular with the band, showing up late and high. Unlike most bandleaders, the laid-back McShann, for the most part, turned a blind eye to drug use in his band, considering what band members did off the band stand was their own business. During off hours, band members divided into two camps. Trombonist Clyde Bernhardt explained, "We all socialized on our time off, only it was in two groups—the Lushies and the Users. Jay, Joe Evans, Freddie Culliver, myself that liked their whiskey, wine, or beer was the Lushies. . . . Charlie Parker, Walter Brown, Little Joe, and some others was in the second group. They didn't drink but was messing with that dope and usually kept to themselves. . . . Jay didn't give a damn what anybody in his band did as long as it didn't get in the way of the job."[32]

Increasingly, Charlie's behavior on and off the bandstand tested McShann's live-and-let-live philosophy. "Bird was with me four years, but he changed in that time," McShann confided. "His heart wasn't like it was at the beginning of our big band. He had got into the habit of going to places like Monroe's in New York with his horn under his arm. There he might blow just a couple of tunes and then step off the stand for a taste. With me, too, his time had been going bad—showing up late, and so on."[33]

To support his habit, Charlie regularly pawned his alto and scammed money from fellow band members. John Tumino dutifully retrieved the horn from hock before the night's performance. In the spring of 1942, an incident at the Savoy led to Charlie's dismissal from the band. "Bird had gone over to Walter Brown's wife and gotten Brown's last five dollars!" Ramey exclaimed. "Brown came over while Bird was on the bandstand and they got into a fight. Each of them was so high, they never made contact. It was like a slow motion picture of a fight. They'd swing at each other and fall down. As a result, a guy from Joe Glaser's [Moe Gale's] office demanded that Charlie Parker be fired immediately. McShann had to let him go, but after a couple of weeks we were getting so many complaints that we got him back."[34] McShann paid Ramey extra to keep Charlie in line.[35]

In early summer 1942, the band embarked on a tour of one-night stands across the South and back up through the Midwest. During the southern leg of the journey, Charlie and Walter Brown landed in jail. "Then we went down South and had a lot of trouble," Ramey remembered.

> In Augusta the operator left with the money at half-time and the cops said we had to pay the rent of the hall, as well as the bouncers and people on the door, or go to jail. In Martinsville, Virginia, the same thing happened, and this time they were not only going to take us to jail but they were going to take our instruments and the bus as well. In Natchez, Mississippi, they put Walter Brown and Bird in jail for smoking cigarettes in a screened porch of the rooming house where they were staying. If they'd been smoking pot, they'd have been there forever, but John Tumino had to go and pay twenty-five dollars each to get them out. When they joined us in Little Rock, they had knots on their heads big enough to hang a hat on. They had really taken a beating.[36]

Other times, Charlie politely charmed the police into escorting the band through racially hostile counties. By the time the band reached Kansas City, Charlie and other band members were ready to quit.

Through the force of his personality, McShann kept the band together and returned to New York. On July 2, 1942, Dave Kapp ushered the band back into the studio for a recording session ahead of a recording ban ordered by James Petrillo, the President of the American Federation of Musicians. Petrillo had long railed against records, jukeboxes, and radio transcription services for costing musicians jobs. During the union's annual meeting in June, he called for a ban on recording beginning on July 30. Decca and other record labels hurriedly recorded to "beat the ban." The band recorded four selections: "The Jumpin' Blues," "Lonely Boy Blues," "Get Me on Your Mind," and "Sepian Bounce." Charlie showed up high and off his game, so McShann had John Jackson take the lead solos for the session. "On 'Lonely Boy' we had two altos that blew the first chorus together," McShann recalled. "Alto solo was taken by John Jackson. I was gonna have Bird blow it but instead I had him and Bird to blow the thing he had written out. Later on, J. J. [John Jackson] did a solo in there. A lot of people thought J. J. was Bird blowin'. But it wasn't, it was John Jackson blowin'. 'Jumpin' the Blues' was on that session and some others." Jackson, whose execution rivaled Charlie's, recreated Charlie's solos note for note, leaving record buyers none the wiser.[37]

In late fall, McShann fired Charlie following an incident at the Paradise Theater in Detroit. Trombonist Clyde Bernhardt recounted the events leading to McShann's firing Charlie:

> The band played its first show that Friday night. After we did Mary Lou Williams's "Roll 'Em," a hell of a band number, Walter Brown sang a blues. When we hit "Cherokee," Parker walked down front as usual and began blowing real hot when all at once he just fell over. Down on the floor, out cold. People in the audience screamed. We kept playing but I was dumb-founded—thought he dropped dead. They pulled the curtain and the stage manager dragged Parker off, put him in a back room, and tried to revive him while we continued the show. After the set we all ran back and Parker was sitting there laughing. "What the hell happened, man?" he was saying. We were wondering the same thing. "Goddamn, must have had too much of that shit." Jay didn't say anything. He was easygoing. The next day some guys [narcotics agents] came up to where Parker and Brown was staying, a rooming house run by a big 250-pound feminine guy, out there on Adams Avenue. Tore the place apart, ripped carpets up, cut open mattresses. . . . Parker played the rest of that

weekend, but on Monday he was high again. The owner of the theater told Jay to get rid of him, and the next day Parker was on his way back to New York."[38]

Charlie hitched a ride with the Andy Kirk band, which happened to be in Detroit.

Charlie briefly rejoined the McShann band when it returned to New York but left in December 1942, when Earl "Fatha" Hines raided the McShann band, taking Charlie and two other band members. Hines, a veteran bandleader, informed McShann that he intended to "make a man" out of Charlie. Hines had no idea what he was getting himself into.

CHAPTER 4

Bebop

A few months after Charlie joined the Earl Hines band, Jay McShann ran into Hines at a jam session on Fifty-Second Street. Hines begged McShann to take Charlie back. McShann chuckled, "He [Hines] threw up his hands when he saw me and said, 'That's the worst man I ever met in my life! He owes everybody money. Come get him!' Earl had bought Bird a saxophone worth four to five hundred dollars, and Bird really had him crying the blues!"[1] Charlie had already pawned the new horn.

During his long career, stretching back before the dawn of jazz, Hines had never met anyone quite like Charlie. Hines grew up in a suburb of Pittsburgh. As a child, he studied classical piano and memorized show tunes while attending theatrical productions and films. He began playing professionally as a teenager, accompanying Lois Deppe, a popular baritone. Dapper, with angular features highlighted by a finely etched mustache, Hines made his recording debut for the Gennett label in 1923 with Deppe's Serenaders.

In 1925, Hines moved to Chicago and joined the Carroll Dickerson Orchestra for a forty-two week tour of the Pantages vaudeville circuit that ranged up the West Coast to Canada. Louis Armstrong joined the band when it returned to Chicago for an engagement at the famed Sunset Club. Armstrong had been freelancing around Chicago while making his groundbreaking Hot Five and Hot Seven recordings for the OKeh label, featuring his wife Lil Hardin Armstrong on piano. Hines and Armstrong became close friends while working together at the Sunset. Armstrong admired Hines's "trumpet style," distinguished by offbeat accents, octaves, and tremolo. In 1928, Armstrong reorganized the Hot Five band and replaced Lil with Hines. Armstrong and Hines made a number of recordings for the OKeh label, including a brilliantly executed duet, "Weatherbird." Hines more than held his own against Armstrong in their tricky musical back and forth.

On his twenty-fifth birthday, Hines launched his career as a bandleader at Al Capone's Grand Terrace Café, one of Chicago's brightest nightspots. Capone lavished $100 tips on the young pianist. The band spent winters at the Grand Terrace and toured nationally during the summer months. The all-star revue at the Grand Terrace featured leading dancers, comedians, and entertainers. Nightly broadcasts from the Grand Terrace over the NBC Network established Hines's reputation nationally. He became known as "Fatha" after the radio announcer began heralding the band with "Here comes Fatha Hines, leading his band out of the deep forest with his little children."[2] The nickname stuck, and Hines, although still a young man, became known as "Fatha."

Hines left the Grand Terrace in 1938, after a dispute over money with the manager, Ed Fox. Despite his long tenure at the Grand Terrace and broadcasts over a national network, Hines earned less money than Duke Ellington, Jimmy Lunceford, and other top bandleaders. When Hines left the Grand Terrace, half of the band stayed behind out of loyalty to Fox.

Hines and music director Budd Johnson rebuilt and updated the band by recruiting young, progressive musicians. Vocalist Billy Eckstine joined the band in Detroit. Eckstine, who hailed from Pittsburgh, modeled his style after Paul Robeson. A strikingly handsome baritone with precise diction, Eckstine favored ballads but gained fame as a blues stylist. While audiences on the East Coast swooned at Eckstine's ballads, fans in the South clamored for the blues in the style of Big Joe Turner. Eckstine, who disdained the blues, hastily sketched out the lyric to "Jelly, Jelly," a risqué, orchestral expression of the blues that became the big hit of 1941. The next year, he scored another hit with "Stormy Monday Blues." Off stage, Eckstine helped Hines scout young talent, bringing Dizzy Gillespie, Charlie Parker, and other modernists into the band.

In November 1942, Eckstine convinced Gillespie to join the band. Gillespie had been dividing his time between leading the house band at the Downbeat Club in Philadelphia, where his mother lived, and sitting in at jam sessions in Harlem, where his wife Lorraine worked and maintained their apartment. Eckstine and other band members lured Gillespie into the band by promising that Charlie would soon join the band. They told Charlie the same thing about Gillespie.

Just before Christmas, Eckstine convinced Hines to hire Charlie. Eckstine recalled how Charlie came to the band:

> There used to be a joint in New York, a late night spot on 138th [*sic*] called Clarke Monroe's Uptown House, where the guys all jammed. . . . Bird used to go down there and blow every night, and he just played gorgeous. Now by this time I was with Earl Hines, who was starting out with his new band. Budd Johnson and myself got this band together for him and it was all young guys—Scoops Carry, Franz Jackson, Shorty McConnell, Little Benny Harris, and guys like that. We sold Hines on the idea to go up and hear Charlie Parker. Now Budd Johnson had left the band and we needed a tenor player. Charlie was playing alto, of course, but Earl bought him a tenor and turned Charlie over on tenor and we got Bird in the band then.[3]

After initially grousing about the size and feel of the tenor, Charlie quickly mastered his new instrument. His tone assumed the richness of Lester Young. Charlie's fleet execution on the tenor at first confounded Ben Webster, a tenor saxophonist who also hailed from Kansas City. After walking into Minton's one night and seeing Charlie on stage, Webster protested "What the hell is that up there? Man is that cat crazy?" Webster, who was a balladeer at heart, strode up to the band stand and snatched the tenor out of Charlie's hand and proclaimed, "That horn ain't s'posed to sound that fast." Later that night, Webster changed his tune, walking all over town telling musicians "Man I heard a guy—I swear he is going to make everybody crazy on tenor."[4] A few months later, Webster rated Charlie second only to Benny Carter in an article published in *Music Dial*, a literary music and arts magazine published in Harlem.[5]

After rehearsing for three weeks at the Nola Studio, the Hines band opened at the Apollo Theater for a weeklong engagement starting on January 15, 1943. The stage review featured the comedy duo Long & Short and the dancing Three Business Men of Rhythm, along with Patterson & Jackson, rotund dancers and entertainers known as "600 pounds of rhythm." The Hines band played to a packed house nightly. After closing at the Apollo, they embarked on a tour across the Midwest booked by Billy Shaw at the William Morris Agency.

While on the road, Charlie and Gillespie challenged each other on and off the bandstand. After hours, they hunkered down in hotel rooms, wood shedding and refining their new musical ideas. "I think they really complemented one another," said Trummy Young, a trombonist with the Hines band. "I think Diz got some things from Bird, and Bird got some things from Diz. But, every time they got on the stand, it was competitive. The two of them. They had blood in their eyes every time. They loved one another. But they would try to extend each other to make a move."[6]

The day after a Valentine's Day dance at the Savoy Ballroom in Chicago, Bob Redcross, the band's road manager, recorded their off-stage fireworks with a Sears Silvertone disc recorder during a jam session at the Savoy Hotel. Oscar Pettiford, who was in town with Charlie Barnet, carried his bass several miles through frigid temperatures to sit in on the session. As Gillespie, Pettiford, and Charlie jammed, Bob Redcross recorded the session on ten-inch metal discs coated with cellulose acetate. On "Sweet Georgia Brown" Gillespie states and embellishes the melody, then, after a pause, improvises on the theme with a staccato burst of notes. Charlie follows with three brilliantly executed choruses. Gillespie answers with three choruses. With time running out on the disc, Redcross flipped the disc over in time to capture Charlie's fluid five choruses urged on by Gillespie, shouting in the background, "Come on, Yard!" After three more choruses by Gillespie, the two take it home in the last eight bars. Night after night, Charlie and Gillespie challenged each other until they came together in what Gillespie later described as "one heartbeat."[7]

The band returned to New York in early March 1943 for a series of dates on the East Coast. During an engagement at Princeton University, Charlie met Albert Einstein. The band arrived early for the dance, so Charlie and saxophonist Junior Williams took a stroll around campus. Charlie spied Albert Einstein walking across campus wearing a black fez and bulky wool sweater. Charlie introduced himself and the two hit it off. Einstein invited Charlie and Williams to his house. The two spent the afternoon discussing the Theory of Relativity and other weighty subjects over tea and crumpets.[8]

While on tour, Charlie married again. During an engagement at the Howard Theater in Washington, D.C., in early April, Charlie married Geraldine Marguerite Scott, an attractive dancer in the stage show. Charlie, caught up in the passion of the moment, exchanged vows with Geraldine while he was still legally married to Rebecca. Years later, Rebecca remembered Geraldine as the other woman in Kansas City who exchanged love notes with Charlie. Trumpeter Bennie Harris recalled how "at times Bird really gave his wife Jerry [*sic*] a hard time. He would always be taking her wedding ring and pawning it or use it as bait to make chicks."[9] Like Charlie, Geraldine loved the nightlife. She soon shared his habit. The newlyweds stayed together for a short time before drifting apart. Years later during the litigation over Charlie's estate, Geraldine observed, "When I married him, all he had was a horn and a habit. He gave me the habit, so I might as well have the horn."[10]

Initially, Charlie's massive consumption of alcohol liberally mixed with a wide array of opiates, nutmeg, marijuana, downers, and uppers did little to dim his brilliance as an improviser or the crispness of his photographic memory. His ability to play from memory baffled Earl Hines. Buddy Anderson disclosed:

> He [Charlie] had a photographic memory. . . . He would sit down and play some altogether foreign music. . . . He would rehearse with the group and read the music [for] the first show; and after that he would close the book. Earl Hines challenged him once about that. He was new to the Hines band and Earl didn't know it. And he closed his book and Earl just stepped up to see what he was doing, to reprimand him about it, apparently. And Earl stood there and the man [Charlie] was playing perfectly and consequently Earl wound up not saying a word. . . . He [Charlie] could go back later, months later, and he could play the same music. And not the first part, the lead, that was easier to remember than the third part, which was what he played.[11]

Other times, Charlie used his amazing gift of recall to nod out on the bandstand, sitting straight up with saxophone to his pursed lips, dark glasses hiding his closed eyes.

As before with the McShann band, Charlie became undependable. "He [Charlie] used to miss as many shows as he would make," Billy Eckstine mused.

> Half the time we couldn't find Bird. He'd be sitting up somewhere sleeping. So often he missed the first show, and Earl used to fine him blind. . . . We got on him, too, because we were more or less a clique. We told him, "When you don't show, man, it's a drag because the band don't sound right. You know, four reeds up there, and everything written for five." We kind of shamed him. . . . Bird says, "I ain't gonna miss no more. I'm going to stay in the theatre all night to make sure I'm here." . . . Sure enough, we come to work the next morning; we get on the stand—no Bird. . . . We played the whole show, the curtains closed, and we're coming off the band cart, when all of a sudden we hear a noise. We look under the stand, and here comes Bird out from underneath. He had been under there asleep through the entire show![12]

Charlie later joked about his chronic tardiness, telling a friend, "My watch don't work that well. I don't show up to all my gigs."[13]

In May 1943, the Hines band embarked on a Blue Ribbon Salute Tour of army bases and dances across the South and back through the Midwest. On the road, the band navigated wartime restrictions imposed by the federal government. As World War II raged on, touring became a logistical nightmare, particularly for African American bands theat traveled great distances between engagements. At the outset of the war, the government rationed gasoline and tires, making it difficult for bands to travel by bus or car. In early 1943, the government began seizing buses for the war effort. Trains, the only other transportation alternative, were unreliable and usually packed with soldiers. Hines managed to obtain a bus for the band by agreeing to play army bases on the tour. In between, the band played dances in small towns along the way.

During the southern leg of the tour, the band encountered racial hostility at every turn. At a dance in Americus, Georgia, white patrons turned off the lights and threw cherry bombs on stage, sending band members scurrying for their lives. After a dance in Pine Bluff, Arkansas, Charlie verbally defused a racially charged altercation between Gillespie and an angry white patron. "I used to sit up on the bandstand during intermission," Gillespie explained.

> We were playing white dances, and during intermission you couldn't go out in the audience, so you stayed backstage. I was sitting at the piano, fooling around with something. Some white guy said, "Hey . . ." to me and thumped a nickel on the stand. And then he said, "When you come back on, play so-and-so." . . . I looked down at the nickel and up at this dude, and picked up the nickel and threw it someplace, and just kept playing. Later on that night, after the dance was over, I thought everyone had left and we could go to the "white" men's room. While they were dancing, all the men's rooms were "white" and the women's too. Anyway, I went in and came out of the men's room, and as I was coming out I saw this shadow behind my head coming down. This bottle was coming at my head. So I just happened to turn, just a little bit, and the guy caught me in the back of the head with this bottle. And boy, I really saw stars! But he didn't knock me out. I reached on the table and picked up one of those big, big bottles, a magnum bottle. I turned around and was just getting ready to hit this guy when about five guys grabbed me. And then Charlie Parker came along. Charlie Parker walked over to the guy who hit me and said, "You took advantage of my friend, you cur!" He called the guy a "cur." The guy probably didn't even know what a cur was, man. That was funny, because I know that peckawood didn't know what a cur was.[14]

Eckstine, Gillespie, Charlie, and other band members were glad to leave the South and return to the East Coast in July.

Shortly after returning to New York, Hines announced plans for another tour. Leery of traveling in the South, Eckstine, Charlie, Gillespie, and seven others quit the band. Eckstine wanted to form a big band featuring Charlie and Gillespie but lacked money to cover start-up costs, so band members went their own ways. Eckstine, who had recently married, worked as a single in the clubs on Fifty-Second Street. Gillespie freelanced, filling in with the Duke Ellington band before joining forces with bassist Oscar Pettiford at the Onyx Club on Fifty-Second Street. The Gillespie-Pettiford group became the first modern group on Fifty-Second Street. Charlie briefly reunited with Geraldine in Washington D.C. before returning to Kansas City.

Back in Kansas City, Charlie moved in with Addie, who had recently returned to Kansas City after spending several years living on a farm in Kansas. Back when Charlie left for New York with the McShann band in the winter of 1941, Addie moved to a farm in northern Kansas with her boyfriend, Augustus Daniels. Rebecca and Leon stayed behind and settled in with her parents in Kansas City, Kansas. Addie, unable to get along with Daniels, returned to Kansas City and bought a spacious, three-story brick house at 1535 Olive Street, right down the street from the house where Charlie grew up.[15] There was plenty of room in Addie's new home for Rebecca and Leon, but they remained in Kansas City, Kansas. Charlie, like his father years earlier, maintained his distance from his wife and son.

Charlie switched back to alto saxophone and quickly found work with a group led by bassist Winston Williams playing an extended engagement at Tootie's Mayfair. Tootie Clarkin, a retired policeman, operated the Mayfair, located at Seventy-Ninth Street and Wornall Road, just past the city limits, in an unincorporated area known as "out in the county." The clubs and roadhouses "out in the county" stayed open until daybreak. When the clubs in town closed at 1:30, carloads of drunken patrons caravanned to Tootie's, Mary's, and other clubs in the area to dance and carouse all night long. A colorful figure, Clarkin fussed over the chickens he raised behind the roadhouse and presided over the evening festivities. Charlie, who had worked for Clarkin off and on over the years, usually brought mischief, but Clarkin hired him time after time.

Clarkin recalled one early incident with Charlie. "When I first knew Charlie, he was getting high on nutmeg. One day I ran into the grocer who said, 'Tutty [sic], you sure must be making a lot of pies over there with all the nutmeg your club has been ordering.' I knew something was wrong and rushed back to the club to check up on the cats. I searched around, but couldn't find any trace of the spice. Finally, I looked under the bandstand and found the floor littered with cans of nutmeg. Later Charlie told me, 'Another sax player and I would chew spices and laugh at each other and our heads would enlarge and shrink. And if we didn't play, there'd be no more reed section.'" Another time after Charlie had been sleeping on a tabletop in the club for three nights in a row, Clarkin looked out the window to see the ground covered by a blizzard of empty white Benzedrine inhalers.[16]

The Williams group at Tootie's featured Charlie "Little Dog" Johnson on trumpet; Charlie's local connection, drummer Edward "Lil' Phil" Phillips; Buddy Anderson on trumpet and Leonard "Lucky" Enois on guitar; along with Charlie's pianist of choice, Edward "Sleepy" Hickcox, a slender, dreamy eyed modernist, who, according to Mary Lou Williams, "played almost as much piano as Art [Tatum], and in the hard keys A natural, B natural, E natural."[17] Buddy Anderson was eager to join the group to work with Charlie. "Leonard Enois offered me a job in his group which had Bird, and I quickly accepted," Anderson reported. "Bird had come out of the Earl Hines band. This group was taken over by Winston Williams for an engagement at Tootie's Mayfair. It was an extremely interesting combo with Little Dog, Bird and another sax, Sleepy Hickcox and Little Phil in the group and Bird writing charts. We soon had a reputation as one of the first bop groups in the country with traveling bands."[18]

Across the country, young musicians were jamming together in small groups, exploring new chord progressions and harmonies that would lead to bebop, the next innovation in jazz. Ironically, it was a big band led by Billy Eckstine that first introduced the new style to the national audience. After leaving the Hines band, Eckstine signed on as a single with Billy Shaw at the William Morris Agency and opened at Chick Goldman's Yacht Club on Fifty-Second Street. To avoid offending Jewish patrons by presenting an African American with a Jewish sounding name, the Yacht Club sensationally billed Eckstine as X-Tine.[19]

The Yacht Club soon closed, driven out of business by a wartime 20 percent cabaret tax recently imposed by the federal government to discourage prostitution. Concerned by the rise in venereal disease among servicemen patronizing taxi dance halls and cabarets where prostitutes often solicited, the government imposed the tax on clubs that featured dancers and entertainers. Instrumental groups were exempt from the tax. Club owners on Fifty-Second Street crowded the dance floors with tables and in protest posted "no tax" signs. The tax proved to be a boon to Gillespie, Charlie, and other modernists. Club owners on Fifty-Second Street turned away entertainers and dancers while opening their doors wide for small ensembles.[20]

Known as "Swing Street" to fans and simply the "Street" to musicians, Fifty-Second Street between Fifth and Sixth Avenues thrived during the war years. Servicemen flocked to the clubs, crowding the basements and ground floors of the dingy, four-story brown stones lining either side of the street, for one last night on the town before shipping out to the European theater. The swank exteriors of clubs, sporting neon signs and colorful awnings jutting out to the curb, belied the close, smoky interiors. Down the short, steep flights of stairs, young jazz fans crowded the bar to avoid paying the minimum charge. Along the sides and down the center of the narrow confines, patrons perched at the postage-stamp–size tables slapped together like dominos. The clubs featured modest bandstands crammed in the back corner next to the service door. Club Downbeat, the Three Deuces, the Spotlite Club, and the Onyx Club anchored the end of the street just west of Sixth Avenue. Beyond the main strip near Seventh Avenue, the spacious Kelly's Stable and the Hickory House, known for its hickory-fired steaks and recessed bandstand behind the bar, catered to traditionalists. Coleman Hawkins, Billie Holiday, Art Tatum, Stuff Smith, Slam Stewart, Ben Webster, Erroll Garner, Harry the Hipster Gibson, and scores of other top stars worked the small clubs up and down the street, disbanding and then regrouping with each change of venue.[21]

When the Yacht Club closed, Eckstine moved across the street to the Onyx Club, where he and Gillespie formed the first big bebop band. Eckstine drew from alumni of the Hines and McShann bands. "First I got Diz for MD [music director], then tried to get most of the other guys that left Earl," Eckstine explained. "Bird, meanwhile, had been working with Andy Kirk and Noble Sissle, but by this time was back in Chicago. I called Bird from New York and asked if he wanted to come in the band. I went into Chicago to get Jerry Valentine, Gail Brockman, Tom Crump and Shorty McConnell and brought Bird back. We came back to New York to rehearse, and we were all buddies . . . we were the clique. We knew the style of music we wished to play."[22] Charlie led the reed section, putting members through their paces with rigorous rehearsals.

Count Basie helped get the new band started by generously loaning Eckstine arrangements from his library. Gillespie rounded out the book with arrangements of his compositions, giving the band a distinctive modern style. "Our breathing and phrasing were different from all the other bands and naturally we sounded different," Gillespie related. "There was no band that sounded like Billy Eckstine's. Our attack was strong, and we were playing bebop, the modern style. No other band like this one existed in the world."[23]

Billy Shaw, who felt the band would fare better on the road playing the-aters and ballrooms than staying on Fifty-Second Street, booked a June tour extending down the East Coast, across the South and back up through the Midwest. Eckstine reluctantly agreed to the southern leg of the tour. Band members traveled in Jim Crow railroad cars, sleeping on hay in baggage cars.

The band stopped off in St. Louis for an engagement at the Plantation Club, a white club operated by the mob. Fed up with towing the Jim Crow line, Charlie, Eckstine, and the others breached the color barrier at the Plan-tation Club by repeatedly entering through the front door and fraternizing with patrons. Drummer Art Blakey recounted how Charlie protested the club's Jim Crow policy by breaking drinking glasses:

> The man told us all to come in through the back door. The guy is wigged. They [band members] all come in the front door havin' a ball. He said, "I don't want you to fraternize with the customers." When Charlie got to the intermission, they all sat at the tables and the guy was about to wig. He told someone, "You gotta get this band the hell out of here." The guys were carrying on something fierce despite the fact that gangsters were walking around with big guns up on their hips. They didn't scare Bird or anyone. Tadd Dameron was drinking a glass of water. Out of one of the beautiful glasses they had to serve the customers. Bird walked over to him saying, "Did you drink out of this, Tadd?" Tadd says, "Yeah." Bam! He smashes it, "It's contaminated. Did you drink out of this one?" "Yeah," Tadd says. Bam! "It's contaminated." He broke about two dozen glasses. A guy was glaring at Bird; he just looked back coolly. "'What do you want? Am I bothering you?" Bird asked him. "Are you crazy?" the guy asks. "Well, if you want to call me crazy," Bird replies. Then once again he turns to Tadd, "Did you drink out of this glass?" Bam. "It's contaminated." They put us out. They put Jeeters-Pillows [Jeter-Pillars] in our place at the Plantation and they sent us to the Riviera, which was a colored club.[24]

While in St. Louis, Charlie made a half-hearted attempt to reconcile with Rebecca. Addie watched Leon while Rebecca took the train to St. Louis. The high-flying Charlie and down-to-earth Rebecca, however, found little common ground. "I thought it was a trip for us to get together, you know, like husband and wife," Rebecca recalled. "But he brought me to this little room after the gig and asked me did I want something to drink. I said no and we took off our clothes and went to bed. Nothing happened. The next morning he gave me the keys to his mother's house. 'Here, take these to ma,' he said. I knew he wasn't coming home then and didn't want to face his mother."[25]

During the St. Louis engagement, Buddy Anderson developed tuberculosis and returned home to Oklahoma. Miles Davis, an intense trumpeter with a lyrical style, replaced Anderson. Davis, a wiry, strikingly handsome, dapper scion of a solid, middle-class family, planned to attend Juilliard in the fall. "That's when Billy Eckstine's band came to St. Louis and I got that chance to play with them for two weeks," Davis recalled. "This really made up my mind for me to go to New York and attend Juilliard. . . . After I had heard and played with Charlie Parker, Dizzy Gillespie, Buddy Anderson . . . Art Blakey, Sarah Vaughan, and Mr. B himself, I *knew* I had to be in New York where the action was."[26]

The Eckstine band's frantic modern style thrilled Davis and other young musicians, but left swing fans cold. "We never had any problems with the young musicians; they loved it; they loved the band," Gillespie explained. "Everywhere we'd go there was a following of young musicians. But the populace, in general, and the powers that be, that booked the bands, and the clubs were used to listening to a certain type of music. They were not thrilled by us coming in; young, wild, crazy young cats playing this style. I remember one place we worked, the man wanted to give me some money to go downtown and buy some stock arrangements."[27]

Dizzy Gillespie set the band's brash, modern tone by stocking the band's library with his compositions and showcasing the all-star trumpet section featuring Howard McGhee, Gail Brockman, and Marion Hazel. *Down Beat*, reviewing the band in Chicago, noted that the "trumpet quartet grabbed the spotlight during the band's stay at the Regal Theater here," adding "the band plays some terrific double-timed specials such as 'Salt Peanuts,' 'Night in Tunisia' and 'Blitz,' all arranged by Dizzy Gillespie."[28] The review mentioned Charlie and other members only in passing. Charlie disdained Gillespie's grandstanding and chafed at the constraints of the big band. Years later he observed, "A big band slows anybody down, because you don't get a chance to play enough."[29]

In August 1944, the band returned to New York. After a September engagement at the Apollo Theater, Selective Service agents appeared backstage and ordered band members to report to the draft board. The next day, Charlie and the others reluctantly reported for duty. "I think most of the guys didn't have draft cards," drummer Art Blakey explained. "The authorities didn't know what to do so finally they got us. They waited until we opened at the Apollo, and then they went down there and sent for all the guys to join the army. They sent for Bird, to come down and join. He went in a phone booth and went to sleep, and he stayed in there all day and then came out and went back to the gig. They didn't want nothing to do with him." In the end, the board rejected Charlie, Blakey, and other band members, sending them home with red cards, advising that they "would be a great risk to the U.S. Forces, never to be recalled."[30]

Charlie left the Eckstine band in September and joined the Ben Webster group at the Onyx Club, one of the top clubs on Fifty-Second Street. The Webster band featured Argonne Dense Thornton on piano, Bill DeArango on guitar, Bill Beason on drums, and Leo Guarneri on bass.[31] Pianist Toy Wilson entertained the audience during intermission. Charlie graciously treated the less-experienced sidemen as equals, and they rose to the occasion. Delighted to have the opportunity to work regularly on Fifty-Second Street, Charlie spent the fall through early winter of 1944 working with the Webster band. Gillespie soon joined Charlie on Fifty-Second Street.

Gillespie left the Eckstine band in early January 1945. He freelanced on Fifty-Second Street and recorded for a number of small, independent labels that sprang up in the wake of the repeal of the recording ban. As the recording ban had dragged on, one by one the labels gave in to the union's conditions, and the ban ended in November 1944. With the major labels Columbia, Decca, and Victor slow to resume production, Manor, Savoy, Musicraft, and other small, nimble labels stepped in to fill the void.

On January 4, 1945, Charlie and Gillespie reunited as sidemen for a recording session led by pianist Clyde Hart, featuring blues shouter Rubberlegs Williams. Like Al Haig, Erroll Garner, and other pianists plying their trade on Fifty-Second Street, Hart absorbed the new style. A rising star known for playing the modern style left handed, Hart won a recording contract with the recently established Continental label, one of a number of small labels capitalizing on the musicians playing on Fifty-Second Street.

During the early morning session, blues shouter Rubberlegs Williams inadvertently drank Charlie's Benzedrine-spiked coffee, sending the already musically baffled vocalist's performance over the top. Trummy Young recounted the incident:

> We had all worked down on Fifty-Second Street, we used to record after work, and everyone was feelin' pretty mellow by then. Teddy Reig, who was running Roost Records then, got us all together. . . . This was all for this blues date with the singer, Rubberlegs Williams. He was a favorite at the Apollo Theatre—he'd dance, kick real high, sing the blues. He was a real big guy, and everybody was real scared cuz he was so big and bad. Anyway we . . . all had coffee and drinks and everything. The coffee was lined up in cups on the table. Charlie wasn't feeling so good that night so he took—well in those days, they had Benzedrine inhalers. . . . everyone of those inhalers was the equivalent of about 70 Benzedrine tablets. So Bird broke open one and put the paper in his coffee, let it sit there. Now Rubberlegs was drinking this *bad* liquor, and he was feeling pretty good. But in the meantime—just before we got started recording—he got ahold of one of the cups of coffee and drank it. But he got the wrong coffee—he drank Bird's coffee! And Bird was drinkin' Rubberlegs' coffee—which had nothing in it—and Bird says, "Damn, this stuff don't move me anymore! My tolerance is gettin' terrible man . . . I don't even *feel* this thing!" . . . We got to playing and Rubberlegs got hot in the studio, with the lights on, because the Benzedrine was making him sweat. He was getting ringing wet, man, and he was hollerin,' "It's too hot in here, what's the matter!?" He was screechin' and his voice was going . . . so Dizzy was playing some flatted fifths behind him. Rubberlegs wasn't used to hearing it, so he said "Stop the music!" and told Dizzy, "If you don't stop playing those wrong notes behind me, I'm gonna kill you!" Now his fists were as big as hams! So he told Teddy Reig, "Turn out all the lights!" It was the funniest thing I ever saw in my life. . . . I don't think they got one decent side out of that date."[32]

The session continued without Williams. Trummy Young took over vocal duties for the remaining four tunes. These mismatched recordings broke no new musical ground, outside of finely crafted solos by Charlie and Gillespie, but they set the stage for future sessions together.

The next week, Gillespie inadvertently coined "bebop," the phrase that defined the new movement during his first recording session as a leader. On January 9, 1945, Gillespie, joined by Oscar Pettiford and Don Byas from the Onyx Club band, recorded four selections for the Manor label, including his own compositions "Salted [Salt] Peanuts" and "Be-Bop," one of the combinations of syllables he used to articulate the structure of his phrasing to his sidemen. "Dizzy tried to hum everything; he had to hum everything to everybody to get them to see what he was talking about," Budd Johnson disclosed.

> It could be hard to explain it. It could be notated, but it was very hard to read, because cats weren't used to reading—he would be writing in double time, but the rhythm would be going [sings rhythm], so you gotta feel a double time feel against a 'one, two, three, four,' say, and then therefore you're looking at sixteenth notes and sixteenth rests and thirty-second rests . . . which the cats were not used to doing. . . . then you gotta get the melodic structure of it, and once you heard how it goes you say, "Oh." So he [Gillespie] would sing, and actually [that's] how I think that it got its name bebop. Because he would be humming this music, and he'd say, "Ooop bop ta oop a la doo bop doo ba," So people said, "Play some more of that bebop" because he would be saying "Bebop." And the cats would say, "Sing some more of that bebop," and actually, I think that's how it got its name, because that's the way he would have to sing it to make you get the feeling that he wanted you to play with.[33]

The recording "Be-Bop" received little critical acclaim, but the phrase stuck. By the summer of 1945, bebop and its variant "rebop" defined the new music.

Many skeptical older musicians and critics scoffed at the new music. Louis Armstrong publicly denounced bebop as "jujitsu music." He strongly criticized the movement and its creators: "Bop is ruining music . . . and the kids that play bop are ruining themselves. Playing bop tears a kid's lips apart in two years. With good tone, a sense of phrasing, and imagination, you can play forever. But these kids won't even learn. They don't care about their appearance, they don't care about nothing."[34]

Howard McGhee received plenty of grief from older musicians for play-ing the new style on Central Avenue in Los Angeles. "The musicians out there hated us, man," McGhee exclaimed. "They thought we were bringin' somethin' there to destroy their kingdom. They hated it. Kid Ory an' them, they hated me. Oh, boy! We went in this joint to work. After we played the first set, Kid Ory stormed out of there. 'I *will* not play with this kind of mu-sic.'"[35] The modernists referred to the traditionalists as "moldy figs."

For their part, younger musicians along with Leonard Feather, Barry Ulanov, and other progressive critics considered the new movement a "bit of fresh air in the otherwise too stagnant swing music of today."[36] In Sep-tember 1945, *Down Beat* weighed in lightly on the controversy. An unnamed critic, with tongue planted firmly in cheek, theorized that the style originated not with Charlie and Gillespie, but in the music of Igor Stravinsky. "Much controversy," the critic wrote, "has arisen over the claims of altoist Charlie Parker and trumpeter Dizzy Gillespie to the origination of their fantastic and exciting 're-bop' style (which is used for the lack of a more appropriate title or description). Those involved in the current question may be interested in the fact that in most all Stravinsky's works, particularly *Rites of Spring* [sic], the basic 're-bop' idea is frequently and obviously scored."[37] Ironically, Charlie was extremely fond of classical music, particularly Stravinsky. While trav-eling with the Hines band, Charlie had pored over Stravinsky's scores and quoted the composer onstage.

In February 1945, Gillespie assembled a small combo for a follow-up ses-sion for the Guild label. Finding Charlie otherwise engaged, Gillespie used Dexter Gordon, a tall tenor saxophonist who bore an uncanny resemblance to boxer Joe Louis. The band recorded two Gillespie originals, "Groovin' High" and "Blue and Boogie," during the makeshift session. Gillespie and Gordon had briefly worked together in the Billy Eckstine band, but they failed to click in the studio. Guild rejected the take of "Groovin' High." Less than satisfied with the results, Gillespie brought Charlie to the next session.

Gillespie and Charlie entered the studio on February 29, 1945, joined by pianist Clyde Hart, guitarist Remo Palmieri, humming bassist Slam Stew-art, and swing drummer Cozy Cole. In quick succession the band recorded "Groovin' High," the popular standard "All the Things You Are," and a new

Gillespie composition, "Dizzy Atmosphere." Gillespie based "Groovin' High" on the chord changes of the pop standard "Whispering." Charlie and Gillespie introduce the theme with a sinuous unison line taken at a bright tempo, punctuated by Hart's percussive piano exclamations. Charlie follows with a brilliantly constructed solo giving way to an oddly out-of-place sawing bass solo by Slam Stewart. Gillespie then takes a muted turn, echoing Charlie's solo, followed by a brief measured solo by Palmieri. Gillespie dramatically wraps things up with a legato nod to Bunny Berigan, a coda later adapted by Tadd Dameron for his composition "If You Could See Me Now." In a more traditional, bordering on danceable, approach to "All the Things You Are," Gillespie, Charlie, Stewart, Hart, and Palmieri trade solos, playing the melody fairly straight in a medium tempo. Charlie and Gillespie launch into "Dizzy Atmosphere," a pure bop romp based on the changes of "I Got Rhythm," with a jaunty chase chorus highlighted by triplets. Charlie and Gillespie settle into the shout chorus, exchanging spirited solos leading to a solo turn on bowed bass by Stewart. The two come back together for the coda with a unison line. These first recordings by Gillespie and Charlie, along with an even more successful follow-up session that produced "Salt Peanuts," "Shaw 'Nuff," and "Hot House" a few months later, led to the formation of their first group.

Charlie and Gillespie, the two recognized leaders in the field, came together in a marriage of convenience, united by their pursuit of a new musical breakthrough but separated by differing personalities and lifestyles. Charlie and Gillespie clicked professionally, but they differed greatly in personality and lifestyle. Gillespie's outrageous wardrobe topped off with a beret and goatee along with his on-stage antics belied his virtuosity and otherwise traditional lifestyle. His clowning onstage and blatant self-promotion gave jazz critics ammunition to blast his credibility as a serious artist. Charlie's cool detachment and control on stage masked his tumultuous personal life marred by capricious behavior and drug use. Socially, they traveled in different circles.

On convergent musical paths since they first met in Kansas City at the corner of Nineteenth and Vine five years earlier, Charlie and Gillespie at last joined forces in the spring of 1945 at the Three Deuces. Their small combo defined and set the standard for the still-emerging style. Gillespie recalled:

The height of the perfection of our music occurred in the Three Deuces with Charlie Parker. He'd gotten in touch with me, played in the [Eckstine] big band, and finally we'd assembled in a setting ideal for our music, the quintet. With Yard and Max [Roach], Bud Powell and Curley [sic] Russell, aw, man it was on fire all the time. . . . Bud Powell was the definitive pianist of the bebop era. He fitted in with us more than anybody else because of the fluidity of his phrasing. . . . Curley Russell started off with us and then Ray Brown took his place. Curley couldn't read well but he could swing. . . . Yard and I were like two peas. . . . His contribution and mine just happened to go together, like putting salt in rice. Before I met Charlie Parker my style had already developed, but he was a great influence on my whole musical life. The same thing goes for him too because there was never anybody who played any closer than we did. . . . Sometimes I couldn't tell whether I was playing or not because the notes were so close together. . . . The enunciation of the notes, I think, belonged to Charlie Parker because the way he'd get from one note to another, I could never. . . . What I did was very much an extension of what Roy Eldridge had done—Charlie Parker definitely set the standard for phrasing our music, the enunciation of notes.[38]

In the same succinct manner that distinguished his style, Charlie explained, "It's just music. . . . It's trying to play clean and looking for the pretty notes."[39]

In May 1945, Gillespie, armed with more ambition than organizational skills, introduced bebop to a broader audience with a concert at Town Hall on Forty-Third Street. The concert, produced in conjunction with popular local disc jockey Symphony Sid Torin under the auspices of the New Jazz Foundation, started off with a bang then fizzled when Count Basie, Teddy Wilson, Georgie Auld, and other advertised jazz luminaries failed to show. Barry Ulanov, reviewing the concert for *Metronome*, reported that

Dizzy's boys played through the first half of the concert unrelieved, and the effect was stunning. "Shaw 'Nuff" (named for booker Billy Shaw), "Night in Tunisia," "Groovin' High," "Be Bop," "'Round about Midnight," and "Salt Peanuts" played in programmed order, were run off magnificently by Dizzy and Charley [sic] in that opening half. Dizzy and Charley played their unison passages with fabulous precision, no easy achievement when your lips and fingers are so tangled up in mad running-triplet figures. Charley's solos almost never failed to get a roar from the audience because of his habit of beginning them with a four-bar introduction in which the rhythm was suspended (as in a cadenza), then slamming into tempo, giving his listeners a tremendous release, an excited relief. Al Haig played pleasant piano in Dizzy's groove and Curley [Curly Russell] and Harold [West] played well; the former with an unusual regard for pitch and a big bass tone; the latter with a good feeling for Dizzy's style, all the more impressive when you realize that he is not his regular drummer.[40]

The second half of the concert fell to pieces when the top-billed stars failed to show, leaving Symphony Sid to hem and haw in hipster jargon on stage, barraged by a chorus of catcalls from concert goers demanding their money back. A second Town Hall concert the following month suffered the same fate when Coleman Hawkins, Slam Stewart, and other headliners failed to show. In a role reversal, Gillespie took the critical heat for the botched productions, while Charlie basked in the limelight.

Charlie's career and personal life flourished. While working at the Three Deuces, Charlie fell in love with an attractive young dancer named Chan Richardson. Born Beverly Dolores Berg, Chan grew up in a privileged home in Yonkers but came of age in the Cotton Club and Fifty-Second Street. Chan came from a show-business family. Her Jewish father produced vaudeville shows and her mother was a former dancer at the Ziegfeld Follies. Chan's father bought her expensive clothes and indulged her every whim. He died when she was a child, leaving the family with a modest insurance settlement, which her mother went through in four years. Forced to go back to work, Chan's mother ran the concessions at the Cotton Club. Chan helped with the stand. Night after night, she watched a parade of jazz stars, including Duke Ellington, Cab Calloway, Sister Rosetta Tharpe, and Ethyl Waters. While hanging around the Cotton Club, Chan grew accustomed to socializing with African Americans and became attracted to musicians. She developed a schoolgirl crush on Cab Calloway.

Chan began dancing professionally as a teen while attending Professional Children's School in New York City. After an ill-fated trip to New Orleans with a chorus line, she hitchhiked back to New York and moved into her mother's apartment at 7 West Fifty-Second at the foot of Swing Street. Chan found work as a checkroom girl and photographer in the clubs lining the street. She spent the rest of her time circulating on the street, checking out the scene. Hip, with exotic features and wavy auburn hair, Chan attracted the attention of musicians and pimps who worked the street. Robert Sylvester crowned her "The Queen of 52nd Street" in an article about the clubs on Fifty-Second Street for *Collier's Magazine*."[41]

Chan first met Charlie when he stopped by her apartment building with some friends. She remembered:

> Someone brought him to 7 West and, although he wasn't handsome or physically attractive to me, his magnetism and experience were different from any of the men I had known," Chan remembered. "He had been married twice, had a young son and an old habit. I liked him. He was sweet, gentle, and always cheerful with me. He soon became my confidant and best friend. Insensitive as I was to his love for me, I would confide my latest passion. He never reproved me. One night I was dozing on the couch in someone's 52nd Street pad. Bird dropped by. He sat on the edge of the couch and whispered the love he had kept silent. It startled me into thinking about him in a different way. It also frightened me because his feelings were deeper than mine. I wasn't ready to get deeply involved, so we kept it light. We hung out. He dropped by or I went to the club. We smoked reefers together and were buddies.[42]

Smitten with Chan, Charlie wooed her with afternoon movies and malts at Belle's, an ice cream shop at 149th and Broadway. Charlie and Chan celebrated her coming-of-age birthday with a nocturnal romp uptown. "On my twenty-first birthday," Chan recalled,

> I went to the Three Deuces around midnight. Bird was working there with Diz, Max, Al Haig, and Curly Russell. During a solo, he spotted me and interpolated "Happy Birthday." Then he grabbed Diz's arm and told him to play "All the Things You Are," which he always called "YATAG." Like all good players, he knew the lyrics of this song, and "You are the angel glow" was his favorite. That was a lovely birthday present. After the gig, we went uptown. First we went to Bird's pad on 149th Street where he rolled a joint as big as a cigar and insisted that I smoke it all. . . . Then we walked along upper Broadway, which was just waking up. A few people were waiting for the trolley to take them to work, sitting on the benches in the island which divided uptown and downtown traffic. . . . Bird lit a railroad flare, which was his special surprise birthday gift for me. I had no idea where he found it, but it set off a startling

light in the early dawn. Mixed couples were apt to be met with hostility, and we were attracting a lot of attention with our hissing cerise torch. . . . Besides, I was stoned. "That's beautiful, Bird. I'd love to have a dress that color, but let's split before the fuzz comes," I pleaded. We ran up Broadway hand in hand, followed by hostile glances from the gray people we left behind to watch my sputtering end of a perfect day."[43]

Their friendship blossomed into romance, and one night they made love in Charlie's apartment on 149th Street. While enthralling Charlie, Chan fell into a side romance with pianist Argonne Thornton. The two rendezvoused in a room Thornton rented from Doris Sydnor, a hatcheck girl on Fifty-Second Street. One evening Chan overslept in Thornton's room and showed up late for a date with Charlie. Doris, who was enamored of Charlie, told him about Chan and Thornton. Stunned by Chan's fickleness, Charlie ended their relationship and took up with Doris.

After a brief courtship, Charlie moved into Doris's apartment at 411 Manhattan Avenue in lower Harlem. The interracial couple raised few eyebrows on Fifty-Second Street, where African Americans and whites mixed freely. Doris, tall and gangly with a buck-toothed grin and dark hair swept up on top of her head, adored Charlie. Like Addie, she doted on Charlie, buying him Broadway pinstripe suits and silk ties. Doris took care of business, paying bills and tending to domestic details, freeing Charlie to concentrate on his career.

Charlie soon split with Gillespie and formed his own band. The quintet abruptly disbanded after closing at the Three Deuces in early July. Gillespie, bucking the national movement to small ensembles, assembled an eighteen-piece big band complete with a floorshow for a tour of the South and West booked by the William Morris agency. Billed as the Hep-Sations of 1945, the show featured Billy Eckstine's wife, June, on vocals, the tap-dancing Nicholas Brothers, along with Patterson & Jackson. Charlie declined Gillespie's invitation to join the band as star soloist. Instead, Charlie capitalized on his growing critical acclaim and formed his own combo on Fifty-Second Street.

Charlie's association with Gillespie and his critically acclaimed performances at the Town Hall concerts caught the attention of more mainstream jazz fans, enabling him to step out for the first time as a leader. As a sweltering heat wave settled over the city in mid-July, the Charlie Parker Quintet featuring Don Byas tenor, Al Haig piano, Curly Russell bass, and Stan Levey drums opened at the Three Deuces on a double bill with the Erroll Garner Trio. Leonard Feather noted Charlie's debut as a bandleader in his column "Manhattan Kaleidoscope" in *Metronome*. "For instance, a month ago the band at the Three Deuces was Dizzy Gillespie's featuring Charlie Parker. . . . This month it's Charlie Parker's band with Don Byas's tenor replacing the Dizzy trumpet; Curly Russell is still on bass and Al Haig is expected back." Feather went on to praise Charlie's genius. "Parker is the most phenomenal and frantic alto man ever. His partnership with Byas in a collection of weird originals, played almost entirely in lightning unison, is as effective as it was with Dizzy, and his solo work is a reminder that if you must play 500 notes a minute, there are two ways of doing it: one as sheer technical display without harmonic imagination or dynamic variation (Jimmy Dorsey, Dick Stabile), two, by making every note mean something (Charlie Parker)."[44] Opening on Fifty-Second Street with his own group, Charlie had truly arrived in New York.

With Gillespie on the road, Charlie became the standard bearer of bop on Fifty-Second Street. The next month he formed a new group and moved down the street to the Spotlite Club, operated by Clark Monroe. *Down Beat* noted the personnel changes and the band's top-shelf status, proclaiming that the "highlight on 52nd Street is Charlie Parker and his combo, which opened last month at the Spotlite club. Charlie's great alto, complemented by drummer Stan Levy [Levey], Sir Charles [Thompson] on piano, bassist Leonard Gaskin, tenorman Dexter Gordon and Miles Davis on trumpet, cannot be outranked by many other outstanding attractions on the street."[45]

Beginning in late 1945, Fifty-Second Street began to change. The bright lights of the clubs lining Swing Street attracted hustlers who worked the crowds, dispensing marijuana and narcotics. Since arriving in New York, Charlie had attracted a growing entourage of jazz writers, hipsters, musicians, poets, artists, sexually curious young women, and drug dealers. Encouraged by Charlie, jazz's most notorious junkie holding court in the heart of Fifty-Second Street, the drug business picked up considerably, catching the attention of the narcotics squad.

In November, New York police, armed with an order charging that Fifty-Second Street served as a "rendezvous for persons engaging in the narcotics and marijuana traffic," swooped down on the clubs, shuttering the Three Deuces, Spotlite, Downbeat, and Onyx.[46] After a few nights of darkness, the clubs reopened with new lineups. Charlie, afraid of losing his cabaret card, which allowed him to work in New York, flew to Toronto, Canada, with Erroll Garner, Slam Stewart, Trummy Young, and other stars of Fifty-Second street for a concert at Massey Hall and a jam session with local admirers. The two-picture spread in *Down Beat* covering the event was the first in-print reference to Charlie as "Bird," a truncation of his nickname Yardbird, earned for his love of chicken while working with the McShann band.[47] At last, Yardbird had taken wing.

Later that month, Charlie made his first recordings as a leader. Shortly after returning to Fifty-Second Street, Charlie recorded for the Savoy label as a sideman with Art Tatum's guitarist Tiny Grimes. Impressed with Charlie's performance on the Grimes date and his growing reputation, Herman Lubinsky, the fireplug-shaped, cigar-chomping owner of Savoy, offered him a chance to record as a leader. Charlie approached the late-November 1946 session with the same spontaneity and disregard for convention that characterized his personal life. He lined up the personnel while composing new material on the fly. A spontaneous improviser, Charlie spun new melodies off the changes of popular standards or the blues, usually only sketching out the first eight bars. "He [Charlie] got a telegram from Savoy in the morning telling him to get a group together and make a recording date," recalled Argonne Thornton, the pianist for the session. "By 10:30 A.M., he had written the two new blues, 'Now's the Time' and 'Billie's Bounce' . . . , and for the other two numbers he planned to use a 'head' of his those fellows were playing then which was called 'Thriving from a Riff' on the record and later called 'Anthropology,' and finally 'Ko Ko'—which is based on the chords of 'Cherokee,' of course."[48] Charlie's method of creating new compositions from popular standards suited Lubinsky, who balked at paying mechanical rights for recording copyrighted songs.[49]

When lining up the band for the session, Charlie initially passed over Gillespie, who had recently returned to New York in the wake of a disastrous tour of the South with his big band, in favor of Miles Davis, a less experienced and more technically limited soloist. When Bud Powell backed out of the date, Charlie hastily recruited Gillespie for the piano slot. While by no means on par with Powell, Gillespie could comp his way through standards and the blues in a pinch. For a backup, in case he needed Gillespie in the front line, Charlie asked Argonne Thornton to stop by the session. Rounding out the rhythm section, Curly Russell and Max Roach supplied the sympathetic modern rhythmic texture lacking during Charlie's previous sessions as a sideman and with Gillespie.

The session proceeded in fits and starts. "Bird was having trouble with his horn," Teddy Reig, the producer for the session, recalled. "We tried everything to get it straight. Bird even poured a pitcher of water into the horn to get the pads wet. We had a big pool of water in the middle of the floor at WOR."[50] Charlie wrestled with the horn while leading the group through the head arrangements in the studio, leading to an inordinate number of takes on each selection. After struggling through three takes of a medium tempo blues in F major Reig dubbed "Billie's Bounce," the band broke the tension by ripping through a warm-up exercise based on the changes to "Cherokee," which Savoy later released as "Warming Up a Riff." Following two more tries, marred by fluffed notes and uneven phrasing by Davis, the band finally came together for the final take of "Billie's Bounce." Four takes of another blues, "Now's the Time," ensued, highlighting Charlie's Kansas City roots and deep feeling for the blues. Gillespie's chord substitutions on "Now's the Time" pushed Davis out of key with flatted fifths and major sevenths. Following a four-bar piano introduction to "Thriving on a Riff," based on the changes of "I Got Rhythm," Davis and Charlie exchanged solos. Rising to the occasion, Davis deftly navigated the passage with a fleet run of eighth notes. Following a stumbling solo by the neophyte Thornton, Charlie and Davis came back together, restating the head.

The session came to an abrupt halt when a union representative arrived to find the nonunion Thornton at the keyboards. Taking advantage of the break, Charlie rushed out to get his horn repaired. Reig, the producer, tagged along to keep an eye on Charlie.[51] Miles Davis, settling in for what appeared to be a long haul, took a nap on the floor. Returning to the studio armed with the retooled horn, Charlie embarked on a lazy improvisation, accompanied by Gillespie on piano, aptly titled, "Meandering," based on the changes of "Embraceable You," before wrapping up the session in short order with two takes of "Ko Ko."[52] Davis, nervous about his ability to navigate the tricky introductory passage of "Ko Ko," drawn from the changes of "Cherokee," deferred to Gillespie on trumpet for the final set. Tired of waiting in the wings, Gillespie wholeheartedly jumped in on trumpet, matching Charlie note for note through the breakneck tempo of the unison and solo statements in the introductory chorus. Serving double duty, Gillespie switched to piano in the bridge, accompanying Charlie's sharply executed solo that bristled with ideas.[53] In a nod to Art Tatum, Charlie delivered a musical one-liner, embellishing the melody of "Tea for Two." Following a melodic half-chorus solo by Roach, Charlie and Gillespie took things home with a tidy coda, restating the original theme. Charlie's haphazard approach to the session—failing to replace Bud Powell with an experienced pianist, using an alto in need of repair, and working through the head arrangements on the spot—undermined his first recording date as a leader. Ironically, when released nationally six months later to lukewarm revues, critics held Charlie blameless, praising his solos while panning the overall result. Reminded of the hassles and responsibilities of being a bandleader at the session, Charlie briefly reunited with Gillespie.

In early December 1945, Charlie and Gillespie bore the banner of bebop to the West Coast, only to be met by indifferent audiences. The William Morris Agency booked Gillespie for a two-month engagement at Billy Berg's supper club in Hollywood. He rounded up Charlie and Max Roach, along with two newcomers, vibraphonist Milt Jackson and bassist Ray Brown, for the trip west. Gillespie, under contract for a quintet, hedged his bets by bringing along Jackson to cover when Charlie failed to make the job. Al Haig, the band's pianist, had already arrived in Los Angeles. With the heat still on the clubs on Fifty-Second Street, Charlie readily joined the jaunt, figuring he could easily find a connection on Central Avenue. Boarding a train at Penn Station, Gillespie, Charlie, and company embarked on what turned out to be a long, hard journey. Fully taking wing in California, twenty-five-year-old Charlie soared above previous jazz conventions, only to plummet back to the ground, brought down by his own excesses.

Charlie with his half-brother John Anthony (Ike) Parker circa 1923. (Used by permission of the University of Missouri–Kansas City Libraries, Dr. Kenneth J. LaBudde Department of Special Collections.)

Charlie, top row, on the far left, and other students in front of Penn School, 1931. (Used by permission of the University of Missouri–Kansas City Libraries, Dr. Kenneth J. LaBudde Department of Special Collections.)

REBECCA RUFFIN
Boosters' Club
Girl Reserve
"Have you seen Charles?"

Charlie as a teenager. (Frank Driggs Collection)

Rebecca Ruffin Lincoln High School senior photo, Lincolnite, 1935. (Used by permission of the University of Missouri–Kansas City Libraries, Dr. Kenneth J. LaBudde Department of Special Collections.)

Musser's Ozark Resort where Charlie came of age musically in the summer of 1937. (Courtesy H. Dwight Weaver)

Charlie recording in Wichita with the McShann Band, November 30, 1940. (Used by permission of the University of Missouri–Kansas City Libraries, Dr. Kenneth J. LaBudde Department of Special Collections.)

Charlie with the Jay McShann band circa 1941. (Used by permission of the University of Missouri–Kansas City Libraries, Dr. Kenneth J. LaBudde Department of Special Collections.)

Charlie on stage with the Earl Hines band, 1943. (Courtesy Norman Saks)

Charlie on stage with Lucky Thompson, Dizzy Gillespie, and Billy Eckstine, Pittsburgh, summer, 1944. (Frank Driggs Collection)

Charlie and Dizzy Gillespie on stage at Town Hall, New York City, May 16, 1945.
(Frank Driggs Collection)

Publicity photo circa 1948. (Frank Driggs Collection)

Dean Benedetti and Max Roach escorting Charlie out the back door
of the Three Deuces, April, 1948. (Frank Driggs Collection)

Charlie and Sarah Vaughan doing an in-store signing at Klayman's Records in Cincinnati during the Jazz at the Philharmonic tour, spring, 1948. (Courtesy Norman Saks)

Birdland, 1956. (Courtesy Frank Driggs Collection)

Publicity photo taken by William Fambrough, Kansas City circa 1952. (Courtesy of William Fambrough, Jr.)

Charlie soloing in front of the Graham Topping Band at Massey Hall Concert, May 15, 1953.
(Frank Driggs Collection)

CHAPTER 5

Relaxing at Camarillo

On the way from New York to Los Angeles, the band stopped off in Chicago to switch to the Super Chief, a sleek express train that made the trip from Chicago to Los Angeles in less than forty hours. During the ten-hour layover, band members stopped by a jam session at a club on the South Side. Despite Gillespie's best efforts to get Charlie and other band members back to the train station on time, they lingered too long at the session and missed the Chief, which made the trip to Los Angeles only once a week. Having missed their connection, the band had to take the South West Limited, a passenger train that delivered mail to small towns along the way, adding two days to the journey.[1]

Charlie ran out of heroin and went into withdrawal during the unexpectedly long journey. As the train paused at a depot in the Nevada desert, Gillespie looked out the window and saw Charlie staggering off on foot in the desert with his saxophone case under his arm, searching for a fix. Not quite believing his eyes, Gillespie woke up drummer Stan Levey and asked, "What the hell is that out there?" Levey replied, "I think it's your sax player." Levey hopped off the train and dashed over to where Charlie was attempting to crawl underneath a barbwire fence. Levey, who was physically fit from his avocation as a boxer, grabbed Charlie and carried him back to the train. Charlie sweated out the last twenty hours of the journey strapped to his bunk, sedated by whiskey.[2]

After finally arriving in Los Angeles, Charlie conned a doctor into writing a three-day prescription for morphine by faking kidney stones. He then connected with Emry Byrd, a portly character in a wheelchair who ran a shoeshine stand on Central Avenue. On the side, Byrd sold records, green Mexican marijuana, and brown heroin. Byrd, who was known on the street as Moose the Mooche, gladly extended Charlie a credit line.[3] The high cost and low quality of heroin available on Central Avenue bode ill for Charlie's stay in Los Angeles.

Gillespie's recordings arrived ahead of the band to the West Coast, only to be met by mixed reviews. The Tempo Music Shop received the Guild recordings in August 1945. Hal Holly, the Los Angeles correspondent for *Down Beat*, reported that "Dorothy (Mrs. Ross) Russell of the Tempo Music Shop, who had been expecting the stork, put a Dizzy Gillespie disc on a turn-table for a customer. After a few bars of Dizzy's horn she exclaimed, 'That did it!' [and] rushed to the hospital to welcome Erica, seven lbs., 12 oz."[4] Ironically, her husband Ross, a gangly, ruddy-complexioned former merchant marine, became a midwife for the new music, recording Charlie and Gillespie for his fledgling Dial label.

Ross Russell, who was at first skeptical of the new music, became a devotee during the band's debut at Berg's. Russell confessed that initially he found the recordings "incomprehensible bewildering. . . . They sold like made [*sic*] within a week we reordered. . . . After a month I was still dubious, but I was fascinated too and had began to listen. More great sides arrived: 'Congo Blues,' 'Ko Ko,' 'Red Cross.' Then came Dizzy's famous small band for a two-month engagement at Berg's . . . one of the greatest small bands of all time. The opening night completed my conversion."[5]

The Gillespie band opened at Billy Berg's Supper Club on a cool Monday night, December 10, 1945. A light green, one-story, frame-and-stucco building, Berg's sat at a right angle off Vine Street just south of Sunset Boulevard in the heart of Hollywood. Harry "the Hipster" Gibson, a trim, blond, fast-talking, frantic boogie-woogie pianist headlined the show. Born Harry Raab in the South Bronx, Gibson attended Julliard while playing Fifty-Second Street. A master at interpolating classical and barrelhouse, he performed at Carnegie Hall. He moved to California in 1945, where he established residency at Billy Berg's. Slim Gaillard, a lanky, jive-talking multi-instrumentalist, and his band featuring Bam Brown on bass supplied entertainment during intermission. The marquee heralded the Gillespie band's debut as "Bebop Invades the West."[6] That afternoon Berg, anticipating a large crowd, hung a standing room only sign on the marquee.

Musicians and hipsters packed Berg's early, crowding the fifty tables spread out in a semi-circle in front of the bandstand and the bar on the east side of the building. As the evening progressed, a line of patrons waiting to gain entrance stretched from the marquee south down Vine. Band members breezed in shortly after 8:00, the scheduled starting time. Milt Jackson arrived first, decked out in a double-breasted suit with a grey flannel shirt. After glancing at the audience, he went straight to the bandstand and started adjusting the settings on his vibes. While Jackson pecked out notes on his vibes, bassist Ray Brown and drummer Stan Levey entered, making small talk and ignoring the crowd. Pianist Al Haig followed, dressed conservatively in a sleeveless V-neck sweater with a starched white shirt and grey tie. Then Gillespie strolled in wearing a double-breasted suit with a rainbow-colored tie, topped off by his signature beret. He worked the room, mugging and greeting patrons. At show time, Charlie was nowhere to be found.[7]

The band mounted the bandstand, backed by sloping tan-upholstered panels, and launched into "Dizzy Atmosphere" at a breakneck tempo followed in quick succession by "Blue 'n Boogie," "Mean to Me," "Shaw 'Nuff," and a blues. The audience, anticipating Charlie's arrival, glanced restlessly at the door. Ross Russell clearly recalled Charlie's show-stopping entrance that evening:

> After the blues the musicians paused for breath, seemed to be on the point of a break, then decided against it. Dizzy looked several times at the doorway. Then Levey put away his sticks, picked up the jazz brushes and began laying down one of his fast shuffle rhythms on the snare drum. It was the fastest tempo yet played that evening. The tune was "Cherokee," the old Basie favorite, only faster. After a few bars the rhythm section was tracking and the horns began riding the sixty-four bar riff that the boppers had

retitled "Ko Ko." Charlie Parker walked through the doorway and through the crowded tables and aisle towards the bandstand.

Charlie was wearing the wrinkled trousers of an old suit, red suspenders, a white shirt, a tie with a thick, square knot and shortened ends, and a handsome new suede jacket. He was strong and chunky, with heavy shoulders, a broad chest, powerful hands and he looked younger than his twenty-five years. He smiled boyishly as he climbed onto the bandstand, fingered the saxophone and joined the ensemble. The band took on a new character. Everything was suddenly bigger, clearer, more authoritative. The music swung more. As good as the band had been without Bird, it was better now. Everything that had been played before seemed as a prelude, just a warm-up. The missing element had been found [and] fitted into place and now the music was whole, complete, inevitable. It was on a new level altogether. Something jazz had been striving towards for several generations of players.[8]

Down Beat noted the band's successful opening, declaring that it "looks like Billy Berg has a big draw in Dizzy Gillespie, to judge by turn-out on opening night."[9] Unfortunately for Berg, crowds dwindled after a few days. Los Angeles audiences were confounded by the new music. Art Tatum, Benny Carter, and other musicians continued attending the club, but the general public stayed away. Stan Levey recalled that, "Nobody got bruised or anything, but the reception was cool to the music. What they were used to in California was 'Slim and Slam,' Eddie Heywood entertainment as opposed to pure music. Everybody was asking, 'Well, where's the vocalist?' That was the thing, 'Who's going to do the singing here? Who's gonna tell the jokes?' That wasn't it. The pure jazz enthusiasts were all there, but the numbers were small."[10]

Gillespie, under pressure from Berg, added vocals. Charlie wrote a few vocal charts for band members. Gillespie also added tenor saxophonist Lucky Thompson, a big-toned tenor saxophonist in the tradition of Coleman Hawkins, to cover for Charlie, who chronically showed up late, high, or not at all. Charlie's continual tardiness strained his relationship with Gillespie. "So their relationship was rough because Diz was all business, and he says, 'We hit at nine-thirty, and goddamit, this is it, man!' 'We gotta hit!'" Levey described, "And Charlie wasn't hitting at nine-thirty. If he got there at eleven, that was good. So that ground their relationship to kind of a halt.

Because it was just unbearable to Dizzy. Dizzy was voracious in his drive to succeed, to get wherever he wanted to get with the bucks and the numbers, or whatever, and Charlie was oriented to drugs, to get his drugs. So there was a problem."[11]

While audiences at Berg's were indifferent to the new music, record buyers enthusiastically picked up on the new sound. The strong sales of bebop at the Tempo Music Store caught Ross Russell by surprise. Located on Hollywood Boulevard, just around the corner from Berg's, the Tempo Music Store opened in July 1945. Russell modeled his operation after the Commodore Music Shop, a small New York record store with a thriving jazz label. "The store became a battleground between 'mouldy figs' and hipsters, with the hipsters coming out on top after a few months," Ross related. "We ended up selling a lot more records by Dizzy Gillespie and Charlie Parker than we did of, say, Duke Ellington or even Benny Goodman."[12]

Based on the strong sales of bebop at his retail outlet, Russell jumped into the modern music field with both feet, only to stumble initially. In January 1946, Russell launched Dial Records with the financial backing of Marvin Freeman, a prominent attorney and professor of law at the University of Southern California. Russell, anxious to record Charlie and Gillespie for Dial before they returned to the East Coast, scheduled a session for January 21 at Electro Broadcast Studios, located on the edge of Forest Lawn Cemetery in Glendale, California.

With no time to waste, Russell skirted rules requiring the local union to sign off on Dial's contract for the session by using, as a proxy, Alex Compinski, the owner of Alco Records, a small label specializing in contemporary classical composers. Compinski let Russell use Alco's contract with the American Federation of Musicians for the session. Russell hired George Handy, a pianist working with Boyd Raeburn, to nominally lead the session. Russell brought along guitarist Arvin Garrison to supplement the lineup from Billy Berg's.

As the band warmed up, Charlie knocked Compinski back with a barrage of notes. Russell related the strong impression Charlie made on Compinski: "I was standing next to Compinski in the sound proof control room . . . in the studio when Charlie Parker attached the saxophone to his neck strap and played a trial scale burst of notes. At the sound of these notes Compinski staggered backwards as if he had [been] hit by a fusillade not of notes but bullets. 'Who's that fellow?' he demanded in an astonished voice."[13]

The session went rapidly downhill. Russell watched in dismay as hipsters who followed the band invaded the studio, causing the session to descend into chaos. "We had the studio for at least three hours, and during that time, we actually recorded one thing that was later released on Dial, a version of 'Diggin' Diz,'" Russell confided. "But the confusion was terrible. The hippies who jammed the studio kept interfering with the musicians and engineers, and I was too inexperienced to get the situation under control."[14] One musician complained to Russell that he found it hard to concentrate after one of the hipsters seduced the musician's girlfriend in the bathroom. Distracted by the hipsters moving in and out of the studio, the engineer left a microphone open, ruining the session.

Russell, undaunted by the chaos swirling around the studio, scheduled a follow-up session for two days later. Handy, put off by the disorder at the rehearsal, bowed out of the second session at the last minute, complaining that a band member called him a "dirty Jew." Russell, unable to locate Charlie, contacted Gillespie to salvage the date. Gillespie rushed the principal members of the band from Berg's into the studio. Getting right down to business, the band recorded six selections, including Charlie's "Confirmation" and Thelonious Monk's "'Round about Midnight," giving Russell enough recordings potentially to establish Dial as a serious player in the small-label field. Unfortunately, Gillespie recorded for Dial while under contract to the Musicraft label, forcing Russell to release the recordings under a pseudonym, the Tempo Jazz Men, featuring Gabriel on trumpet. Those in the know sought out the new releases, but casual fans passed over the discs, not noticing Gillespie's arranger credit in the fine print.

While mainstream acceptance eluded the band in Los Angeles, wider recognition arrived from the East. Charlie and Gillespie, having ranked in the 1945 *Down Beat* readers poll, joined an all-star lineup for the *Down Beat* Award Winners Concert in Philharmonic Auditorium in Los Angeles on January 28, 1946.[15] Norman Granz, who had vigorously denounced Charlie, Gillespie, and the New York scene in general just six months earlier in *Down Beat*, produced the concert. The event sold out, filling the auditorium to the brim and turning away two thousand eager fans. Charlie and Gillespie jammed with an all-star aggregation featuring Charlie Ventura, Willie Smith, Mel Powell, Nat Cole, Lester Young, Arnold Ross, and Howard McGhee, egged on by the roaring audience.

Backstage, after the first set, Gillespie, feeling rejected by West Coast audiences, groused to Barry Ulanov, jazz critic for *Metronome*, that his stay in Los Angeles "should have been a lot shorter," then left early.[16] Charlie, mindful of his humiliation years earlier at the Reno Club, stayed to show Lester Young what he had learned in the ensuing years. Ross Russell recalled Charlie's stunning climax. "Then Charlie Parker, following the man [Lester Young] who had been his idol, topped the whole performance," Russell declared. "His solo on *Lady Be Good* is one of his greatest improvisations. Of the improvisation, John Lewis, musicologist and director of the latter-day MJQ [Modern Jazz Quartet], said, 'Bird made a blues out of *Lady Be Good*. That solo made old men out of everyone onstage that night.'"[17]

During the final week at Berg's, a misunderstanding between Gaillard and Gillespie culminated in a brawl. Mrs. Gaillard overheard Gillespie commenting on how many "Uncle Toms" he had come across in Los Angeles. She assumed the remark was directed at her husband and took umbrage. A melee ensued that ended with Gillespie decking Gaillard then fending off Gaillard's wife with a chair when she came after him with a butcher knife.[18]

The Gillespie combo closed at Berg's on Monday, February 4, 1946, to the relief of all parties concerned. "We hit some grooves on the bandstand at Billy Berg's that I'll always remember, but the audience wasn't too hip," related Gillespie. "They didn't know what we were playing, and in some ways, they were more dumb-founded than the people down South. Just dumb-founded."[19] Berg, seeking to rid his club of the dead beats who followed the band, steered the music policy to mainstream by bringing in accordionist Milton Delugg. *Down Beat* reported that "Dizzy Gillespie was too much for the Hollywood 'hep-cats' who frequent Billy Berg's. The spot has been generally crowded during Dizzy's stay but too many were professionals."[20]

The next Saturday, Gillespie, Al Haig, and Stan Levey flew back to New York. Charlie, Ray Brown, and Milt Jackson stayed behind in Los Angeles. While Jackson and Brown gave Gillespie ample notice of their intent to remain in Los Angeles, Charlie, true to form, vanished at the last minute. Unable to locate Charlie the morning of the flight, Gillespie gave Charlie's ticket to Stan Levey, who spent the better part of the morning searching for him—to no avail. Gillespie finally gave up and left Charlie's ticket and pay at the desk of the Civic Hotel. Charlie cashed in the ticket and stayed in California.

The trip to Los Angeles ended one of the most creative musical partnerships in the history of jazz. Charlie and Gillespie remained friendly, but they never again worked together on a regular basis in a group. While they continued to share the bandstand at concerts occasionally, offstage they drifted apart creatively and socially.

The steadfast Howard McGhee and other fans helped Charlie get established in Los Angeles. "Diz and he had split up," McGhee stated. "Gillespie went back to New York, and Bird stayed on scuffling. He used to come by where I was playing at a place called The Streets of Paris, and I used to give him a little bread to keep him going."[21] Charlie joined as a regular member when the McGhee band switched to the Finale Club located downtown near the corner of First and San Pedro Streets in the area that had been known as Little Tokyo before the Japanese residents were rounded up and packed off to internment camps.

The Finale, a narrow, crowded, after-hours haunt perched at the top of two flights of stairs, operated as a bottle club, where patrons brought their own liquor and purchased soft drinks and mixer set-ups. McGhee's wife, a stunning blond and former model, collected a cover charge at the door, stashing the money in a cigar box. McGhee led the band, featuring Charlie as the star soloist. Young progressive musicians flocked to the late-night sessions at the Finale, jamming into the next morning. "The Finale soon became a West Coast Minton's," Russell observed. "The low ceiling made for excellent acoustics, and Charlie's presence acted as a magnet for resident and visiting jazzmen, among them Stan Getz, Zoot Sims, Miles Davis, Gerry Mulligan, Red Rodney, Hampton Hawes, Serge Chaloff, Shorty Rogers, Ralph Burns, Johnny Bothwell, Gerald Wilson, Sonny Criss, and Charlie Ventura. Sessions at the Finale Club were probably the finest in the country in 1946, Minton's and the Street notwithstanding. When the music at the Finale had settled into its three-o'clock groove, Foster Johnson [the owner], a slender man of effortless movement, would spring lightly onstage and improvise steps to 'A Dizzy Atmosphere' or 'Now's the Time.'"[22]

On off nights, Charlie made the round of jam sessions, encouraging younger musicians along the way. Pianist Hampton Hawes and other up-and-coming players worshiped Charlie. "When Bird opened at Billy Berg's, I made the scene that night. I was seventeen and it changed my entire life," Hawes explained. "Bird played a bridge on 'Salt Peanuts' that was so strong that I was stamped for life, right there, like a piece of clay. A few weeks later I was jamming with Gene Montgomery and some others at the Bird-in-the-Basket when Bird came in and one of the musicians on the stand said, 'Let's play bebop.' I thought they meant the tune, not the style, as I had just learned the riff and the chords off Dizzy's record of it for Manor, so I began playing 'Bebop.' Bird's face lit up and he sent out to the car for his horn and came and sat in with us. 'That's crazy!' he said 'You young cats really know the tune!'"

"I saw a lot of Bird after that," Hawes recalled. "He was wonderful to me, like a big brother. I played with him at the Finale and after the Finale folded at the Hi-De-Ho with the Howard McGhee band. Bird could never get enough of jamming. It was a habit he picked up in Kansas City. If he couldn't find musicians in a spot he would go around waking them up."

But Hawes added, "Bird was unpredictable in his moods. Sometimes he'd say nothing for hours. Another time he'd talk up a storm. He lectured me about keeping my music pure and being my own man and not getting hung up on narcotics. He told me that he had gotten hooked with a habit as a kid in Kansas City and that he couldn't stop. 'Do as I say' he would tell me, 'not as I do'"[23] Unfortunately, Hawes and others ignored Charlie's warning about using narcotics and suffered the consequences.

Young musicians and hipsters from across the country filtered into Los Angeles to check out Charlie. In February, Chan Richardson, who was two months pregnant from an affair with a sportswriter in Canada, arrived in Los Angeles. Chan had been dancing with a revue in Chicago, when she met a Hollywood producer who offered her and a girlfriend jobs and a place to stay in Los Angeles. Eager to see Charlie again, she took the producer up on his offer and caught a train packed with soldiers to Los Angeles. Chan quickly located Charlie at a house he was sharing with tenor saxophonist Gene Montgomery. "The day I tracked him down, he was alone, playing his horn, and I followed the sound," Chan related. "We had a tender, friendly reunion. . . .

Now I had to tell him not only that I had had another affair, but that I was carrying a child. Bird put down any thoughts of resuming our romance when I told him I was pregnant."[24]

Charlie urged Chan to have an abortion and move in with him. Instead, she chose to stay in Los Angeles and have the child on her own. She slipped easily into the nightlife swirling around Hollywood and Central Avenue, making friends with Wardell Gray, Sonny Criss, and other African American jazz musicians. She frequently stopped by the Finale Club where Charlie was playing. Charlie remained friendly with Chan, but kept his distance. Three months later, when she called Charlie to tell him that she was returning to her mother's apartment in New York to have the child, he coolly replied, "Have a nice trip."[25]

The evening of February 26, Charlie unexpectedly showed up at the Tempo Music Shop and apologized to Russell for not making the Dial session. Russell, a self-professed intellectual who aspired to be a hipster, was completely charmed by Charlie, the ultimate hipster and con man. Russell confided:

> Charlie apologized for the costly Glendale fiasco; he had not wanted to record with George Handy. Nor did he want to record any more with Dizzy; the Guild sides had completed their collaborations. It was time for new modes. The trumpet player of his choice would not be a virtuoso capable of fireworks, but a different sort of musician, someone who played a relaxed legato style, with a warm tone, in the lower and middle registers, someone like Miles Davis, who would be arriving in Los Angeles within a week or two. Charlie spoke of his future and frustrated ambitions. . . . He planned to compose seriously. He would write a beautiful mood piece, similar to his "Confirmation" for the first Dial record date. Names of musicians that Charlie would like to use, and who were available on the Coast, were discussed, as were social and political ideas. . . . The discussion lasted for an hour, and before Charlie left we had drawn up a hand-written agreement."[26]

Russell generously gave Charlie a one-hundred-dollar advance from the store's cash register.

A few days later, Russell's partner, Marvin Freeman, drew up a contract to record twelve sides with an option to renew. Charlie signed the contract and then disappeared. Russell finally managed to locate him a few days before the session, scheduled for March 28. Charlie hastily assembled a band for the session. Lucky Thompson along with Miles Davis, who had recently arrived from the East Coast with the Benny Carter Band, eagerly signed on for the session. Once again, Russell brought guitarist Arvin Garrison to the recording date.

While the front line came together easily, Charlie had to patch together a rhythm section after alienating pianist Joe Albany and bassist Red Callendar, regular members of the Finale Club band. The sensitive Albany walked off stage at the club after taking offense at a remark by Charlie. Dodo Marmarosa, a progressive pianist with a large bird-like head, replaced Albany. Influenced by Teddy Wilson and Art Tatum, Marmarosa soloed in an intense angular style, switching easily to comp behind the soloists. Callendar left in disgust during the rehearsal the night before the session after Charlie disappeared for several hours to connect with Moose the Mooche, leaving Russell and other band members in the lurch. Vic McMillan, who was grumpy and unkempt from being called at the last minute, replaced Callendar. Drummer Roy Porter from the Finale Club band rounded out the rhythm section. Porter, an enthusiastic timekeeper, was known for "dropping bombs," a technique distinguished by an irregular syncopated beat with a bass drum flourish.

The loose, unrehearsed aggregation had to learn the tunes in the studio, causing the scheduled three-hour session to run into a six-hour marathon that produced only four takes. Charlie arrived early for the session at Radio Recorder studio in Hollywood on March 28, 1946, ready to get down to business. Unfortunately, band members were ill equipped to follow. Nominally making good on his promise to create fresh, original compositions for the session, Charlie sketched out "Moose the Mooche," named in honor of his drug connection, Emry Byrd, and based on the changes of "I Got Rhythm" along with "Ornithology," drawn from "How High the Moon," in the car on the way to the session. "Yardbird Suite," originally written for the McShann band, and Gillespie's "A Night in Tunisia" filled out the final takes recorded during the session.

The band's unfamiliarity with the originals and the difficulties in navigating Gillespie's "A Night in Tunisia" generated multiple false starts and takes of each selection. "The interesting thing of the unsuccessful takes was that Charlie Parker always played well," Russell explained. "Errors of execution which resulted in rejection of early takes were always the fault of one side-man or another. Charlie always knew what he was going to play and deliv-ered a complete and valid solo. If the engagement had been entirely up to him we could have packed up and gone home with four sides in less than an hour." Russell, awed by Charlie's virtuosity, recorded every note, attentively documenting each take for posterity. Charlie stopped after each selection, monitored the result, and carefully chose the final takes.[27]

During the session, Charlie relaxed the tempo, achieving a new lyricism as a composer and soloist. Marmarosa introduced the medium tempo theme of "Moose the Mooche," leading to an ensemble passage playing the melody in unison. Then at the head, Charlie artfully stated variations on the distinc-tive rhythmic motif of the melody.[28] Following half-chorus solos by Davis and Thompson, Marmarosa jumped in on the bridge, omitting the first six-teen bars. The ensemble then restated the theme before ending with a string of codettas, lightly delivered by Charlie, Thompson, and Marmarosa.

"Yardbird Suite" reveals Charlie's increasing lyricism. Marmarosa in-troduced the bright theme with a rolling eight-bar solo buoyed by McMil-lian's pedal point bass segueing into a sixteen-bar statement of the catchy melody by the band. At the bridge, Charlie took charge with a lilting melodic solo, echoed by the ensemble playing the closing eight-bars of the theme. Charlie improvised off his own changes in the second chorus, engaging in a musical dialogue with himself. Davis and Thompson followed, exchanging two confident solos each, spilling sixteen bars over into the fourth chorus. Garrison then took the chorus out with a sixteen-bar solo, remaining faith-ful to the melody. Running out of the three minutes allotted for each take, Marmarosa omitted the first sixteen bars, beginning his nimble solo at the bridge. Tidying things up with a flourish, the ensemble returned to the theme in the last eight bars.

"Ornithology" was a work in progress. Only recently introduced at the Finale Club, the band had yet to set the structure or work through the changes.[29] Instead of a piano introduction, drummer Porter set the tempo for the statement of the theme by the ensemble, concluding with a round of quick triplet codettas heralding Charlie's thirty-two-bar solo gliding on eighth notes. Following solos by Davis and Thompson, the ensemble re-turned to the theme, concluding with a second set of codettas.

The group ended with a kicker, Dizzy Gillespie's "A Night in Tunisia." Highly original and tightly structured, "A Night in Tunisia" began with an introduction followed by the theme statement and a twelve-bar segue lead-ing to Charlie's legendary four-bar break. During the initial take, Charlie's lightning pass through the break totally lost the band. "Couldn't anyone count the break because Bird was doubling, tripling, quadrupling and everything else on what he played in those four bars," drummer Roy Porter exclaimed. "It was throwing all of us! Finally, Miles Davis said he would go in the corner and listen and bring his hand down on the first beat of the fifth bar. That's how the rhythm section came in right on time."[30] After two more tries, the band finally managed to keep pace with Charlie and arrive at a final take.

Russell hurried the masters into production for release in early April. Ostentatiously looking out for his best and only client's interest, Russell set up a publishing company for Charlie's compositions and drafted a contract paying him two cents per side for recordings of his original compositions. Charlie readily signed the royalty contract but failed to follow through on the publishing agreement, leaving his compositions in limbo. The next week, he signed over half the royalties for all contracts with Dial to Emry Byrd in exchange for heroin.

On the heels of the Dial session, Charlie returned to the Finale Club. As in the case of Fifty-Second Street the year before, the hipsters and musi-cians crowding the Finale Club drew the attention of local law enforcement. Charlie and other band members arrived for work one night to find the club shuttered. Worse yet, the narcotics squad rounded up the dealers working Central Avenue, creating a shortage of heroin. Emry Byrd landed in San Quentin, the judge taking no pity on his physical condition.

The undertow of panic engulfing Central Avenue swept Charlie from the scene. Howard McGhee managed to find Charlie holed up in an unheated garage using an old overcoat for a blanket, nursing jugs of wine to ease the pain of withdrawal. Ironically, Charlie tolerated heroin better than alcohol. McGhee took the disheveled Charlie into his own home, a stucco bungalow on West Forty-First Street. Like Gene Ramey earlier with the McShann band, McGhee assumed responsibility for the strung-out Charlie.

McGhee soon learned the extent and cost of Charlie's addiction to heroin. He related that " [Charlie] told me that he had a problem and that he was sick, and that he had to have a certain amount of heroin a day to keep operating. And that's when I really realized that the man was strung and he was really sick. But I had to try [to] step in and try to help him the best way I could, but he was draining my loot fast as I could get it. He was taking it all, you know, and I couldn't afford that."[31] McGhee helped Charlie get a room at the Civic Hotel.

In May, Charlie opened with the McGhee band at the Hi-De-Ho Club. Charlie continued drinking heavily over the next few months. His health declined rapidly, manifested by mental disorientation and sudden jerky movements of his limbs. McGhee alerted Russell to Charlie's quickly deteriorating condition. Russell ushered Charlie, accompanied by the principal members of the McGhee band from the Hi-De-Ho Club, back to the recording studio for a late-night session on July 29. Finding the star of the session in no shape to record after downing a quart of whiskey, Russell and Freeman brought in Freeman's brother, Richard, a psychiatrist, to monitor Charlie's condition.

Drunk and exhausted, Charlie broke down in the studio. According to Russell, "Someone suggested 'Max Is Making Wax,' a Fifty-Second Street favorite. Dull-eyed, with clumsy fingers, Charlie hooked the saxophone to the neck strap and took his place at the microphone. . . . The band began recording 'Max Is Making Wax.' Much too fast," Russell judged. "The rhythm section was shaky, the men in it unnerved by the tension. The alto wobbled into the ensemble line uneven and out of focus. . . . The alto was drifting on and off mike. Jordan [the engineer] rode the gain knobs to keep the dynamics at a constant level. Saxophone phrases came in short bursts, like gunfire. The take ran a bare two and a half minutes, and was obviously worthless."[32] During a brief break, Richard Freeman attempted to quell Charlie's spasms with six phenobarbital tablets.

Overwhelmed by the medication, Charlie became musically incoherent and confused. "Charlie nodded vacantly and said that he would like to try 'Lover Man,'" Russell remembered, "The rhythm section began running down the chord changes, and Howard cleared the valves of his trumpet. . . . There was a long, seemingly endless piano introduction as Jimmy Bunn marked time, waiting for the saxophone. Charlie had missed the cue. The alto came in at last, several bars late. Charlie's tone had steadied. . . . Charlie seemed to be performing on pure reflexes, no longer a thinking musician. . . . There was a last, eerie, suspended, unfinished phrase, then silence. Those in the control booth were slightly embarrassed, disturbed and deeply affected."[33] When Charlie veered off-mike during the last bars of "Lover Man," Russell wrapped his arms around him and squeezed out the last few notes. Russell later described it as a "ghoulish business."[34] After struggling through two more selections, "The Gypsy" and "Be-Bop," Charlie collapsed in a chair, overcome by the combination of exhaustion, alcohol, and phenobarbital. A reporter covering the session for *Billboard* later described the sad spectacle, in a fictional account published in *Harper's*, as "a record of a guy going nuts."[35]

Russell and Freeman sent Charlie back to the Civic Hotel in a cab accompanied by Slim, the band boy for the session. Slim managed to get Charlie in bed and then left. Later that evening, Charlie grew restless and strolled downstairs stark naked, across the lobby, past the incredulous night manager, out the front door, and climbed on top of a car where he sat Buddha like. The police had already arrested Charlie by the time Howard McGhee arrived at the Civic.

McGhee followed Charlie's trail through the system and finally located him confined to a local hospital and in a surprisingly good mood. "So like I said, when I walked in there," McGhee described, "Bird was smilin' and laughin' and talkin'—'Maggie [McGhee], what are you doin'?' . . . I said 'Gee, I expected to see you laid out, man.' He said, 'No, I'm fine, man.' He said, 'Get me my clothes; I'm ready to go.' I said, 'Well, it ain't quite like that, Bird. I can't get you out like that. You have to go to court and all that shit."[36] Charlie was now a ward of the California's mental health system. He soon discovered that once committed to the system, it was difficult to get out.

Ross Russell and Marvin Freeman advocated on Charlie's behalf. Unable easily to extract him from the mental health system, they steered the case to a liberal judge, who sentenced Charlie to a minimum of six months in Camarillo State Hospital, a "country club" mental institution.[37]

State mental health workers escorted Charlie to the hospital, located forty-five miles north of Los Angeles, near the town of Camarillo. Nestled in a coastal plain at the foot of nearby mountains, Camarillo was surrounded by orange, lemon, and walnut groves. The facility featured separate campuses for men and women. The spacious Spanish revival buildings with tile fountains and cloistered hallways faced vast open courtyards. A bell tower anchored the cavernous dining room. For vocational therapy, patients worked in the hospital's vegetable fields or the dairy farm. Charlie settled into the routine, tending to a lettuce patch and playing in the band on Saturday nights.

In September, Doris Sydnor moved to Los Angeles to be close to Charlie. She rented a small, furnished apartment and found a job as a waitress. Three days a week, she took the bus up the coast to visit Charlie. She found him in good shape physically, but mentally unsteady. "He was really kind of inside of himself," Doris observed. "I think he was looking at his life. . . . There were people there that were very disturbed, and I think he—that was a time when he was looking at how their life affected them. . . . And Charlie said, you know, it really made him think, you know, maybe it's not good to lose yourself in one thing; that you need a more rounded life. You need, you know, you need other things in your life. Because . . . music was his whole life."[38]

After a few months, doctors approved passes for Charlie to leave the hospital for short stretches with Doris. They picnicked in the fruit groves surrounding the facility, strolled hand in hand around the city of Camarillo located nearby. On several occasions, Charlie broke down and had some drinks. During one trip, Doris became concerned about Charlie's mental state and rushed him back to the hospital.

By winter, Charlie became eager to leave Camarillo. Doris related that Charlie told her how "this man used to get up every morning and eat breakfast and go stand—look out on a hill. And so, for about three mornings, Charlie had gone out and watched him. And all of a sudden, he had a mental vision of, like, ten years from now there would be this man, and him and whoever was behind him, watching them to see what they were looking at. He said that was when he panicked, and he felt he had to get out of there."[39]

On December 1, 1946, Charlie dashed off a terse note to Ross Russell urging him to "get me out of this joint. I'm about to blow my top."[40] Charlie's nonresident status complicated matters. Usually, nonresident patients were shipped back to their state of residence every six months. Richard Freeman searched the state mental hygiene code and found that, with the approval of the Department of Mental Hygiene, Charlie could be released to the custody of "an approved California resident." Doris, a nonresident, was ineligible, so Russell agreed to take responsibility for Charlie.[41]

On December 12, Charlie appeared before a board of staff members for "consideration of parole." The board rejected Charlie's request for release. Two days later Russell appealed to Doctor Hammond on Charlie's behalf. In a letter to Russell dated December 24, 1946, the superintendent of the hospital, Thomas W. Hagerty, M.D., informed Russell that "the staff felt that a release from the hospital at this time was not considered best for Mr. Parker. On the other hand, he is a non-resident of California, and unless we could discharge him as recovered, it will be necessary for us to obtain permission from the Department of Mental Hygiene, Deportation Division, for his release. We are writing to this Agency, and as soon as we hear from them, we will be better able to advise you concerning possibilities of his release."[42]

Before releasing Charlie, the doctors prescribed electric shock therapy, a common treatment of the day where a series of electric shocks were administered to the brain, sometimes with disastrous consequences to the patient. Russell and Richard Freeman intervened and blocked the procedure. "At one point it was up to us [Russell and Freeman] to decide whether Parker would be given a series of electric shock treatments," explained Russell. "The opinion of the staff, one of the staff members, at the hospital was that such a series of treatments would probably serve to completely disorganize Parker's personality, with the subsequent reassembly of the personality, a matter of chance. It was further believed that the treatment would impair or slow down his reflexes and if continued sufficiently perhaps produce a fairly docile and perhaps predictable human being. I opposed such treatment.... I felt that the experiment, whatever its value in social therapy, might very probably impair or kill musical genius. In any case, these treatments were not carried out and Bird was shortly thereafter released, in my custody."[43]

Russell's interest in Charlie's welfare was not entirely altruistic. Before signing the release papers, Russell pressured Charlie into signing a year extension to his Dial contract. Russell had recently sold the Tempo Music Shop and become sole owner of Dial Records. Dial's first release, "Dynamo A" backed by "Dynamo B" by Gillespie, released as the Tempo Jazz Men featuring Gabriel, sold well in Los Angeles but received little distribution elsewhere. The follow-up release by Charlie's Septet, "A Night in Tunisia" backed with "Ornithology," fared little better.

Russell, like other small-label owners across the country, lacked a distributor to market Dial releases nationally. Big record outlets sold few bebop records, but small specialty record stores like the Tempo Music Shop were beginning to sell respectable numbers of recordings by Dizzy Gillespie, Charlie, and other beboppers. Russell, determined to build his own distribution circuit one shop at a time, starting on the West Coast, loaded four hundred discs by Charlie and Gillespie into the trunk of his new 1946 Chevrolet and headed for San Francisco. He returned to Los Angeles with an empty trunk and orders for more discs. He soon found outlets in Chicago and New York. Russell, seeking to cash in on bebop's growing popularity and establish Dial Records nationally, became very interested in Charlie's well-being.

Once back in Los Angeles, Russell gave Charlie six hundred dollars raised by fans and friends during a December benefit. Given a margin of comfort, he moved in with Doris and enjoyed a stable home life for the first time since leaving his mother's house. Charlie had gained forty pounds and his skin, renewed by his hiatus from drugs and alcohol, assumed a healthy deep chocolate hue. Freed from the burden of his addictions, Charlie reverted to his naturally playful, boyish self. During a party at the beach with Doris, Ross Russell, and friends, Charlie plunged fully clothed headlong into the surf, ruining his brand new suit and shoes.[44]

As part of the release agreement with Camarillo, Charlie was required to return to New York. Russell contacted Chan Richardson, who had moved back in with her mother at 7 West Fifty-Second Street, about helping Charlie find work in New York. In the letter dated February 1, 1947, he warned Chan, "Medical opinion is unanimous that the present situation is most critical—if Bird goes back on narcotics, or even more than passing indulgence in charge [heroin] and alcohol he is bound to break up rapidly. During recent paroles and even since his release he has been both drunk and on charge. At such times he is so impossible his best friends must throw up their hands. Also a lucrative tour of one-nighters around Chicago which a local agency had lined up with Charlie and Howard McGhee had to be cancelled by the booker when he heard what Charlie had been doing." Chan contacted Sammy Kaye, owner of the Three Deuces. Kaye offered seven hundred dollars per week for a sextet led by Charlie. Chan and Russell continued corresponding about Charlie. Like two schoolgirls with a mutual crush, they confided their devotion to Charlie and concern for his future.[45]

Charlie lingered in Los Angeles for the next two months. He played a month-long series of Sunday matinees at Billy Berg's and then joined the Howard McGhee band at the Hi-De-Ho Club. Dean Benedetti, a tenor saxophonist and bandleader, recorded Charlie's solos at the Hi-De-Ho and other clubs around Los Angeles. Born in Utah to Italian immigrant parents, Benedetti moved to Los Angeles in 1943. Swarthy, with matinee-idol looks topped by a shock of thick black hair, Benedetti hoped to break into the movies. He gigged around Los Angeles and hung out at the Tempo Music Shop. Benedetti introduced Russell to bebop and took him to Gillespie's opening night at Berg's. Awed by Charlie's virtuosity, Benedetti gave up playing his saxophone and followed Charlie from club to club.

Benedetti became inspired to record Charlie after watching someone record a jam session featuring Charlie at Chuck Copely's home using instantaneous cut disc technology.[46] This technology was first developed in the mid-1930s for use by radio stations and recording studios. After World War II, smaller, portable consumer recorders became widely available at reasonable prices. Benedetti bought a disc-cutting machine and asked Charlie's permission to record him on the bandstand. Benedetti, who was interested only in Charlie's solos, set the microphone up directly in front of Charlie and turned the microphone on before Charlie's solos and abruptly turned it off after the last note. Benedetti then transcribed Charlie's solos note for note, seeking to capture the essence of his genius.

Like Benedetti, Ross Russell was eager to record Charlie again. Charlie, who was upset with Russell's reluctance to sign his release papers from Camarillo without first obtaining a Dial contract extension, unenthusiastically recorded two more sessions for Dial before leaving for New York. At the first session on February 19, 1947, Charlie insisted Russell include vocalist Earl Coleman, a slender baritone, formerly with Jay McShann and Earl Hines. Charlie and Coleman, who were friends from the heyday of Eighteenth and Vine, had renewed their acquaintance on Central Avenue. Coleman often accompanied Howard McGhee to visit Charlie at Camarillo. During one of their visits, Charlie promised Coleman a recording date. Once released, he made good on his promise—to the chagrin of Russell, who wanted nothing to do with vocalists, let alone one who specialized in ballads. Joined by the Erroll Garner Trio, Charlie and Coleman recorded two ballads, "This Is Always" and "Dark Shadows." Russell, eager to cut to the chase and record Charlie, squirmed through the four takes of each ballad. Getting down to business, Charlie threw together two originals, on the spot, "Bird's Nest," based on the chord patterns of "I Got Rhythm," and "Cool Blues," a variation on his solo phrase from "Yardbird Suite," wrapping them up in a half hour.[47]

Under pressure from Russell, Charlie returned to the studio on February 26, fronting an all-star septet that featured Howard McGhee; tenor saxophonist Wardell Gray, a rising star from the Eckstine band; pianist Dodo Marmarosa; guitarist Barney Kessel; bassist Red Callender; and drummer Don Lamond, who was then working with Woody Herman. Charlie almost missed the date after getting drunk and passing out fully clothed in a bathtub. Rousted by McGhee, the foggy Charlie sketched out one of four fresh compositions promised to Russell in a cab en route to the recording date. Howard McGhee took up the creative slack, rounding out the session with three originals. Charlie, frustrated at the band members' inability to decipher his handwritten notation, picked up his alto and ripped through the theme several times, aptly maneuvering its innovative melodic and rhythmic structure, built on three notes.[48] Working for an hour in the studio, the band finally mastered the tricky passages after five takes. Once released, the twelve-bar blues, dubbed "Relaxing at Camarillo" by Russell, won Charlie his first international acclaim, the prestigious Grand Prix du Disque award in France.[49]

Tired of Los Angeles and Ross Russell's pressure to record for Dial, Charlie returned to New York in early April 1947, stopping off on the way for an Easter Sunday Concert at the Pershing Ballroom in Chicago and a string of club dates. Back in New York, Charlie's career careened like a roller coaster, lifted to new heights by his charisma and brilliance as an improviser, only to derail and crash from drug abuse and capricious behavior.

CHAPTER 6

Dewey Square

When Charlie and Doris returned to New York City on Easter Monday, April 7, 1947, they moved into the Dewey Square Hotel at 201 and 203 West 117th Street. One of the largest hotels in Harlem, the Dewey Square Hotel featured 250 luxurious rooms. That evening friends and fans threw a welcome home party for Charlie at Small's Paradise. The next night Charlie stopped by the Savoy Ballroom and sat in with the Dizzy Gillespie big band. After the show, Charlie asked Gillespie if he could work with the big band while he assembled a quintet for the Three Deuces. Gillespie feared Charlie would bring drugs in the band. Despite having much to lose from being associated with a possible drug bust, Gillespie hired Charlie anyway.

As Charlie's career crashed in California, Gillespie's had soared nationally. After returning to New York from the engagement at Billy Berg's in February 1946, Gillespie emerged as a top bandleader and established bebop with mainstream jazz audiences. In March, he formed a seventeen-piece big band, featuring Thelonious Monk, Ray Brown, Milt Jackson, and Kenny Clarke. Gillespie recorded prolifically and toured nationally, capped off by a December swing across the South with Ella Fitzgerald. Unlike the earlier southern tour with the Hep-Sations of 1945 revue, the band and new music were well received—thanks to Ella Fitzgerald. Her popularity and strong draw at the box office validated Gillespie and the bebop movement. In turn, she received a new musical language, bebop.[1]

The next week, Charlie confirmed Gillespie's worst fears by showing up high for the band's opening night at the McKinley Theater in the Bronx. Miles Davis recalled how Charlie's debut with the band ended on a sour note. "On the night we opened at the McKinley, Bird was up on stage nodding out and playing nothing but his own solos. He wouldn't play behind nobody else. Even the people in the audience were making fun of Bird while he was nodding up there on stage. So Dizzy, who was fed up with Bird anyway, fired him after that first gig."[2] Arranger Gil Fuller and Davis urged Gillespie to give Charlie another chance, but Gillespie remained adamant.

For the next couple of weeks, Charlie made the rounds, sitting in on late-night jam sessions in Harlem and on 52nd Street. Word of Charlie's return spread swiftly throughout the hipster community. *Metronome* heralded Charlie's triumphal return and renewed vigor:

> The Bird came back to New York in April, after more than a year on the West Coast, came back to a musician's community wildly eager to see and hear him again. The night he arrived in town the word went around from one club to another, from one bar to another. "Bird's back in town!" whispered in sepulchral tones, usually reserved for religious leaders and revolutionaries. Every session he appeared at for the next few weeks was ballyhooed days in advance among the beboppers as another Bird-letter day and attendance was compulsory for those who wished to continue in the bebop school. Happily, in spite of strong reports to the contrary, the Bird showed up in New York in good health. Forty pounds heavier than usual, still a brilliant musical thinker, still the most influential bebopper of them all if not yet in full possession of his technique, tone and taste.[3]

Tales of Charlie's exploits passed from hipster to hipster. Embellished with each retelling, his legends assumed mythic proportions.

Charlie handpicked the group for the Three Deuces. He chose Miles Davis as his foil in the front line. Unlike Gillespie, who challenged Charlie at every turn, Davis played under his flowing solos. Charlie built the rhythm section around Max Roach, a melodic percussionist who set a steady pulse on the ride cymbal, creating a flowing carpet of sound. This freed Roach to create a polyrhythmic texture with the high hat and bass drum.[4] Meeting the demands of Charlie's abrupt rhythmic shifts fully realized Roach's textured approach. Charlie rounded out the rhythm section with Tommy Potter, former bassist with the Billy Eckstine band, and Duke Jordan, the pianist in the house band at the Three Deuces. Charlie called for daily rehearsals and then failed to show up, leaving Davis to rehearse the group at Teddy Reig's apartment or the Nola Studios.

Charlie's charisma and celebrity created a demand for the quintet. Fifty-Second Street, after declining during the war years, underwent a renaissance, sparked by the popularity of bebop. Miles Davis explained, "The two records Bird had recorded for Dial out in Los Angeles had been released. . . . They had been released in late 1946 and were now big jazz hits. So, with 52nd Street open again and Bird back in town, the club owners wanted Bird. Everybody was after him. They wanted small bands again and they felt Bird would pack them in. They offered him $800 a week for four weeks at the Three Deuces. . . . He paid me and Max $135 a week and Tommy and Duke $125. Bird made the most he had ever made in his life, $280 a week."[5] For the first time, Charlie and Doris enjoyed a degree of financial security. Doris put money in the bank and bought Charlie a new wardrobe of Broadway pinstripe suits, shoes, shirts, and silk ties.

In late April, the quintet opened at the Three Deuces opposite the Lennie Tristano trio to overflow crowds. Charlie, glad to be back on Fifty-Second Street, graciously worked the room, charming patrons and musicians alike. Pianist Tristano, who had been blind since infancy, fondly recalled Charlie's professional courtesy and thoughtfulness. "I can say that [Charlie] has been nicer to me than anybody in the business," Tristano judged. "My group was opposite his at the Three Deuces. He sat through my entire first set listening intently. When it was all over, the two fellows I was playing with left the stand, leaving me alone. They knew I could get around all right, but Bird didn't know that; he thought I was hung up for the moment. He rushed up to the stand, told me how much he liked my playing, and subtly escorted me off the bandstand."[6] Crowds packed the Three Deuces, cementing Charlie's reputation as the "High Priest" of bebop.[7]

After closing at the Three Deuces, Charlie signed with the Moe Gale Agency, which also represented Gillespie. Billy Shaw, the agency's vice president, personally represented Charlie, giving his career a boost. He booked Charlie into six Monday night performances of Jazz at the Philharmonic at Carnegie Hall starting on May 5. Charlie's participation in the Jazz at the Philharmonic at Carnegie Hall concerts initiated an association with Norman Granz, a relationship that later paid off handsomely for both men.

Charlie wasted no time getting back into the recording studio for the Savoy label. Bud Powell, Charlie's pianist of choice, replaced Duke Jordan for the session. Before hiring Jordan, Charlie had offered Powell the job at the Three Deuces. Powell, who was mentally unstable and personally disliked Charlie, refused the offer. Charlie repeatedly pleaded with Powell to work with him, only to be turned down. The inscrutable Powell finally relented and agreed to sit in for the Savoy session.

On May 8, the band recorded four selections: "Donna Lee," "Chasing the Bird," "Cheryl," and "Buzzy." As usual, Charlie composed out of necessity rather than by design. He sketched out the first section of each selection in the studio then worked through the changes with the band until arriving at a final take. Miles Davis contributed "Donna Lee," a new composition. "Donna Lee" captures Charlie at the top of his game, effortlessly spinning inventive solos with unexpected twists and turns of phrasing. The band rises to the occasion, matching his imaginative phrases note for note. Kicking off "Donna Lee" at a bright tempo, Charlie and Davis introduce the intricate theme, peppered with eighth notes, in unison, giving way to two masterfully conceived and executed choruses by Charlie. Davis confidently jumps in with a fiery first-half chorus middle-register turn, revealing a new mastery of technique and wealth of ideas. Bud Powell then takes charge of the second half of the chorus, artfully accenting clustered notes with space. Charlie and Davis revisit the theme in the out chorus, taking things home to a photo-finish ending.

When the records were released, Ross Russell notified Savoy of Dial's exclusive contract with Charlie. Herman Lubinsky, the owner of Savoy, countered by producing a handwritten agreement with Charlie for a total of twelve sides, predating the contract with Dial.[8] The flustered Russell, feeling like a "mere babe in the woods" surrounded by "a jungle of larceny," complained,

"Charlie had been silent on the matter. Savoy claimed no prior knowledge of the exclusive Dial contract and was legally blameless," he explained. "The musicians Union refused to intervene. The Moe Gale agency took a dim view of Charlie's recording for either label."[9]

Russell hired attorney Alan J. Berlan to take Savoy to court—to no avail. After researching the case, Berlan informed Russell:

> The attorney for Savoy advised the N. J. attorney that Parker had signed a contract with Savoy on November 19, 1945, in which Parker gave an option for eight additional recordings. As they predate you, they claim no responsibility. They claim same is in writing and that they have a written statement from Parker. I checked with Mr. Ricardi of AFM, to ascertain whether the contract was filed. To date I have not heard. You have to write and wait. The implication I received was that if it was not filed, it is still legal, but if the parties got in trouble, then they are on the spot with the AFM. If Savoy's contention is correct and he has a prior contract, we feel that you may be out of luck on the eight recordings.[10]

Russell, who was in no position financially to call Lubinsky's bluff, let the matter ride.

The legal dispute between Savoy and Dial became a moot point when Billy Shaw suspended all recording sessions for either label to clear the way for a deal with Mercury, a leading independent label. Shaw's intervention came at an inopportune time for Russell, who was in the midst of moving Dial's operation to New York. A few months earlier, Russell had bought out Marvin Freeman and incorporated Dial, leaving the label strapped for cash. Russell desperately needed new recordings by Charlie to build Dial's catalog and generate a profit. For his part, Charlie wanted as little as possible to do with Russell.

Rumors of Charlie's renewed drug and alcohol abuse began circulating in the jazz community. He countered the allegations by publicly acknowledging his past drug use in an interview with jazz critic Leonard Feather published in *Metronome*. Imploring Feather not to make him out to be a "moralizer or reformer," Charlie candidly addressed his drug addiction. "It all came from being introduced too early to nightlife," Charlie divulged. "When you're not mature enough to know what's happening—well you goof." Describing his addiction, Charlie explained, "I didn't know what hit me . . . it was so sudden. I was a victim of circumstance. . . . High school kids don't know any better. That way, you can miss the most important years of your life, the years of possible creation. I don't know how I made it through those years." Charlie added how the rejection of his music contributed to his breakdown. "I became bitter, hard, cold. I was always on a panic—couldn't buy clothes or a good place to live. Finally out on the Coast last year I didn't have *any* place to stay, until somebody put me up in a converted garage. The mental strain was getting worse all the time. What made it worst of all was that nobody understood our kind of music out on the Coast. They hated it." Expressing his great admiration for classical music, Charlie compared his lack of acceptance to the rejection of Beethoven. "They say that when Beethoven was on his deathbed he shook his fist at the world: they just didn't understand. Nobody in his own time really dug anything he wrote. But that's music." Weighing in on the continued controversy swirling around bebop, Charlie dismissed the label and modestly downplayed his contribution. "Let's not call it be bop. Let's call it music. People get so used to hearing jazz for so many years, finally somebody said 'Let's have something different and some new ideas began to evolve. Then people brand it 'bebop' and try to crush it. If it should ever become completely accepted, people should remember it's in just the same position jazz was. It's just another style. I don't think any one person invented it. I was playing the same style years before I came to New York. I never consciously changed my style." Charlie wrapped up the interview on an up beat, declaring, "Let's get straight and make some music!"[11]

Charlie played a July engagement at the New Bali Restaurant in Washington, D.C., and then returned to the Three Deuces on a double bill with Coleman Hawkins. While playing at the Three Deuces, Charlie participated in two battles of the bands broadcast over the Mutual Broadcasting System. The battles pitted modernists against traditionalists and were broadcast as part of the *Bands for Bonds* program sponsored by the Treasury Department. *Metronome* columnist and reviewer Barrry Ulanov fielded the modernists led by Charlie and Gillespie. Rudi Blesh, the host of the radio series *This is Jazz,* assembled an all-star New Orleans band featuring Baby Dodds drums, Edmond Hall clarinet, Pops Foster bass, and Danny Barker guitar. Like the jazz camps they respectively represented, modernists and moldy figs, Ulanov and Blesh were at odds over the merits of bebop versus traditional jazz.

The two bands faced off in the studio of radio station WOR. Ironically, WOR did not carry the program, so listeners in New York had to listen over WICC, Bridgeport, Connecticut. During the first broadcast the all-star New Orleans group led off with "Sensation Rag," "Save It Pretty Mama," and "That's-a-Plenty." The modernists countered with "Hot House" and "Fine and Dandy." For the next broadcast, the two bands shared the same set list of standards: "On the Sunnyside of the Street," "How Deep Is the Ocean," and "Tiger Rag." While the traditionalists stuck closely to the melody, the modernists played off the changes. In the end, the broadcasts helped heal the rift between two jazz communities. Ulanov, covering the battles in *Metronome* observed, "Notes are still better than words to settle differences of musical opinion. When they are blown by the greatest representatives of the warring sides, the schisms of the jazz community assume a dignity, of which all of us are jealous, for which we intend to fight hard."[12] The rehearsals and broadcasts briefly reunited Charlie and Gillespie.

On September 29, Charlie and Gillespie played a concert at Carnegie Hall. Gillespie and Leonard Feather, taking a cue from Norman Granz's Jazz at the Philharmonic series, staged a concert at Carnegie Hall showcasing Gillespie's big band, Charlie and Gillespie with a small combo, and Ella Fitzgerald accompanied by the big band. Kicking things off with the big band, Gillespie unveiled a chamber work by pianist John Lewis, "Toccata for Trumpet," and "Cubano Be, Cubano Bop," a new Latin composition he composed with pianist George Russell, to mixed reviews. Barry Ulanov, usually supportive of new directions in jazz, gave the band and the two new compositions a lukewarm review in *Metronome*: "Dizzy's band was generally clean in its Carnegie performance, remarkably adroit in its negotiation of a new little nothing called the *Afro-Cubano Drums Suite*, a little less at home with the improperly named but most provocative piece of the evening, John Lewis's *Toccata* for solo trumpet and orchestra."[13]

Charlie joined Gillespie during the second half of the program and stole the show. He outplayed Gillespie at every turn, egged on by his fans on the front row of the packed house. The long-simmering rivalry between the two erupted into a musical free for all, running through a set of bebop standards including "A Night in Tunisia," "Dizzy Atmosphere," "Groovin' High," "Confirmation," and "Ko Ko." At one point, Charlie teased Gillespie by quoting "Be Bop," the title of Gillespie's early recording which critics used to define the new music.[14] Reviewing the concert, *Down Beat* hailed Charlie's brilliant onstage victory. "In the quintet numbers with Charlie, Gillespie was appreciably bested. Charlie's constant flow of ideas, his dramatic entrances and his perky use of musical punctuation was a revelation to an audience too often satiated by tenors."[15] Ross Russell, who was in the audience that evening, confirmed *Down Beat*'s account: "At the Carnegie Hall concert where he [Charlie] was featured guest artist with Dizzy Gillespie he gave an incredible exhibition of altosaxology deliberately designed to cut Dizzy to pieces and prove himself the greatest jazz musician living. . . . The town is still talking."[16] A hard act to follow, Charlie exited to thunderous applause, leaving Gillespie on stage to clown and dance through Ella Fitzgerald's set.

Impressed by the concert overall, but put off by Gillespie's antics during Fitzgerald's performance, a reviewer in *Down Beat* groused, "One thing throughout the concert was completely inexcusable. Dizzy demands consideration from musicians and writers as a serious leader of a good musical band. No one, not even in Carnegie Hall, would want him to work without the showmanship so necessary to appeal to large crowds. But this doesn't mean that he has license to stand on the platform doing bumps and grinds and in general often acting like a darn fool. . . . Gillespie is too fine a musician to have to indulge in shoddy tricks like this to garner attention. Showmanship is one thing. Acting like a bawdy house doorman is another."[17] While Gillespie took a critical beating for his distracting antics, Charlie received musical honors for his virtuoso performance, establishing his credentials as a concert artist, leading the way for his future participation in Jazz at the Philharmonic.

Economic necessity compelled Charlie to record again for the Savoy and Dial labels. On October 17, James Petrillo, the president of the American Federation of Musicians, announced a ban on recording by union members effective December 31, 1947, declaring, "I know of no other industry that makes the instruments that will destroy that industry and believe me when I say that records sooner or later will destroy musicians."[18] Billy Shaw, judging that recordings for small, independent labels were preferable to no recordings at all, reversed course and directed Charlie to fulfill his contracts with Dial and Savoy before the ban took effect.

Shaw then renegotiated Charlie's deal with Dial. Russell recalled that Shaw "called me into the Gale office and in a masterful mix of brag and con worked out a new deal for Bird with Dial. The deal was: one hundred dollars a side, cash in front, three sessions to be done that fall. The royalty matter was now a forgotten matter. Nobody seemed to give a damn about royalties, least of all Bird. In fact, the royalty situation was so messed up that a copyright attorney couldn't have set it straight."[19] Russell, still short of capital, invested his life savings, borrowed against his car, and wrote his mother pleading for a loan to finance the sessions.

Charlie recorded twenty-four new selections for Dial before the ban took effect. Just before the first session, Billy Shaw reconsidered and upped Charlie's price per side to include royalties. Russell readily accepted Shaw's offer. "Naturally I went along with Shaw's proposal and Bird produced the Three Deuces quintet, more or less in residency there by this time, and the sessions were made," Russell explained. "These sessions went like clockwork. The musicians were playing together every night, had all of the originals in hand and all the useful ballads run down. Six sides were made at each session and no session ran more than about 2½ hours. The time would have been less than that except for Miles's frequent fluffs."[20]

The sessions gave Russell two years' worth of releases, enough to carry Dial through the recording ban. At the end of 1947, Russell quit paying Charlie royalties, alleging he breached his contract with Dial by recording for Savoy and Mercury. Russell wrote a note to himself based on a conversation with his legal counsel Morris B. Rauscher: "Do not pay further royalties. At the end of each quarter send C. P. [Charlie Parker] a registered letter with statement of royalties due him for that quarter and deducting total of same from the sum C. P. owes Dial records from advance royalties. When the debt is repayed [*sic*], Dial Records should contend that C. P. broke his contract by recording for other companies, etc., and thereby is not entitled to further royalties, inasmuch as the contract is no longer in force. If he sues, it will take about eight to ten months for the case to come up in court, during which time it is most probable that C. P.'s lawyer would attempt a settlement."[21] In a royalty statement issued on January 25, 1948, Russell claimed cash advances to Charlie totaling $1,689.50. Russell then deducted the advances from Charlie's subsequent royalty statements. By 1950, Russell quit issuing royalty statements to Charlie altogether. Charlie never forgave Russell for not paying royalties and for releasing "Lover Man," from the July 1946 session, chronicling his break down in the studio. The disputes ended their association.

The 1947 annual *Metronome* readers' poll marked a changing of the guard, with Charlie and Gillespie leading the way. Across the board, modernists, including Leo Parker, Howard McGhee, Kai Winding, J. J. Johnson, Lennie Tristano, Ray Brown, Max Roach, and Milt Jackson successfully challenged entrenched traditionalists. *Metronome* noted that "throughout, with rare exception, the votes are to the young, the modern, the progressive voices in jazz."[22] Dizzy won top trumpet honors. Charlie edged out Johnny Hodges for the top alto slot and won the coveted Influence of the Year Award, remarkable accomplishments considering his hasty return from exile just seven months earlier.

After noting Charlie's fall from grace, *Metronome* praised his amazing comeback:

> But Charlie wasn't through. He came back to New York and showed us. He played better than ever before. He elicited more enthusiasm and more imitation than ever before. He took over as the major influence of the year in jazz. Perhaps the greatest compliment that can be paid this imposing musician is an accurate description of his talent. Where other purveyors of bebop, more and more a formularized expression, stick closely to the cadence, changes and rhythmic devices which identify their form, Charlie goes further and further afield. If any man can be said to have originated bop, Charlie Parker did it." Concluding by predicting further breakthroughs by Charlie, *Metronome* added, "If any be bopper can break away from the strictures of his style, utilizing its advances and advancing beyond them, the Influence of the Year, Charlie Parker, will do it.[23]

In January 1948, Charlie embarked on a two-month tour of the Midwest, playing clubs and ballrooms in Chicago and Detroit. The quintet returned to New York in late March for a two-week stand at the Three Deuces. On the second night of the engagement, Dean Benedetti, equipped with a new paper-based, open-reel tape recorder, recorded two sets before being thrown out by the management for not buying drinks. On a number of occasions, Benedetti helped carry Charlie, who had gotten too high on heroin and liquor, out the back door of the club.

In early April, the narcotic squad cracked down on residents of the Dewey Square Hotel, singling out Charlie as a person of interest. Charlie and Doris promptly moved to the Marden Hotel, located at 142 West Forty-Fourth near Times Square, conveniently located between WOR studios and Fifty-Second Street, where Charlie recorded and worked. Charlie was pleasantly surprised to find that his hero, Lester Young, also lived in the Marden.

Charlie spent the spring through early summer on the road. On April 18, Charlie and Sarah Vaughan joined the Jazz at the Philharmonic tour. Since Jazz at the Philharmonic's inception in Los Angeles four years earlier, it had grown from a freewheeling jam session into an institution, playing stately halls and auditoriums across the country. Norman Granz, relying on a proven formula, presented top jazz soloists accompanied by all-star rhythm sections in concert settings. Giving jazz the same dignity afforded to classical music, Granz paid musicians well and insisted they be respected as artists and individuals, regardless of the color of their skin. Uncompromising, Granz bypassed municipalities and venues unwilling to relax Jim Crow practice.[24] Finding few venues below the Mason-Dixon Line agreeable to his terms, Granz usually passed over the South.

Granz, impressed by Charlie's meteoric rise in the reader's polls and stunning performance at Carnegie Hall, recruited him, along with Sarah Vaughan, to headline the spring 1948 Jazz at the Philharmonic tour. The twenty-six-day tour featured Vaughan, her pianist Jimmy Jones, guitarist Barney Kessell, along with tenor saxophonists Flip Phillips and Dexter Gordon. Charlie wanted to take the quintet from the Three Deuces on the road, but Miles Davis and Max Roach declined to join the tour. "Soon after," Davis recalled, "When Norman Granz came and offered me and Max fifty dollars a night to go with Jazz at the Philharmonic with Bird, I said no. . . . Max was mad because Norman didn't like or take the kind of music we normally played seriously, and the money wasn't right."[25] Unlike Davis and Roach, Tommy Potter and Duke Jordan enthusiastically joined the tour.

Charlie hired Red Rodney and Stan Levey to replace Davis and Roach. Rodney, trim with wavy red hair, launched his career during the waning days of the big band era, passing, in quick succession, through the bands of Tony Pastor, Jimmy Dorsey, Les Brown, Gene Krupa, Georgie Auld, and Woody Herman. Originally inspired by Harry James's sweet style, Rodney became a devotee of bop after hearing Gillespie and Charlie on Fifty-Second Street and at Billy Berg's in Los Angeles.

Jazz at the Philharmonic played two dates in Kansas City, a concert in the art deco Music Hall on Tuesday, April 27, followed by a date the next night at the Municipal Auditorium for a racially mixed audience. Sarah Vaughan enchanted the audiences with her cool, sinuous vocals on ballads. As a counterpoint, Charlie heated up the hometown audience with fiery solos. The *Kansas City Call* reported that "Charley [sic] 'Yardbird' Parker, a Kansas City, Kas., [sic] born alto saxist, was terrific and won resounding applause for his Be-bop mastery. He heated up the house to the boiling point every time he appeared on stage. The guy actually crowded so many eighth and sixteenth notes into a measure that it seemed his horn would burst."[26]

While in Kansas City, Charlie and Rodney stayed at Addie's home. After the show, they sat in with Bud Calvert and His Headliners at the Playhouse, a popular nightclub located "out in the county" at 2240 Blue Ridge. The nightly floorshow at the Playhouse featured a band, dancers, and singers. The Calvert band played from 9:00 P.M. to 5:00 A.M. Tenor saxophonist Charlie White and other white musicians who jammed with Charlie years earlier when he was a member of the Buster Smith band stopped by to renew old acquaintances.

Charlie White, who was a professional pilot, flew Charlie and Rodney in his private plane to the next Jazz at the Philharmonic stop in Saint Louis. During the trip, Rodney found that White, like Charlie, delighted in living close to the edge. "We were with Norman Granz [and Jazz at the Philharmonic] and had played K.C. and stayed over night at Bird's mother's home," Rodney recalled. "The fellow named Charlie White was an airline pilot (T.W.A.) and also had his own plane—with which he offered to fly us to St. Louis for the next concert. During the very rough and bumpy flight in the small aircraft Bird decided he would like to operate the plane and Mr. White allowed [Charlie to take the controls] over my screaming protests."[27] During the Jazz at the Philharmonic tour, Charlie and Rodney became fast friends. Charlie affectionately referred to Rodney, who was born Robert Chudnick, as Chood.

Back in New York in early July, Charlie opened at the Onyx Club, one of the few clubs on Fifty-Second Street still booking jazz combos. Since the beginning of the year, Fifty-Second Street had declined dramatically, taking on a tawdry atmosphere. Strippers and drag queens replaced small combos in the clubs lining the street until only the Three Deuces and the Onyx featured jazz. The owners of the Spotlite abandoned its well-established music policy in favor of snake dancer Zorita and her Python and Camille's Six Foot Sex, the King Size Glamour Girl. Following the skin trade, prostitutes worked the street. Pushers, back on the street after the cleanup a few years earlier, openly peddled their wares.

Leonard Feather wrote Fifty-Second Street's obituary in the April 1948 issue of *Metronome*. "Fifty Second Street, which all over the world is recognized as a symbol of jazz—Fifty Second Street, which has provided musicians with more great kicks and more good jobs than any other block of buildings in the world in the past fifteen years, now seems to be headed for oblivion." After running down a litany of club changes and closings, Feather pinned the blame on indifferent management, prostitution, and narcotics:

> There can be no doubt that the average non-musician who might be interested in an act or band at one of these places is repelled by the poor value, poor service and watered liquor, and is even more depressed by the unsavory atmosphere created by the characters that hang around. . . . What was once a healthy meeting place for musicians and fans, a street on which racial barriers were broken down, by 1945 had turned into something that parallels the notorious Barbary Coast of San Francisco. . . . The truth is that today marijuana is kid stuff compared with what's been going on along The Street. Marijuana, though illegal, is not a dangerous habit—dangerous drug, in the opinion of most doctors. But heroin, morphine and cocaine are other and far graver matters. Their use has spread like a vile disease among an increasing clique of musicians, involving, alas a number of Streeters.

Feather concluded with an oblique reference to Charlie's renewed drug use. "It's not a pretty sight when your favorite horn man, after taking a terrific chorus, sneaks off to a secluded spot, hypodermic needle in pocket, and returns twenty minutes later glassy-eyed, completely out of the world."[28]

Taking up the slack from the decline of Fifty-Second Street, a string of clubs on Broadway between Forty-Seventh and Forty-Ninth Streets began featuring jazz. Shortly after the publication of Feather's article, the Royal Roost, a roomy club and restaurant located on Broadway at Forty-Seventh Street, right across from the Strand Theater, initiated a weekend bebop policy at the urging of Symphony Sid Torin, a popular disc jockey and impresario.

Originally from Newport News, Torin's family moved to Brooklyn when he was a child. As a teenager, Torin worked in record shops in Manhattan. He set up the famed record department at the Commodore Music Shop, which then mainly sold radios. Milt Gabler, a teenager who would later own Commodore, worked side by side with Torin. He received his nickname Symphony Sid while hosting a popular music show over a classical radio station.

Three years later, Torin moved to WHOM, where he hosted an all-night jazz show starting at 11:00. Torin's show, which prominently featured African American musicians and bands, became a hit with listeners in Harlem. During his off hours, Torin hung around Clark Monroe's Uptown and Jimmy's Chicken Shack, befriending Lester Young, Roy Eldridge, and other jazz greats. A tireless self-promoter, Torin emceed concerts and hosted dances, where he played his favorite 78 discs for thousands of dancers. Torin broadcast live from the Roost opening night, inviting listeners up and down the east coast to stop by the "metropolitan bopera house."

Crowds of fans accepted Torin's invitation. The Roost quickly became a popular gathering spot for celebrities, visiting bandleaders, and Café Society. Jazz fans of lesser means huddled at the bar. Younger fans perched on the bleacher seats in the milk bar or peanut gallery on one side of the spacious room. Lucky Thompson, Allen Eager, Tadd Dameron, Miles Davis, and other top modernists attended the late-night sessions at the Roost. Charlie directly moved his headquarters around the corner to the Roost, holding court between tours across the Midwest for the Moe Gale Agency. According to Ross Russell, "Billy Shaw promised Charlie a Cadillac, home and bank account by Christmas if he stays straight."[29]

That fall, Charlie toured with Jazz at the Philharmonic. After opening at Carnegie Hall on November 6, Jazz at the Philharmonic, featuring Charlie along with Howard McGhee, Coleman Hawkins, up-and-coming alto saxophonist Sonny Criss, tenor saxophonist Flip Phillips, and trombonist Tommy Turk, embarked on a thirty-five-city tour stretching to the West Coast and back to New York. Doris accompanied Charlie on the tour.

The morning before the Jazz at the Philharmonic concert at the Municipal Auditorium in Long Beach on Saturday, November 20, Charlie and Doris drove to Tijuana, where they were married. According to Doris, she "had no strong desire for marriage, but Charlie was going through a jealousy period, a romantically insecure stage with me; so I said yes."[30] Charlie and Doris returned to Long Beach in time for the concert that evening.

Two days later the Jazz at the Philharmonic tour arrived in Los Angeles for a concert at the Shrine Auditorium. During the tour Norman Granz did his best to shield Charlie from drug dealers. Concerned about the Los Angeles concert, Granz hired an off-duty African American detective with the police department to chauffer Charlie around and keep an eye on him. The detective checked Charlie into a motel on the outskirts of the city. Charlie gave the detective the slip and disappeared into Central Avenue. "Apparently," Granz explained, "Charlie said he was going to go to sleep, and I think the young detective thought he could sack out, too. When he woke up, Charlie had taken the keys to the car and gone."[31]

Granz learned of Charlie's disappearance a few hours before the concert. If Charlie failed to show, the program would have to go on without him, and Granz would have to refund some ticket holders' money—a financially disastrous situation. Jazz at the Philharmonic made enough money in larger metropolitan areas like Los Angeles to cover for less profitable dates at smaller locations like Salt Lake City. Tenor saxophonist Teddy Edwards, who knew the Los Angeles scene, located Charlie, who was passed out. Edwards managed to get Charlie to the Shrine Auditorium while Jazz at the Philharmonic was in full swing. Granz sobered Charlie up and shoved him onstage for the last two numbers, satisfying his obligation to ticket holders. "He was really out of it," Granz confided. "There was no way for Charlie to go on effectively. Coleman was playing, and I kept signaling when Coleman would finish a number that finished his set. I'd say, 'One more, one more.' Poor Hawk was out there interminably, it seemed." Granz stuck Charlie's head under a cold running faucet and told him, "'Charlie, I'm gonna kill you if you don't get yourself together.' . . . He got himself together, and went onstage. I think he played one or two numbers, and I brought the curtain down. They had seen Charlie Parker, so technically I was okay. I didn't blame him for that. If you're taking someone out on tour, you know whom you are taking. I mean, there were a lot of musicians I knew who were not straight. As long as they did their show, it wasn't up to me to tell them what to do and what not to do offstage."[32]

An anonymous critic reviewing the concert for *Down Beat* roundly panned Charlie's performance. "Complete disappointment of the evening was the performance—or nonperformance—of Charlie Parker, who came on late in the session to a screaming stomping ovation and then blew virtually nothing but clinkers and meaningless, disconnected passages that sounded as though they had tumbled from a dream—almost completely alien to the architectural structure of the compositions attempted." The reviewer, who was quite familiar with Charlie's career, added, "It was hardly the talents of the Charlie Parker of Dizzy Gillespie, Earl Hines or Jay McShann days."[33]

Ironically, despite Charlie's transgressions and irresponsible ways, he got along famously with the no-nonsense Granz. Like Howard McGhee and Gene Ramey earlier, Granz looked out for the unreliable Charlie, taking more than a passing interest in his career.

Mercury records sponsored the fall Jazz at the Philharmonic season, requiring the tour to stop in every city with a Mercury distributorship. Anticipating an end to the recording ban by the end of 1948, Mercury hired Granz to build a roster of top bebop musicians. James Petrillo finally relented and lifted the nearly year-old ban on recording effective in mid-December 1948. Granz swung into action, lining up stars from his Jazz at the Philharmonic not already signed to other labels.

On the heels of the fall Jazz at the Philharmonic tour, Granz recorded Charlie and Flip Phillips with Machito's Afro-Cuban orchestra. By no means a bop purist, he opted to record "danceable bop," pairing bop soloists with Latin groups.[34] Granz had become enamored of Afro-Cuban jazz after seeing Chano Pozo, the great conga player, with the Dizzy Gillespie orchestra at Carnegie Hall in 1947. Critics referred to the hybrid as Cubop.

Granz featured Charlie's soaring solos against the backdrop of the highly rhythmic Machito band, creating a striking contrast of styles. Once released, "No Noise part 2" and "Mango Mangue" were well received. Granz signed Charlie to a long-term contract with Mercury, enabling him to exert considerable influence over Charlie's recording career.

In early December 1948, Charlie reformed the quintet and opened at the Royal Roost. Miles Davis and Max Roach rejoined the band, and Al Haig replaced Duke Jordan. An irresponsible bandleader, Charlie consistently failed to pay band members on time. Later that month, long-simmering tensions between Davis and Charlie exploded at the Royal Roost. Davis, feeling slighted after asking for two weeks' back pay, lost his temper and threatened to kill Charlie. Quickly exiting, Charlie returned with half of Davis's money. The next week Charlie came up short again. "About a week later . . . we were playing at the Royal Roost. Bird and I had an argument about the rest of the money he owed me before we went on stage to play," Davis disclosed. "So now Bird is up on the stage acting a fool, shooting a cap gun at Al Haig, letting air out of a balloon into the microphone. People were laughing and he was, too, because he thinks it's funny. I just walked off the bandstand."[35]

Davis left the quintet for good, complaining that "Bird makes you feel like you are one foot high."[36] He recommended Kenny Dorham, a capable soloist with a lyrical style, as his replacement. Having come into his own, Davis moved in a different musical direction, joining arranger Gil Evans, alto saxophonist Lee Konitz, baritone saxophonist Gerry Mulligan, and pianist John Lewis in founding what soon became known as the cool school, a new orchestral expression of jazz emphasizing space and lyricism, the extension yet antithesis of bebop. Davis defined the new style with a series of recordings for the Capitol label, later reissued as *Birth of the Cool*.

Charlie began 1949 on an up note, again winning the number-one alto slot in the *Metronome* readers' poll, outpolling Johnny Hodges 1,058 to 393. *Metronome* noted Charlie's contribution to the bebop tradition and influence on subsequent generations of jazz musicians:

> Charlie Parker won his position in this year's poll with the greatest of ease. His pre-eminence as one of the founding fathers of bop, as the definitive exemplar of the medium on alto, and as a fount of new jazz ideas, in or out of the idiom associated with him and Dizzy Gillespie, has, at this point, carried him to the very top of his profession. Today, very few jazz instrumentalists born since the first World War play without a decisive Parker influence. . . . His work can be heard, in some small measure at least, in almost all the alto

men who placed near him except those trained in an earlier music: listen to Art Pepper, George Weidler, Sonny Stitt, Charlie Kennedy, Lee Konitz [and] you will hear at least a warble of Bird music.[37]

At the first of the year, Billy Shaw left the Moe Gale Agency to form his own agency. Located in the RCA building, the Shaw agency represented Charlie, Miles Davis, clarinetist Buddy DeFranco, organist Milt Buckner, and Lionel Hampton. Charlie became Shaw's most important client. Shaw celebrated their new affiliation by buying Charlie a new black Cadillac sedan. On Max Roach's wedding day, Charlie showed up with his Cadillac and a driver to chauffer the happy couple around town.

Charlie spent the late winter and early spring alternating between the Royal Roost and tours of the Midwest. In early May, he made his international debut, headlining the eight-day Jazz Festival International 1949, produced by writer Charles Delaunay and the Hot Clubs of France at the Salle Pleyel, the main concert hall in Paris. The twenty-five thousand jazz fans passing through the concert hall over the course of the festival divided into two camps: traditionalists following Hugues Panassie and modernists led by Delaunay.[38] One-time allies, the two bitterly split over bebop. On stage, Sidney Bechet, Jimmy McPartland, along with Lips Page and Don Byas, led the traditional charge. Charlie and the quintet with Tadd Dameron's group featuring Miles Davis, James Moody, and Kenny Clarke championed the modern style. British, French, and Swedish groups rounded out the bill, making it a truly international event.

The Tadd Dameron group featuring Davis and Moody opened the festival, confounding the audience with its fiery bebop style, judged by Marian McPartland in *Down Beat* as "some of the most controversial music of the day." Traditionalists then took over, dazzling the audience with their showmanship and artistry. Lips Page, always a crowd pleaser, brought down the house with his onstage antics and spirited Kansas City–style solos. Soprano saxophonist Sidney Bechet, representing the New Orleans tradition, charmed the audience with his dazzling performance of "Summertime." Cornetist Jimmy McPartland, who was accompanied by a pickup band, paid tribute to Bix Beiderbecke and the Chicago school.

Hitting the stage for the finale, Charlie astonished the audience, modernists and traditionalists alike, with his endless fountain of ideas and precise

execution. Marian McPartland breathlessly reported how Charlie's brilliance brought the audience to the front of their seats, then to their feet for
a standing ovation. "The band had a tremendous beat, and Charlie, dis-
playing his prodigious technique and originality of ideas, wove in and out
of the rhythmic patterns laid down by Max Roach to the accompaniment
of ecstatic cries of '*Formidable!*' from the fanatics."[39]

Charlie created a sensation in Paris. "The reception in France was lavish,"
Tommy Potter recalled. "Autograph-signing parties in record shops and lots
of press coverage topped by a press party in Bird's hotel room. Charlie ordered
a bottle of champagne, and he tipped the waiter generously; and well he might,
because he had that waiter make five trips for five buckets of champagne."[40]
Throngs of admirers mobbed Charlie in clubs. At Club Saint Germain, Charlie
met existentialist philosopher Jean Paul Sartre. Introduced to Sartre by the
writer Simone de Beauvoir, Charlie quipped, "I'm very glad to have met you,
Mr. Sartre. I like your playing very much."[41] While in Paris, Charlie attended
a concert by guitarist Andres Segovia and met his hero, classical saxophonist
Marcel Mule. The toast of the town, Charlie dined at the estates of aristocrats.

Like Charlie at the Paris jazz festival, bebop gained acclaim with mainstream jazz fans. Club owners, musicians, and critics quickly capitalized on
bebop's popularity. In mid-April, the owners of the Royal Roost opened Bop
City, a smart, eight-hundred-seat nightclub a few blocks north on Broadway.
Bop City, a bebop venue in name only, opened with Artie Shaw's forty-piece
symphony orchestra with strings, Ella Fitzgerald, and trombonist Kai Winding's sextet. Billie Holiday and other celebrities seated in the reserved section gave the club a cachet. Fans of more modest means lined up for several
blocks, eagerly waiting to pay the five-dollar admission fee to mill around
the bar or huddle in the bleacher section, sipping milkshakes. In the lobby,
management set up tables with signs offering to explain to the uninitiated,
"What is bop?" At one of the tables, Leonard Feather hawked his first book,
Inside Be-Bop.

An early champion of the new music, Feather chronicled the history of
bebop, profiled those responsible for its development, and analyzed bebop's
contribution to the jazz tradition, citing key recordings. Concluding his history section, Feather expressed the need to break free of bebop's stylistic
limitations and create a fresh movement:

Now that bebop has been absorbed into the mainstream of jazz, the major question that remains is how it will expand, escape its limitations and clichés, lead the way into something still richer in musical texture and finer in artistic concept. If jazz is to remain a separate entity at all, the element of swing, the implied steady beat and tempo, will still be a vital part of every jazz performance, as will the art of improvisation on a given set of chord patterns. With these confines it may still be possible to develop fertile new ground, as the incorporation of Cuban rhythms has shown. A wider range of instrumentation, with full use of strings and woodwinds, may be one solution; greater variety in thematic bases, and in the tone colors of orchestration, are bound to come.

In a direct reference to Charlie's penchant of conjuring new melodies based on the chord changes of popular standards, Feather predicted the need to transcend the limitations of the technique. "It seems doubtful that jazzmen will be satisfied, a few years from now, to base half their melodies on the chords of 'I Got Rhythm,' 'How High the Moon' or the blues."[42]

Writing in *Metronome* later that year, Barry Ulanov echoed Feather's assessment of the state of bebop and jazz, concluding with the hope Charlie would, by example, lead the way to a new breakthrough. "I have a sneaking suspicion that Bird has been aware of all these things for some years, no matter what he says in his interviews. Certain it is that he began the pruning process and the building activity a long time ago. If change in jazz must come now through imitation of the present-day Charlie Parker, a musician of great talent, a man with a beat, one of the founders of bop, but today much too big to be called a bopper."[43]

For his part, Charlie felt creatively exhausted. Lennie Tristano confided that in 1949, "Bird told me that he had said as much as he could in this particular idiom. He wanted to develop something else in the way of playing or another style. He was tired of playing the same ideas. I imagine it was brought to his attention strongly by the repetitious copying of his style by everybody he met. His music had become stylized. He, of course, played it better than anyone else. In his great moments, it was still fresh. It had to be inspired. I don't think he had this inspiration often after a time. It was a question of saying what had been already said."[44] Charlie, having reached a creative plateau, rested on his hard-won laurels.

Charlie spent the summer touring the Midwest, then joined the fall Jazz at the Philharmonic tour. In October, Charlie re-formed the quintet and opened for a six-week run at the Three Deuces. Before opening night, Charlie replaced Kenny Dorham with Red Rodney. Like Miles Davis, Rodney initially felt overwhelmed by the thought of playing alongside Charlie. "Bird came over to me and offered me the job," recalled Rodney. "And, naturally, I wanted it, but I said, 'My God, man, there's so many people who are much more deserving than me.' And I mentioned Kenny Dorham, for one, who had worked with him for a while. And Bird said, 'Hey let me be the judge of that. I want you. I think that you're the player that I want in my band.' And I still thought that, 'Well gee this is really nice and all, but he likes me personally, that's why he's doing it. I'm not worthy.' . . . I was really frightened, I didn't think I belonged."[45] Just as he had with Miles Davis, Charlie patiently brought his new protégé along, working out the rough spots on the bandstand of the Three Deuces.

In late November, Norman Granz recorded Charlie with strings, realizing Feather's idea of broadening bebop's palette with orchestration. Charlie excitedly embraced the project, feeling that recording with strings legitimized his music. Sticking closely to the thirty-two-bar popular music form, Charlie recorded six of his favorite standards accompanied by a chamber ensemble and a jazz rhythm section. In a near complete musical turnaround, Charlie, with the exception of his solo on "Just Friends," played the melody straight instead of improvising on the changes. His tone assumed a new lyricism. Granz, convinced the formula would introduce Charlie to a new audience, rushed the masters into production for release in early 1950.

In mid-December, the quintet opened at Birdland, a new nightclub on Broadway at Fifty-Second Street, named in Charlie's honor. Originally scheduled to open in September 1949, the club opened on December 15, 1949. Patrons entered under a canopy and descended a flight of stairs to a landing where they paid a seventy-five cents admission fee. Another flight of stairs down led to a dark, smoky "table-crowded" room that held just under five hundred fans. A long bar stretched along the left wall. To the right of the bar in the peanut gallery several lines of chairs faced the bandstand. Serious fans crowded this area, nursing drinks while listening intently to the music. A fence separated the peanut gallery from the main listening area with tables and semi-circular booths lining the right wall. Murals of leading jazz artists adorned the walls. Initially, cages of finches lined the room, but the smoke and noise soon killed the birds. Charlie was flattered to have a regular gig at a club named in his honor.

Birdland opened with *A Journey through Jazz*, a program chronicling the evolution of jazz from New Orleans to the still emerging cool movement. Riding high on the postwar Dixieland revival, Max Kaminsky's band launched the program, satisfying the traditionalists in the audience. Covering the middle ground, Lester Young and Hot Lips Page presented a set of swing, Kansas City style. Charlie and company delivered a brilliant performance that defined the bop movement. The Lennie Tristano Quintet articulated the latest movement in jazz, which later became known as the third stream. Gathering for a group picture, Kaminsky, Young, Page, Charlie, and Tristano picked up their instruments for what John S. Wilson in *Down Beat* considered "the most fantastic cacophony ever heard."[46] From his home base at Birdland, Charlie branched out, playing top clubs in New York and theaters across the country with his rhythm section and the string ensemble.

Right before Christmas, Charlie received a new alto from the King Instrument Company in exchange for his endorsement. He picked up a new King Super-20 with a sterling silver bell at Manny's Music Store, not far from Times Square. As if they knew of Charlie's penchant for pawning his alto, workmen at King personalized the horn by engraving his name on the ring that attached the silver bell to the brass horn and attaching a nameplate to the case. Charlie gave the horn a ringing endorsement in *Metronome*, proclaiming, "King really came up with *THE* horn."[47]

In February 1950, Mercury released *Charlie Parker with Strings*, to strong sales but mixed reviews. *Down Beat* praised the recordings, but *Metronome* roundly panned the concept and Charlie's performance: "Bird with strings may have seemed like a good idea, and *Just Friends* proves that it could have been. But the club labeled 'Play the melody!' that was evidently brandished over Charlie's head is all too obvious, and we can't take the emasculated alto sounds that are all too like Rudy Weidoft on a bad day. . . . 'Just Friends,' however, is Charlie's bid for freedom of interpretation. Save for a tasteless interpolation of 'My Man,' it's the usual deft Charlie performance of skill and inventiveness, for which it's almost worth acquiring the other five sides."[48]

Ironically, the popularity of the 78-rpm album set, quickly issued on the new long play 33⅓-rpm format, sparked a new trend in jazz by inspiring other musicians to record with strings.

Red Rodney, finding himself the odd man out—often passed over in favor of the string section—left the quintet and joined tenor saxophonist Charlie Ventura's group. Charlie and Rodney remained friends. A few months later, Charlie saved Rodney's life. While working with Charlie, Rodney had picked up a heroin habit. Rodney, who was trying to kick cold-turkey, mistook the pain from an appendicitis attack for withdrawal symptoms. "I was attempting to kick my first habit at the time—and not knowing the physiological reactions—thought that the terrible pain was due to this effort," confessed Rodney. "Unable to bear the pain any longer I went to his [Charlie's] home and told him my story—he quickly fixed me—and easily informed me that my pain was not due to withdrawal and we were going to the hospital. On the way I passed out and the doctors credited Bird with saving my life."[49]

In early 1950, Charlie and Chan renewed their romance. Charlie began stopping by Chan's apartment near Central Park on his way to score drugs in Spanish Harlem. Charlie courted Chan, who was initially coy, and they became lovers again. They first appeared together in public at the St. Nicholas Ballroom in mid-February. Over the next few months, Charlie spent more time with Chan than Doris.

Doris, chagrined by Charlie's affair with Chan and suffering from ill health, moved in with her mother in Rock Island, Illinois. "The parting was a combination of things," revealed Doris. "I was in no physical condition to cope with the erratic life of a jazz musician. I was nervous and bothered by low blood pressure and anemia. I just couldn't take the anxiety of wondering where he was the nights he came home very late or not at all. Visions of him hospitalized or in jail would come into my mind."[50]

In late-May, Chan and her daughter Kim moved into Charlie's apartment at 422 East Eleventh on the Lower East Side. Charlie embraced Kim as his own, winning her over with his uncanny ability to relate to children. Charlie, who wanted more children, delighted in family life. Chan assumed Charlie's name, but they never married. Not one to stand on ceremony, Charlie remained married to Rebecca, Gerri, and Doris while living in a common law marriage with Chan.

The next month, Charlie opened at Café Society. Charlie charmed the elite audience, tailoring sets to suit even the squarest dancers. *Metronome* noted the change in Charlie's onstage demeanor and style:

> Charlie Parker played a dance date at Café Society in June and early July and added another shining gem to his already glittering diadem. In the show, which Bird emceed with great charm, he restricted himself to a couple of tunes from his recent album. . . . "Just Friends" and "April in Paris," which to these ears at least sounded far more effective with rhythm section backing than with the tritely scored strings. Between shows the bright Charlie quartet . . . polished off dance sets, with Bird's horn settling comfortably on show tunes and jazz standards, shuffling off rumbas and generally keeping a lovely sound and a bumptious beat going which were, to coin a phrase, the swinging end. In all, this engagement was a delightful reminder of what used to be an accepted fact, that a distinguished jazz band inevitably plays the best sort of dance music."[51]

While generally playing it straight, Charlie could not help giving the well-heeled audience a taste of pure bebop or spontaneously joining Art Tatum, who shared the bill, in a little "Tea for Two." After closing at Café Society, Charlie spent the summer playing Birdland and the Apollo Theater. That fall he toured leading clubs and theaters across the country, accompanied by his trio and a string ensemble.

In late November, Charlie returned to Europe, starting with a seven-day tour of Scandinavia, sponsored by the jazz journal *Estrad*. Before leaving on the tour, Charlie kicked his habit out of respect for Scandinavian audiences. Greeted as visiting jazz royalty by school children and jazz aficionados alike, Charlie played concert halls accompanied by trumpeter Rolf Ericson and Sweden's top bop musicians. American expatriate Roy Eldridge, then living in France, joined in on four dates, relishing the opportunity to jam with Charlie. Truly treated like an artist, Charlie reciprocated by serenading his late-night audience with flowing solo improvisations, weaving popular standards and his own compositions. Charlie loved the easy ambience of Sweden. All-night jam sessions followed the concerts, laced with liberal amounts of schnapps.

The nonstop revelry took its toll on Charlie's already fragile health, exhausting him by week's end. After wrapping up the tour of Sweden, Charlie moved on to Paris for an appearance at Charles Delaunay's upcoming First International Jazz Fair. While in Paris, Charlie stayed with drummer Kenny Clarke and his pregnant fiancée, vocalist Annie Ross. In the post–World War II period, Clarke and scores of other jazz musicians, who were fed up with racism in the United States, moved to Europe, where they were treated with dignity denied to them in their own country. Charlie considered joining the growing ranks of expatriate jazz musicians in Europe, but circumstances cut his trip short, bringing him back to the United States.[52]

Following three days of carousing in the jazz clubs in Montmartre with Clarke and Don Byas, Charlie fell ill, stricken by peptic ulcers. Sick and desperate to get back home, Charlie hastily booked a flight to New York and quietly left Paris without making good on his obligation to play the festival or bothering to return Delaunay's advance. Back in the states, Charlie appeared on Leonard Feather's radio program and apologized to his French fans on air.

Several days later, Charlie entered Medical Arts Hospital, in Manhattan. Alarmed by Charlie's immediate condition and health in general, doctors put the thirty-year-old on a special diet under twenty-four-hour care. Feeling better after a week of rest, Charlie stole out of the hospital and caught a cab to Birdland, where he perched at the bar in his pajamas, downing scotch mixed with milk on the rocks, proclaiming the concoction his new health drink. Finally, management convinced the errant Charlie to return to the hospital, where he slipped back into his room by the fire escape, leaving the staff none the wiser. He convalesced for another week before being discharged with strict orders to stay away from alcohol and maintain a bland diet.

Ignoring doctor's orders, Charlie returned to his old ways, eating and drinking voraciously while dulling the pain of his ulcer with increasing quantities of heroin.[53] "Although he was constantly told by doctors how sick he was, I don't think even he believed it," Chan judged. "Bird had such a huge appetite for life that it was impossible to believe he wasn't immortal."[54] Accolades and awards followed for the next few years, but they came fewer and further apart as Charlie's prodigious alcohol and drug consumption strained his physical and mental health.

CHAPTER 7

Parker's Mood

The year 1951 began with great promise for Charlie—professionally and personally. Billy Shaw lined up a series of engagements with the string group stretching through the spring, and Chan was pregnant with their first child. "Bird was joyous," Chan recalled. "My having his baby assured him of my love. Before Pree was born we moved to a large apartment on Avenue B. For the first time in his life Bird had a stable family life. He played his role as husband and father to the hilt. He adored Kim and took his paternal duties seriously."[1] The three-story Gothic revival brownstone apartment building at 151 Avenue B was located across from Tompkins Square Park in an ethnically mixed neighborhood on New York's lower eastside. Their spacious apartment spanned the ground floor. The back entrance opened onto a concrete courtyard with a swing set, where Kim played with other children who lived in the building.

With a growing family to support, Charlie spent most of 1951 on the road, capitalizing on the popularity of his string recordings. In early February, he launched a tour of the Midwest with a ten-piece string section, headlining a mismatched bill featuring rhythm-and-blues pianist Ivory Joe Hunter and his band along with vaudeville veterans Butterbeans and Susie. Charlie rose to the occasion as a bandleader. Pianist Walter Bishop recalled, "Bird conducted himself beautifully on the tour. He fronted the band impressively and with dignity."[2] Off the bandstand, Charlie reverted to his old ways.

Caught short of marijuana on the tour, Charlie revisited neighborhoods where he had scored during earlier tours with the McShann band. As Walter Bishop explained,

> I remember one time we were in St. Paul, Minnesota, and looking for marijuana. Bird and I got in a cab. We couldn't find any in St. Paul. We went all the way to Minneapolis. We got out of the cab, walked a few blocks, and Bird stopped. He looked around and I said, "What's the matter, Bird?" "God damn, Bish, you know one thing. I stood on this very same corner thirteen years ago, looking for the same thing. I guess a man never learns." Sure enough he found some old cronies, old numbers men, pimps, hustlers, old-time racketeers who were still on the scene since the time thirteen years ago when he came through with Jay McShann.[3]

While on tour, Charlie usually managed to find a source for marijuana, but he often had difficulty scoring quality heroin at a reasonable price, particularly in smaller cities. An addict since the age of sixteen, Charlie needed heroin to maintain his habit and dull the pain of his chronic ulcer. "You know" he explained to Bishop, "there's quite a number of things wrong with me. I go to this heart specialist, you know, give him a hundred dollars for the relief of my heart. He treats me, don't do me no good; my heart is still messed up. I go to the ulcer man, give him seventy-five dollars to cool my ulcers out; it don't do no good. There's a little cat in a dark alley around the corner. I give him five dollars for a bag of shit; my ulcer's done, my heart trouble gone, everything gone, all my ailments."[4]

In between tours, Charlie headlined shows at the Apollo Theater, Birdland, and other nightclubs scattered across New York. Like other musicians working in New York nightclubs, Charlie carried a cabaret card permitting him to perform in the city's cabarets and nightclubs. The city enacted the cabaret card system after the repeal of Prohibition to protect nightclub patrons from criminals and prostitutes. Musicians, entertainers, and dancers had to line up at the police station alongside bartenders, waitresses, and busboys to register for their cards. The card system gave the police considerable control over musicians working in New York. Musicians whose cards were revoked for narcotics or other violations were barred from playing New York City clubs. Billie Holiday and other banned musicians who made their home in New York were forced to play out-of-town dates to earn a living, costing them both financially and creatively.

In early July 1951, the police department revoked Charlie's cabaret card. After years of playing cat and mouse, the narcotics squad finally snagged him. "Bird had taken a bust," Chan explained. "At his trial, the judge said, 'Three months, suspended sentence.' And a lecture followed, 'Mr. Parker, if you ever have the urge to stick a needle in your arm again, take your horn out into the woods somewhere and blow.'"[5]

At the same time that Charlie lost his cabaret card, New York State launched an investigation into drug use at the Apollo Theater, Birdland, and other jazz clubs in New York City. Local tabloids picked up on the story, and radio station WNYC broadcast the lurid details of a woman musician who was forced into prostitution by her habit. According to *Down Beat*, "She mentioned Birdland specifically as a place where dope was sold, claiming that addicts and peddlers visited the spot, particularly when name musicians were there."[6] Charlie abruptly left New York for Kansas City, ostensibly to spend time with Addie.

Charlie seldom visited Addie, but he called her every Sunday evening without fail. When Addie had graduated from nursing school a few years earlier, Charlie sent her a watch and three hundred dollars for uniforms with a promise to visit soon. Finally making good on his pledge, Charlie spent most of July with Addie in Kansas City. Chan, who was nine months pregnant, stayed behind in New York with Kim.

Shortly after arriving in Kansas City, Charlie became stranded by the great flood of 1951. Heavy rains across the Midwest in May and June swelled the Missouri and Kansas Rivers to record levels. A series of thunderstorms rolled across the area from July 9 to July 13, pushing the Kansas River out of its banks. Early in the morning of July 13, the river crested as it flowed into the Missouri River just west of Kansas City. The surge of water breeched the levies in the Armourdale district in Kansas City, Kansas, and the Central Industrial District in Kansas City, Missouri, wreaking havoc on the area. The flood washed away stockyards, meat-packing plants, railroad tracks, and nightclubs in the area known as the West Bottoms. Fortunately, the flood spared clubs located downtown and "out in the county."

Since Charlie's last visit to Kansas City, the late-night jazz club scene "out in the county" had shifted from south Kansas City east to U.S. 40 Highway in unincorporated Jackson County. Tootie Clarkin moved the Mayfair Club from Seventy-Ninth and Wornall to 40 Highway just past the city limits. A roomy, stucco building with large, painted-over front windows, the New Mayfair served steaks, fried chicken, hamburgers, and other home-style favorites along with all the fixings. Operating outside the jurisdiction of Kansas City, Tootie's featured music from 9:00 P.M. to 4:00 A.M.

As usual, Tootie hired Charlie on short notice for an engagement at the Mayfair Club. When in Kansas City, Charlie liked to work with Sleepy Hickcox, a dreamy-eyed pianist who played in all the hard keys. Hickcox was unavailable, so Charlie had to settle for the pianist with the house band. Charlie, who was usually very supportive of fledging musicians, clashed with the pianist who dragged the time and played off key. Charlie complained about the pianist to Tootie. The next evening, Tootie, who loved playing practical jokes, placed an egg on the piano before the band arrived. The pianist assumed that Charlie left the symbol of disapproval. Outraged, he told Charlie, "You think you're big stuff, but you ain't so much Bird." Charlie coolly looked at the pianist and replied, "I ought to go out, get my gun and shoot you in the mouth."[7]

On July 21, the Woody Herman band opened a weeklong engagement at the Pla-Mor Ballroom. Herman band members, excited to find Charlie in town, flocked to the Mayfair to jam all night long. While races mixed freely at Tootie's, African Americans were denied access to the Pla-Mor and other white venues around Kansas City. However, African Americans could attend events at the Municipal Auditorium, Kansas City's largest civic entertainment venue. When white bands came to town, they usually played an engagement at a white ballroom followed by a mixed-race dance at the Municipal Auditorium. That Sunday, the Herman band played a dance at the Municipal Auditorium with Charlie as the featured soloist for the evening.

A few hours before show time, the promoter Francis M. Spencer died unexpectedly, casting a pall over the event. Woody Herman, who doubled as

turned down offers to record for other labels. Charlie's recording projects for Norman Granz paid well but came at a creative cost.

Granz exerted undue influence on Charlie's choice of sidemen and material. Drummer Roy Haynes, a regular member of the quartet, later publicly protested being excluded from recording dates by Granz. "The reason I never made many records with Charlie all the time I was with him . . . was Norman Granz," Haynes complained to *Down Beat*. "Bird was under record contract to Norman. Before a session, he'd show Norman the list of musicians he'd like to use. Everything would be all right until he got to my name. 'You mean you'd like to use Roy instead of Buddy Rich?' Norman would ask. The answer was on the paper, but Buddy always wound up on the date—except for one album I finally made."[13]

Granz took charge of the sessions, selecting the songs and groups that accompanied Charlie. The first session on January 23 featured Charlie with strings augmented by a big jazz band. The next week, Granz recorded Charlie performing a set of Latin standards backed by a septet featuring conga and bongos players. The third session on March 25 featured Charlie with a big band playing standards.

The recordings from the sessions met with mixed reviews. Critics praised the big band sessions but panned the string recordings. A reviewer in *Down Beat* noted Charlie's creative stagnation. "The resplendent sheen of novelty and excitement that coated Bird's string experiments, back in the days when they were experiments seems to have worn off. Whether because the freshness has worn off or because the arrangements are logey and a little pretentious, there's no real excitement here. Charlie's tone is loud and unsubtle and the only mild surprise is the insertion of a couple of solos by other horns, for the first time in this series—a trombone bit here, a trumpet there. Charlie should have made that first fine album with strings and then moved on to something new. He is too great a musician to get into a rut."[14]

The string section became a musical albatross, overshadowing Charlie professionally and creatively. Charlie's tours with strings, which paid handsomely, undermined the already precarious stability of his quintet. Red Rodney explained, "Whenever Bird worked with strings I had to find other employment and usually did much better financially. But, he always talked me into returning to the quintet after the strings finished their work."[15] While Rodney always returned, other members drifted away.

Unable to sustain a working quintet, Charlie toured as a soloist, playing with house bands and pickup groups. Tenor saxophonist Ray Turner recalled Charlie's frustration at playing with less skilled musicians night after night:

> Bird was a star, and they sent him out as a single, throwing him in with different outfits. It was like an actor appearing in a different play every night. Bird was under a strain. One night he appeared slightly alcoholic and in a vile mood. The band he was supposed to play with was not of a caliber he deserved, but it was to their credit that they tried hard. Bird just stood off to the side listening, and at one juncture, he tore off the neck of his horn and threw it into the bell. After a little while, due probably to Bird's presence, the band came alive, and they really started to wail. Parker grabbed his horn to join in and for a few seconds he seemed disconcerted and puzzled, for it was a horn without a neck and mouthpiece—he had forgotten, but he quickly assembled it and himself musically.[16]

In the spring of 1952, Charlie toured the West Coast as a soloist. Billy Shaw booked the club dates on the tour and advanced Charlie money for airfare. In turn, Charlie signed an agreement to have a small percentage of the advance deducted from his weekly pay. Chan, who was pregnant again, stayed behind to care for Pree and Kim.

Charlie traveled light, playing with local pick-up bands. Left to his own devices, he careened up the West Coast from one misadventure to another, alienating club owners along the way. He arrived in Los Angeles in early May for a two-and-a-half week engagement at the Tiffany Club, one of the leading jazz spots in Los Angeles.

Since Charlie's last visit to Los Angeles, the jazz scene in California had come into its own. California jazz musicians moved beyond bebop to create a new cool style, distinguished by restrained execution, orchestration with an emphasis on lyricism and melody. From San Francisco to Los Angeles young musicians championed the new mode pioneered by arrangers/composers Gil Evans, Gerry Mulligan, Miles Davis, pianist Dave Brubeck, trumpeter Shorty Rogers, and saxophonist Jimmy Guiffre. A freewheeling Sunday jam session at the Lighthouse at Hermosa Beach fostered the new

West Coast style that reflected the casual beach culture in Los Angeles and other coastal cities.

The Shaw agency hired pianist Donn Trenner to help Charlie assemble a band for the engagement at the Tiffany Club. Trenner rounded out the rhythm section with drummer Lawrence Marable and bassist Harry Babasin. Charlie auditioned a number of trumpet players before selecting Chet Baker during a jam session at the Trade Winds Club.

Baker, a young white newcomer with boyish good looks, had grown up in Oklahoma. A restless youth, he dropped out of high school and joined the army. A naturally talented musician who played by ear, Baker faked his way into the Sixth Army Band stationed at the Presidio in San Francisco. On the weekends he jammed at the Black Hawk and other clubs in the Bay Area. An officer soon discovered that Baker could not read music and transferred him to the military band at Fort Huachuca near the Mexican border. Fighting off boredom, Baker and a group of kindred souls smuggled green marijuana across the border and stayed high all day long. Baker faked a psychological disorder to get out of the military and settled down in Los Angeles. Like Miles Davis and Red Rodney before, he was at first a little intimidated playing alongside Charlie.

The hastily assembled quintet opened at the Tiffany Club on May 29, 1952. Charlie mentored Baker on and off the bandstand. "He treated me sorta like a son," Baker judged. "I can see now how helpful and understanding he was. He stayed with the tunes I knew well, and he avoided the real fast tempos he used to like so much."[17] Charlie enjoyed Baker's clear tone, which reminded him of the Bix Beiderbecke records that he listened to as a youth in Kansas City. While Charlie coolly surveyed the audience while soloing, the less confident Baker pointed his horn toward the floor, avoiding eye contact.[18]

During the day, Baker chauffeured Charlie around town, showing him the sights. Charlie loved the cliffs at Palos Verde overlooking the South Bay of Los Angeles. He found a rare moment of peace, standing on the windswept cliffs gazing at the waves rolling onto the beach below.[19]

Before shows, Baker watched Charlie down fifths of Hennessy cognac and snort spoonfuls of heroin. Charlie no longer had to visit Central Avenue to score heroin; dealers followed him from club to club. He warned Baker to stay away from heroin. When the dealers who shadowed Charlie made overtures to Baker, Charlie pulled the young trumpeter aside and told him, "You got nothin' to say to him. Don't fuck with these guys."[20] By the end of the engagement, Baker was scoring for Charlie.

Charlie's voracious appetite for alcohol, drugs, and food began compromising his already fragile health. During the previous couple of years, he had put on considerable weight, steadily growing from pudgy to portly. His binge drinking and narcotics abuse while in Los Angeles caused his weight to balloon. Charlie's considerable girth strained the top button of the jacket of his white suit, wrinkled by nights spent sleeping on couches in apartments of friends and acquaintances. He looked considerably older than thirty-one.

The tour also cost Charlie financially. The expense of maintaining a home in New York while living on the road led to financial disaster. The small amounts of money he sent to Chan by Western Union barely covered household expenses let alone the medical bills for Pree. His spendthrift ways and voracious appetite for heroin compounded matters. Charlie habitually squandered his pay and demanded advances from club owners. His persistent financial scams against club owners, sidemen, and the Shaw Agency led to a flurry of charges and countercharges mediated by the American Federation of Musicians.

When the owner of the Tiffany Club, Chuck Landis, deducted the agreed amount to repay the advance Charlie owed the Shaw Agency, Charlie disparaged Shaw and threatened to walk out. Landis relented and paid Charlie the full amount of $750 per week. Feeling caught in the middle, Landis contacted Shaw. The conflict followed Charlie up the coast to San Francisco.

After closing out at the Tiffany Club on June 14, Charlie played a date with the Harry Babasin All Stars at the Trade Winds Club in Inglewood and then headed to San Francisco for an engagement at the Say When Club. A letter from Billy Shaw greeted Charlie's arrival at the club. In the letter dated June 16, 1952, Shaw, who felt personally betrayed, detailed Charlie's financial transgressions and disregard for the Agency:

Dear Charlie:
    I understand that you are back to your old tricks again, making various promises, and not living up to them.

When you were in my office, you signed deduction orders, and asked me to have your money sent here; now, I understand you threatened to walk out if there were any deductions, etc. Also understand you made some very ugly remarks about me.

In the first place, Charlie, rest assured I will not take your word again in the future; as a matter of fact, we do not have to worry about anything but our own monies. We advanced you transportation money to California, and you only allowed them to deduct our commissions, plus the $15.00 per week on the old balance. I am sending a copy of this letter to Cliff Aronson.

Charlie, you are indebted to us in the sum of $734.98. You promised to give us $15.00 a week towards the balance; since you are getting $750.00 a week, I am sure you can spare a stinking $15 per week. In the event you give Cliff Aronson any more trouble with regarding the deductions orders, we will be forced to take this up with the Federation. As far as I am concerned, your word doesn't mean a thing to me anymore; we have tried to help you in every way, but to no avail. I am tired of always getting a run around.

Sincerely,

Billy Shaw[21]

Events that followed ended Charlie's association with the Billy Shaw Agency. During the engagement at the Say When Club, Charlie estranged the club manager, Dutch Neiman, and the local union. One of the leading clubs in San Francisco, the Say When featured a house band led by drummer Cuz Cousineau that accompanied visiting musicians and entertainers. The Cousineau band featured clarinetist Vince Cattolica and guitarist Eddie Duran. Charlie surprised Nieman by showing up with Chet Baker and a drummer from another union, insisting he would only work with them. Opening night, Charlie gave the Cousineau band the benefit of the doubt. The next day, he hired a local pianist and bassist and refused to work with the house band. Tenor saxophonist Flip Philips, the co-headliner, concurred with Charlie's opinion of the house band and left after the first week. Charlie showed his displeasure with the Say When by showing up late and sitting in after hours at other clubs.

Charlie frequented the late-night jam sessions at Bop City which featured drummer Art Blakey, Curly Russell on bass, and Kenny Drew on piano. One night when Charlie showed up wobbly drunk, Blakey and the others took their revenge on him for shorting them on money at the last date they played together. Under pressure from Blakey, Charlie reluctantly sat in with the band. Blakey called "52nd St. Theme," and the band launched into the bop standard at a breakneck tempo, leaving Charlie behind. After several false starts and fluffed notes, Charlie, who was reminded of his humiliation years earlier at the Reno Club, told the band "Give me an hour, I'll be back." Saxophonist Jerome Richardson recalled, "No one knows how he did it, but in one hour, he returned cold, deadly sober. There was no tune too fast, too slow, too unfamiliar. He played till seven in the morning."[22]

Charlie's late night and onstage antics irritated the no-nonsense Neiman. *Down Beat* detailed how the booking at the Say When descended into chaos:

> The heralded Charlie Parker–Flip Phillips battle-of-the-saxes at the Say When disintegrated into one of the most miserable foul-ups in local history. Both instrumentalists were salty at having to work with the house band and Parker finally brought in a unit of his own. Flip and the club parted company after the first week, both being wholeheartedly dissatisfied. Charlie remained for part of the next week, but that ended in a class 'A' hassle. After appearing twice on the Cerebral Palsy TV marathon, Charlie took up a collection in the club, asked club op [operator] Dutch Neiman for a contribution, was refused (because Neiman said he had already contributed), took the mike, called the house 'cheap' and then Neiman and the Bird engaged in a gentle shoving contest with Parker losing. Neiman refused to pay him off and Bird was stranded in town for almost a week. The mix up was still being batted around at the union at press time.[23]

In truth, the TV Marathon had ended by the time Charlie decided to take up the collection at the club.

After the fracas with Neiman, Charlie sat in with tenor saxophonist Vido Musso's band at the Black Hawk. Opening night, Charlie sent word to patrons of the Say When that he was at the Black Hawk. Incensed, Neiman refused to pay Charlie for the three remaining nights of the contract. Charlie later filed a complaint against the Say When for nonpayment with National Federation of Musicians. The complaint brought a strong rebuttal from Neiman and the San Francisco Musicians Union, Local 669. During the engagement at the Say When, Charlie failed to file a contract with the local and pay the 10 percent surcharge levied against visiting bandleaders. In a letter to the national union, A. V. Forbes, the secretary of Local 669 complained that "He [Charlie] not only intended to ignore the Local, but was most insulting to the officers, and created a scene which was unprovoked. As for his conduct both at the club, and the Local, it was without precedent. The man appeared to be constantly under the influence of something."[24]

On the way back to New York, Charlie stopped off in Kansas City to visit Addie and hustle up some nightclub dates. Charlie opened at Tootie's Mayfair on July 17 and abruptly closed a few days later. "In 1953 [1952] he came out to the club one night in an open convertible with some white girl he'd picked up in town," Tootie Clarkin remembered. "We got word somehow that she was trying to frame him on a narcotics charge for the government. He only had time to play eight bars of 'How High the Moon' when we motioned him off the bandstand. . . . I got up and said, 'The Bird goofed,' and the audience understood." According to Clarkin, the girl later framed two other musicians.[25]

The next week Charlie opened at the El Capitan in the heart of Eighteenth and Vine. Fans and musicians jammed the El Capitan to see Charlie playing on Eighteenth Street, where he had launched his career years earlier. The *Kansas City Call* reported that on opening night, "the place looked like celebrity nite."[26] Jay McShann stopped by to sit in with Charlie. Bringing their careers full circle, the two led off with "Hootie Blues." Charlie, out of respect for Jay, played his solo from the original recording note for note. He proved to be such a gracious crowd-pleaser that management added a second matinee and held him over the next week. Off hours, Charlie spent time with Addie and old friends at Eighteenth and Vine.

After playing three weeks of steady engagements in Kansas City, Charlie returned to New York with some money to show for the tour. He arrived just in time for the birth of his second child with Chan. As Chan labored in the hospital, Charlie walked off his nervousness in Tompkins Square Park. That rainy evening, Charlie first met Robert Reisner, a wiry, bearded young jazz enthusiast who taught art history at the New School for Social Research. Reisner distinctly remembered meeting Charlie. "I had been at a party on the East Side of New York City. It was around 12:30 [A.M.] when I saw a large, lumbering, lonely man, walking aimlessly. I recognized him and was amazed and thrilled, but what in the devil was he doing in this poor Jewish neighborhood, walking by himself in the soaking rain. 'You're Charlie Parker,' I said. 'I'm Bob Reisner. What are you doing by yourself?' There was absolutely no one around but him and me. He smiled a big, warm, brown smile. He said, 'My wife is having a baby, and I'm kind of walking off my nervousness and waiting to call back.'"[27] The two struck up a friendship that led to their future association. Inspired by the chance meeting, Reisner later booked Charlie in a Sunday jazz series and became the first to chronicle his life.

Early the next morning, Sunday, August 10, Chan delivered a healthy boy Charlie named Baird. The baby so closely resembled Charlie that he proudly bragged to have "spit him out."[28] Out of concern for Chan, Charlie stayed close to home for the next few months. Since moving into Avenue B, Charlie had spent little time at home. Now Chan found it hard to adjust to having Charlie around for long stretches. She was surprised by his fairly conventional attitudes about family life and motherhood. Charlie loved hosting Sunday dinners. Chan cooked a pot roast and relatives gathered around the treble clef–shaped dining room table for a family meal. He rebuked Chan for dressing immodestly in public and walking around the house naked in front of Baird. Charlie spent weekdays hanging out in neighborhood taverns, drinking and talking politics with the old ethnic men huddled at the bar. They had no idea of Charlie's celebrity, and that suited him.

Financial reality soon interrupted Charlie's domestic idyll. He remained on the Shaw Agency roster, but in name only. After the fiasco at the Say When, Billy Shaw quit booking club dates for Charlie, and the Say When dispute came back to haunt Charlie. Club owners who were already well aware of Charlie's reputation for unreliability declined to book him. Dutch Neiman pressed his case with the union, forcing Charlie to respond in kind. Charlie paced around the kitchen dictating to Chan, who diligently typed his response. In the end, Charlie lost the dispute with Dutch Neiman and had to pay one hundred dollars in damages. Charlie worked little that fall and winter, playing mainly concert dates as a solo.

While Charlie and Chan enjoyed the trappings of the middle class, driving a Cadillac and employing a maid to tidy up the apartment, they sank deeper in debt, sucked down by his habits and inability to work in New York. They applied for assistance from the Aid to Dependent Children board only to be rejected. Desperate for money, Charlie pawned his custom King alto and started playing an English Grafton acrylic saxophone given to him by a factory representative. Since the Grafton held little value to pawnbrokers, Charlie managed to keep it on hand for use when the King was in hock. It mattered little to Charlie, who routinely played borrowed horns. Red Rodney believed that Charlie "could play a tomato can and make it sound great."[29]

In early February 1953, Paul Bley, a brash, lanky young pianist from Montreal, turned up on Charlie's doorstep. A year earlier, Bley and other local musicians had established the Jazz Workshop, a jazz series administered and funded by musicians, held on Saturday afternoons at the Chez Paree, a leading Montreal club. After a series of successful concerts, Bley and other members of the Jazz Workshop decided to book Charlie.

Bley frequently traveled between Montreal and New York, where he attended Julliard. On a whim, Bley knocked on Charlie's door and asked him to play the Jazz Workshop that weekend. Charlie readily accepted the invitation. Well aware of Charlie's reputation for unreliability, Bley recalled, "He was totally out of work, totally without funds. And the money was right. . . . The question was not whether he would accept the gig, but whether he would show up for it."[30] Charlie pleasantly surprised Bley and the Jazz Workshop.

On February 5, 1953, Charlie flew to Montreal for an appearance on a CBFT television program coincidently called the Jazz Workshop, followed by a Saturday Jazz Workshop concert at the Chez Paree. He arrived late and missed the rehearsal for the television show, putting everyone involved with the show on edge. The producer, Bley, and the other musicians waited nervously for Charlie in the studio. At the time, television shows were broadcast live, so if Charlie failed to show, the broadcast would have to go on without him. Eager to be on television, Charlie arrived on time to an excited studio audience and relieved musicians.

The Paul Bley trio kicked off the program with a modern rendition of George Gershwin's "'S Wonderful." Next, guitarist Russell Garcia joined the trio for his composition "Johann Sebastian Bop." The announcer Don Cameron then introduced Charlie. After exchanging pleasantries with Cameron, Charlie called "Cool Blues." Bassist Neil Michaud recalled how "when Bird went on he just called over his shoulder 'Cool Blues in C.' He called every tune from that point on. I think we ended about half a second out from where we started. And the producers were ecstatic; first of all they were freaking that he was just calling everything from the front, and then of course in the end they were delighted because it had run so perfectly."[31]

Charlie spent the next day wandering around Montreal trying to score heroin with no luck. That evening, a pair of jazz fans, Hugette Rajotte, a young bohemian woman who was secretary of the Emanon Jazz Society, and Willie Lauzon, a fellow Emanon member, tracked down Charlie—holed up in his hotel. Charlie graciously invited them up to his room, which was sparsely furnished with two beds and a nightstand. Sweating profusely, he talked with his guests for several hours and then dozed off. Rajotte stayed in the room and worshipfully watched Charlie sleeping. She was surprised when he began whistling "April in Paris" in his sleep.

After breakfast the next morning, Charlie politely informed workshop members that he needed to get "straight" before he could play. Bassist Neil Michaud and Alfie Wade Jr., a young jazz fan, escorted Charlie to the apartment of pianist Steep Wade, where he scored some heroin.[32] Charlie was all business during the transaction, but in no hurry to get to the concert scheduled to begin at 2:00 that afternoon. The concert needed to end promptly at 5:00 P.M. to leave enough time for the staff to set the room up for Frank Sinatra. Michaud recalled, "We had a hell of a time getting him [Charlie] to the concert."[33]

They managed to get Charlie and Steep Wade to the concert after 4:00. Tenor saxophonist Brew Moore was on stage when Charlie arrived. Quickly assembling his Grafton, Charlie took charge of the session. He called "How High the Moon," then segued into "Ornithology." The pianist Valdo Williams rushed the tempo, throwing off other band members who were doing their best to follow Charlie. After an up-tempo version of "Cool Blues," Charlie called a short break and replaced Williams with Steep Wade. Perhaps as a nod to his newfound connection, Charlie launched into "Moose the Mooche," written for Emry Byrd, his Los Angeles connection years earlier. With time running short, Charlie quickly wrapped up the concert with the ballad "Embraceable You" and "Now's the Time" from the Savoy sessions. Later that night, Charlie sat in at the Latin Quarter with the house band. The next morning, he boarded a flight home to little fanfare, leaving behind a lasting impression.[34]

Aside from the heroin scored during his brief visit to Montreal, Charlie conducted himself with great dignity and set new musical standards for local musicians. Bley and the others who accompanied Charlie were both humbled and elated by the experience. Bley judged that "Everybody didn't know how badly they played until that performance. He [Charlie] defined the centre of the aesthetic and left all of us wanting." Bill Graham compared accompanying Charlie to "riding a fire engine around a corner at 90 miles an hour—you're just hanging on by the tips of your fingers."[35] For his part, Charlie was glad to be respected as an artist and to have the opportunity to make some money.

Faced with financial and professional disaster, Charlie resumed playing in New York clubs without his cabaret card. On February 13, 1953, Charlie opened at the Band Box, located next door to Birdland. Metronome hailed the Band Box as the "newest, biggest and most exciting night club to open in years."[36] Charlie shared the bill with the Duke Ellington orchestra featuring Charles Mingus on bass. Charlie and Mingus became friendly while working at the Band Box, setting the stage for their future association.

A few days after Charlie's debut at the Band Box, liquor control agents showed up and pulled him off the stage for performing without a cabaret card. Outraged, Charlie wrote a heartfelt letter to the State Liquor Authority pleading for the return of his card:

> My right to pursue my chosen profession has been taken away, and my wife and three children who are innocent of any wrongdoing are suffering. . . . My baby girl [Pree] is a city case in the hospital because her health has been neglected since we hadn't the necessary doctor fees. . . . I feel sure when you examine my record and see that I have made a sincere effort to become a family man and a good citizen, you will reconsider. If by any chance you feel I haven't paid my debt to society, by all means let me do so and give me and my family back the right to live.[37]

Shortly afterward, the state liquor board reinstated Charlie's card, just in time to hold off total financial disaster. Charlie worked steadily through the spring, alternating between the Band Box and Birdland, filling out his schedule with a series of Sunday concerts booked by Bob Reisner at the Open

Door in Greenwich Village. Reisner, tired of studying and talking about jazz, decided to "get his hands dirty" and learn more about jazz by becoming a concert promoter. The management of the Open Door turned Sunday nights over to Reisner, who was determined to bring modern jazz to the strip of jazz clubs in the Village which otherwise featured Dixieland. Vocalist Dave Lambert approached Reisner about booking Charlie at the Open Door. Surprised to find Charlie available, Reisner drew up an agreement. Reisner paid the sidemen scale and Charlie a percentage of the door. Charlie made his debut at the Open Door on April 26, 1953.

Charlie gave Reisner a crash course on jazz promotion, challenging him at every turn. Reisner related:

> [Charlie] was one of the most difficult individuals I have ever met. He was suave, cunning, urbane, charming, and generally fiendish—too much. He could butter me up, lull me into position, and then bang!—a great betrayal. I have seen managers quit on him in succession like horses shot under a great general. Musicians feared and loved him. Like the comedian who wants to play Hamlet, Bird fancied himself a business expert and virtually assumed command of the business end of the Sunday sessions in which he appeared. He was pretty shrewd about it. I always gave him the first numbered ticket on the roll, and he would match it against the last ticket to check the take. Something would always be wrong; he saw to that. Anything to start a fight, to accuse me of treachery, of cheating him, even though I never did—and I'm sure he never really felt I did—but, nevertheless, he went to preposterous lengths in his farcical belligerence.[38]

On May 15, 1953, Charlie joined Gillespie, Powell, Roach, and Charles Mingus for the first annual Festival of Creative Jazz Concert at Massey Hall in Toronto, giving his career and spirit a needed boost. The concert was produced by The New Jazz Society (NJS), a loose-knit organization that met at members' apartments to listen to jazz recordings. Dick Wattam, a parts clerk at General Electric, and other members of the NJS produced a successful concert featuring the Lennie Tristano Quintet. As a follow-up, they decided to put on a concert featuring Charlie, Dizzy Gillespie with Max Roach, and an all-star bebop rhythm section. They scheduled the concert for May 15, a date with no apparent conflicts.

On January 23, 1953, Wattam, Art Granatstein, and two other NJS members drew up contracts for the concert and drove all night to New York City where they contacted Charlie, Gillespie, Roach, and Mingus. They found Charlie at a recording session. During breaks in the session, Wattam and Granatstein pitched their idea to Charlie, who immediately agreed to participate. Granatstein recalled that "Bird was really the pussycat of them all. He was really desirous of getting together [with the others], and expressed it by signing up as readily as he did. He was a sweet guy, and he really went for it, really liked the whole bag."[39] After traveling as a solo playing with local bands, Charlie looked forward to an evening playing with his peers.

The other musicians were less enthusiastic and more businesslike. Gillespie and Roach, who were contacted in their homes, quizzed the young Canadians about the financial details of the agreement. Their questions about guarantees, travel arrangements, lodging, and other conditions caught the neophyte promoters off guard. Although they had yet to work out the details or raise the money for the concert, Wattam and Granatstein assured Gillespie and Roach that the finances for the concert were in place. In actuality, they planned to borrow enough money to cover initial expenses and then use the profits from the concert to pay the musicians. Gillespie and Roach reluctantly signed on. Mingus, who was a member of the Duke Ellington band, expressed little interest in the concert.

A few months later, Ellington fired Mingus for getting into an onstage altercation with trombonist Juan Tizol. The racially charged incident culminated with Tizol pulling a bolo knife on Mingus, who scrambled offstage and returned with a fire ax in hand, chasing Tizol off the stage. After the show, Mingus became the only musician ever to be personally fired by Ellington. Suddenly available, Mingus signed up for the Toronto concert.

The NJS booked Bud Powell through the Moe Gale Agency. At the time, Powell was receiving in-patient treatment at Creedmor Psychiatric Hospital in Queens, New York. Oscar Goodstein, the manager of Birdland and Powell's legal guardian, agreed to accompany him to the concert. By booking the musicians individually, NJS inadvertently left the concert leaderless.

The morning of the concert, the musicians met at LaGuardia Airport for the flight to Toronto. When Charlie failed to show at the appointed time,

Dizzy located him and the two caught a later flight. Once in Toronto, Charlie slipped away from Gillespie. He later pleasantly surprised Gillespie by showing up on time for the concert, sober and in a good mood. Right before the concert, Charlie told Dick Wattam he needed a drink before taking the stage. Wattam steered Charlie to the Silver Rail bar across the street and watched in amazement as he downed a triple scotch in one gulp.

The New Jazz Society needed to sell fifteen hundred tickets to break even. When the NJS scheduled the date there were no conflicting events on the horizon. Unfortunately, the Rocky Marciano–Jersey Joe Walcott World Heavyweight Championship, originally scheduled for April 10, was rescheduled for the same night as the Massey Hall concert. The long-anticipated fight was broadcast over television to United States and Canadian audiences, drawing significantly from the Massey Hall concert. By curtain time, the concert had sold only half the tickets necessary to cover expenses. The cavernous concert hall, soaring three stories with two balconies, accentuated the sparse attendance.

A hastily assembled sixteen-piece band led by trumpeter Graham Topping opened the concert with a forty-five-minute set of jazz standards and Topping originals. During the Topping band's set, Charlie, Gillespie, and other band members could be heard squabbling backstage about the money, set list, and who would lead the session.

Gillespie took charge of the concert, fronting the band and calling the tunes. He prudently selected standards that band members knew well. The band members came together and gave a freewheeling performance reminiscent of the late-night cutting contests uptown in Harlem during the early days of bop, less than a decade before. Roach explained that "just prior to going on the bandstand, we decided what we're going to play on that particular concert. So it was pure spontaneity. That's the thing about that date. It wasn't like, 'O.K., we'll rehearse two or three hours here,' we just went onstage, and things began to happen."[40]

In the first set, Gillespie led the band through "Perdido," "Salt Peanuts," and "All the Things You Are." While Charlie was all business, Gillespie clowned onstage. During "Perdido" Gillespie's onstage antics caused the audience to break up during Charlie's solo. Gillespie then teased Charlie by quoting

"Laura," a popular standard Charlie had recorded with a string section. For his part, Charlie remained focused and gave a masterful performance.

During intermission, Charlie, Gillespie, and Roach went across the street to the Silver Rail bar to watch the Marciano and Walcott fight. Gillespie and other African American fight fans counted on Walcott to reclaim the title he had lost to Marciano on September 23, 1952. Much to Gillespie's dismay, Marciano knocked out Walcott with a flurry of punches delivered in the first two-and-a-half minutes of the first round.

After intermission, the concert resumed with Roach alone on the massive stage improvising an extended solo that later became known as "Drum Conversation." Then Powell and Mingus joined Roach onstage for a set featuring the trio. Powell hunkered down at the piano and gave a brilliant performance. After a seventy-five minute break, Gillespie and Charlie returned to the stage for three more selections: "Wee," "Hot House," and "A Night in Tunisia," wrapping up with a "52nd Street Theme" coda.

The Graham Topping Band concluded the concert with a set of standards. Topping and the other soloist in the big band dutifully took their appointed solos well aware that they paled in comparison to the spirited exchanges between Charlie and Gillespie in the previous set. Charlie, Gillespie, Roach, and Mingus joined the Topping band for an encore.

In the end, the concert proved to be an artistic success but a financial disaster for all concerned. After the concert, Dick Wattam confessed to Charlie, Gillespie, and the others that the NJS lacked sufficient funds to pay them. Charlie became agitated, insisting that as a family man, he should be paid in full. Ironically, months earlier, Charlie had been paid an advance.

Wattam assured the chagrined musicians that in the future they would profit from tapes of the concert. Charlie and Gillepsie were taken aback to learn the concert had been recorded. Roach and Mingus arranged with NJS to tape the concert without informing them. The NJS borrowed a new Ampex open reel tape recorder, and Mingus brought along reels of a new formula Scotch recording tape available only in the United States to record the concert. Mingus and Roach intended to issue recordings of the concert on their fledgling Debut label. Charlie protested that he was under exclusive contract to Mercury.

Later that night, Mingus, Wattam, and other members of the NJS met at radio station CKFH to audition the tapes. Mingus was outraged to find the recording equipment failed to record his bass. "Mingus nearly exploded," declared Wattam. "You couldn't hear his bass at all." Mingus seized the tapes. Concerned that Mingus intended to destroy the tapes, Wattam sent a telegram to Barry Ulanov, the editor of *Metronome*, pleading "DO NOT LET MINGUS ERASE TAPES. STOP. DO NOT LET MINGUS ERASE TAPES. STOP. HE IS UNBALANCED."[41]

The next morning, NJS members paid Charlie, Gillespie, Powell, and Roach with checks drawn on their personal accounts. They paid Mingus in cash after he threatened to sell his bass, which would have forced NJS to forfeit its custom bond posted for the instrument. Charlie cashed his check at Premier Radio, a local business that sold tickets for the concert. Later, the owner, who was a jazz fan, had the check framed and hung it in his store. Gillespie waited to cash his check until he returned to New York. According to Gillespie, "It bounced, and bounced and bounced like a rubber ball."[42]

Although few outside of Toronto had heard about the Massey Hall concert, it became a legendary performance after Mingus issued three 10" LPs from the tapes of the session on his Debut label. "Jazz at Massey Hall" volumes one and three featured the Quintet, and volume two featured the Bud Powell trio. Having been left out of the mix in the original recordings, Mingus took the tapes into the studio and overdubbed his bass line for the LP releases. Charlie had Mingus list him as Charlie Chan in the lineup of the quintet as a nod to Chan and to avoid possible litigation by Norman Granz.

Energized by the Massey Hall concert, Charlie signed with the Moe Gale Agency and formed a new quintet featuring Bud Powell and Charles Mingus. That summer, Charlie played a series of steady engagements at Birdland, the Open Door, and the High Hat in Boston. An interview with John McLellan on WHDH in Boston captured Charlie in a thoughtful mood looking toward the future. When asked what would be the basis for his musical future, Charlie replied philosophically, "Hm. That's hard to tell, too, John. See, like, your ideas change as you grow older. Most people fail to realize that most of the things that they hear, either coming out of a man's horn ad lib, or else things that are written, you know, say, original things, I mean, they're just experiences. The way you feel, the beauty of the weather, the nice look of a mountain, maybe a nice fresh cool breath of air. I mean, all those things you can never tell what you'll be thinking tomorrow, but I can definitely say that the music won't stop. It'll be—keep going forward."[43]

Just as Charlie's career underwent a revival, his personal life fell apart. Chan, who was pregnant again, suffered from chronic ill health. The two frequently fought. One row caused Chan to flee with the children to her mother's apartment on Fifty-Second Street. "In 1953," Chan recalled, "Baird was less than a year old and Pree was just two. Bird and I were having problems with our relationship, and I was pregnant again. I was not in good health: I weighed 103 pounds, had chronic bronchitis, and was working on my sixth pneumonia. . . . Bird was drinking heavily. After a bad scene, I took the children and fled once again to my womb [her mother's house] on 52nd Street. Three days later, Bird sobered up and realized the physical condition I was in."[44]

Chan's condition worsened after she was bitten by the family cat, Orpheus. She had to be hospitalized when the puncture wound became infected. Chan's mother convinced Charlie that she was too weak to have the baby. Charlie, who wanted the child, reluctantly arranged for Chan to have an abortion at his drug connection's apartment. The abortion went awry, and Chan landed back in the hospital with gangrene. After returning home, Chan asked Charlie to take Orpheus to the Society for the Prevention of Cruelty to Animals and have him tested for rabies. A few hours later, Charlie returned without the cat. When Chan asked what had happened to Orpheus, Charlie confessed he had ordered that the cat be killed. Chan called just in time to save Orpheus. When pressed by Chan why he wanted the cat destroyed, Charlie replied cruelly, "You killed my son, didn't you?"[45]

Increasingly at odds with Chan, Charlie spent most of the fall and winter on the road. On October 12, Charlie opened for a weeklong engagement at the Latin Quarter in Montreal. The owner, Morton Berman, had the Gale agency specify in the contract that Charlie would be accompanied by his working band. Instead, Charlie showed up with a pickup group of musicians who were unprepared for the engagement. The drummer arrived without a drum set and had to borrow one from a local drummer. On opening night, the sidemen, particularly the pianist, failed to rise to the occasion. Charlie's ulcers flared up, making him difficult on and off the bandstand.

After three nights, Berman fired Charlie and refused to pay him for the final four days. Incensed, Charlie filed a suit against the Latin Quarter with the musicians union. In response, Berman complained to the union that "Their performance was pitiful; Mr. Parker personally did his best but the others, especially the pianist, didn't match him at all; the piano-player was always in a fog; half of the time he didn't play; one of the men in the band remarked 'the pianist is way off . . . is bad.'"[46] Customers walked out in mid-set. Morton further claimed that Charlie stopped in mid-tune to announce the breaks, constantly chewed lemon peels which he spat out in the back of the bandstand, and threatened the master of ceremonies, Al Cown.[47]

On the heels of the fiasco at the Latin Quarter, Charlie joined Chet Baker for a tour up the West Coast from Los Angeles to Eugene, Oregon. After being introduced to heroin during his last association with Charlie, Baker began using heavily. On the road, the two spent off hours getting high. After wrapping up the tour on November 8, Charlie returned home to respond to the counter charge filed by Morton Berman, owner of the Latin Quarter. In a lengthy response, Charlie rebutted Berman's account of the incident paragraph by paragraph, indignantly defending his good name and reputation. Charlie could ill afford to lose the union judgment.

That winter, Charlie toured the Midwest and New England, spending Thanksgiving and Christmas on the road. On January 28, 1954, he joined the Festival of Modern American Jazz Tour with the Stan Kenton Orchestra, June Christy, Dizzy Gillespie, the Errol Garner Trio, Lee Konitz, and Latin percussionists Candido. Charlie replaced Stan Getz, who had recently been arrested for possessing heroin and attempting to rob a pharmacy in Seattle.

The tour led to professional and personal disaster for Charlie. The first leg of the trip covered the South, ranging from Wichita Falls, Texas, to Raleigh, North Carolina. Charlie usually avoided touring the South. He still bore scars from the beating he suffered years earlier as a member of the Jay McShann band. Riding on the tour bus across the South, he found that little had changed since then. Alto saxophonist Dave Schildkraut recalled, "In one Southern town, a restaurant would not serve Negroes, so Bird had to wait on the bus while the rest of us were wolfing down steaks. Finally, after persuasion, the eatery relented. Dizzy and Erroll Garner left the bus, but Charlie held out and refused to go in and eat. I brought him out a big steak sandwich, and he grumbled, 'What, are you trying to be good to me?' and he put it aside. But I noticed that, as soon as the bus moved on, he fell on that sandwich and devoured it."[48]

After leaving the South, the tour swept up the East Coast, with dates in New York and Washington, then across the Great Lakes region with stops in Detroit, Toronto, and Chicago. After wrapping up an engagement at the Rainbo Club in Chicago, band members caught a charter plane for the final leg of the tour covering Seattle, Eugene, Oakland, and Los Angeles. The grueling schedule featured two shows nightly. While on the road, Charlie's ulcers flared up, compelling him to drown the pain with huge amounts of alcohol and heroin. High and in constant pain, he performed unevenly. Bill Perkins recalled Charlie as being "so out of it after the job that he'd fall down on the floor. I always remember even when he was out of it he played well. But on those rare nights when he was fairly straight—Dizzy would always be in the wings listening and on those rare nights, maybe one out of five, it was absolutely amazing.[49]

Charlie arrived in Los Angeles mentally and physically exhausted. He was eager to head home after the final concert of the tour at the Palladium. Unfortunately, the Gale Agency had booked a weeklong engagement at the Tiffany Club, starting the next evening. Jack Tucker, the manager of the Tiffany Club, showed up backstage at the Palladium and insisted that Charlie rehearse with the Joe Rotondi Trio the next morning at the club. Worn out from the tour, Charlie rebuffed Tucker's demand. Tucker called the Gale Agency and indignantly complained about Charlie's refusal to cooperate. After a call from Tim Gale, Charlie showed up at the club the next afternoon, rehearsed with the band for fifteen minutes, and then abruptly left.

Opening night at the Tiffany Club began on a sour note. Charlie played two brief sets and then left the club to get a sandwich. While on break, he called Chan to check on Pree, who was suffering from severely declining health. Charlie tried to comfort Chan, who was at her wits' end. On the way back to the club, the police picked up Charlie on suspicion of being a narcotics user. Unable to prove the case for narcotics, the police booked him on a drunk and disorderly charge. The next evening, Charles Carpenter of the Gale Agency paid the ten-dollar fine to get Charlie out of jail just in time for the engagement at the Tiffany Club.[50]

Over the next three days, Jack Tucker and Charlie clashed on and off the bandstand. Tucker dogged Charlie at every turn, clocking his time spent on stage and dutifully noting his every transgression of house rules. While on the job Wednesday night, Charlie learned that doctors had put Pree in an oxygen tent, in a final attempt to save her life. Charlie, grief stricken and suffering from ulcers, drank heavily on the job, downing triple Brandy Alexanders with double scotches on the side until the bartender finally cut him off. Tucker fired Charlie after a row on Thursday night and refused to hire him back Friday morning.[51]

Pree died Saturday evening, March 6, 1954. After learning of his daughter's death early the next morning, Charlie drank himself into a stupor with quadruple Brandy Alexanders and then sent Chan a series of increasingly confused telegrams. 4:11 A.M.:

> MY DARLING MY DAUGHTER'S DEATH SURPRISED ME MORE THAT IT DID YOU DON'T FULFILL FUNERAL PROCEEDINGS UNTIL I GET THERE I SHALL BE THE FIRST ONE TO WALK INTO OUR CHAPEL FORGIVE ME FOR NOT BEING THERE WITH YOU WHILE YOU WERE AT THE HOSPITAL YOURS MOST SINCERELY YOUR HUSBAND CHARLIE PARKER.

4:13 A.M.:

> MY DARLING FOR GOD'S SAKE HOLD ON TO YOURSELF
>   CHAS PARKER

4:15 A.M.:

> CHAN, HELP
>   CHARLIE PARKER

7:58 A.M.:

> MY DAUGHTER IS DEAD. I KNOW IT. I WILL BE THERE AS QUICK AS I CAN. MY NAME IS BIRD. IT IS VERY NICE TO BE OUT HERE. PEOPLE HAVE BEEN VERY NICE TO ME OUT HERE. I AM COMING IN RIGHT AWAY TAKE IT EASY. LET ME BE THE FIRST ONE TO APPROACH YOU. I AM YOUR HUSBAND. SINCERELY, CHARLIE PARKER.[52]

The telegrams meant to assure Chan had the opposite effect. As Chan recalled, "I was in deep shock as the telegrams, some of them strangely dispassionate, kept arriving, each one opening the wound even more."[53]

The next morning, Charlie poured a bottle of scotch down the toilet, gave away his heroin, and left for home sober. Before leaving, he confided in Julie MacDonald, a sculptor and friend who took him to the airport, "I hope I can be a good husband . . . at least until after this is over."[54]

Chan and Charlie buried Pree in Mount Hope Cemetery in upstate New York where Chan's father was interred. Later they discovered that the cemetery buried Pree in the Negro section rather than next to her grandfather in the Jewish section. Standing firm as a rock throughout the funeral, Charlie crumbled afterward, wracked by guilt for not being there when Pree was born or when she died. Charlie never forgave himself. Chan, grieving for both her child lost in an abortion and for Pree, pulled away from Charlie. Kim observed, "Bird detached from things to save himself, which meant that in a way the sadness between them was very powerful. I've seen very sad photographs of them . . . shortly after Pree's death and there's just a complete space between them and I think it was just the beginning of the end, really."[55]

That summer, during a month-long family vacation at the seashore, Charlie began acting strangely, shaving his head, ostensibly to get rid of sand fleas, then dramatically snatching up Baird in the middle of the night and threatening to return to New York. Spooked by Charlie's odd behavior, Chan withdrew emotionally and physically, spending more time with a girlfriend in New Hope, Pennsylvania, and at her mother's apartment than at the apartment she shared with Charlie on Avenue B.

Returning from a tour of New England and the Midwest in early August, Charlie became more difficult than usual. After spending long stretches on the road high on whiskey, heroin, and pills, Charlie became abusive when he returned home. "Beside using shit, Bird was drinking heavily," Chan recalled. "The combination made him a crazy man, evil and violent. When it got to be too much for me, I would take the children and flee to my mother's apartment. My friends began calling me 'Portia' after the heroine of the popular soap opera 'Portia Faces Life.' In fact it was more of a tragedy."[56]

In the early morning hours of August 18, Charlie sent Chan a Western Union Telegram at her mother's apartment, with an oblique reference to suicide:

MY DARLING I JUST WANTED TO LET YOU KNOW REGARDLESS OF THE THINGS WE HAVE TO EXPERIENCE IN LIFE I WANT YOU TO KNOW THAT I AM IN THE GROUND NOW I WOULD SHOOT MYSELF FOR YOU IF I HAD A GUN BUT I DON'T HAVE ONE TELL MY WIFE THE MOST HORRIBLE THING IN THE WORLD IS SILENCE AND I AM EXPERIENCING SAME. IM TIRED AND GOING TO SLEEP

CHARLES PARKER[57]

Moved by Charlie's telegram, Chan returned home.

On Thursday, August 26, Charlie opened at Birdland for a three-week engagement with the string group on a bill with Dizzy Gillespie and Dinah Washington. The next Sunday, on his thirty-fourth birthday, Charlie imperially dismissed the entire string section and repaired to the bar, downing shot after shot of whiskey. The manager of Birdland, Oscar Goodstein, furious at the uproar, banished Charlie from his namesake club. With tears streaming down his face, Charlie walked around the corner to the Basin Street and drank himself into a stupor.[58]

Returning home in the wee hours, Charlie calmly assured Chan that he only wanted to pick up a few things and be on his way. Walking back to the restroom and quietly closing the door, Charlie attempted suicide. "I found Bird in the bathroom. He had swallowed iodine," Chan reported. "There were open bottles of aspirin and other pills in the sink. My reaction was cold: 'That was stupid. Now I'll just have to call an ambulance.' As I was calling Bellevue, Bird wandered to the corner as if he didn't know what to do next. The ambulance arrived at the same time as the *Daily News* press car, and Bird was photographed in his long Bermudas being helped into it."[59]

Bellevue staff assigned Charlie to the ward for agitated patients. The hospital file on Charlie reported that he "exhibited a passive dependency and proved ingratiating and friendly to all physicians. Psychometric testing indicated a high average intelligence with paranoid tendencies. Evaluation by psychiatrists indicate a hostile, evasive personality with manifestations of primitive and sexual fantasies associated with hostility and gross evidence of paranoid thinking. Psychoanalytic diagnosis latent schizophrenia." After being discharged under a doctor's care on September 10, Charlie resumed drinking. Later that month, Charlie readmitted himself to Bellevue, feeling depressed and fearing "for his own safety."[60]

After being discharged on October 15, Charlie moved with Chan to New Hope. He commuted for outpatient treatments and work in the city, temporarily regaining a sense of normalcy. Charlie enjoyed playing the square, riding the train into the city surrounded by businessmen, poring over newspapers. Around Christmas, Charlie resumed drinking heavily again, driving Chan away for good. Cut loose from his domestic anchor, Charlie drifted off into the New York nightlife, drinking excessively and sleeping wherever and whenever he could. When he could not find shelter, Charlie rode the subways all night long.

Ahmed Basheer, a young devout Muslim with an air of gentle dignity, literally picked Charlie up off the street and put him up in a spare room in his cold-water flat on Barrow Street in the Village. It took Basheer and three friends to maneuver Charlie upstairs to the apartment and lay him out on the bed. As Charlie's rescuers hovered over the bed, he feverishly expressed a desire to die. He told them, "I know you fellows are trying to keep an eye on me because you don't want me to kill myself, but regardless of what you say or do, I'll have to die, and that's all there is to it. It won't be anything to it; it will be very easy. I'll just simply maybe jump off a bridge or something some night, and you fellows will hear about it."[61] Charlie stayed with Basheer during the last four months of his life.

Leonard Feather witnessed Charlie's swift mental and physical decline, starting in early 1955:

> I saw Charlie three times after that. The first time playing, a Town Hall concert, he looked healthy, talked sensibly, played magnificently and told me he was commuting daily between New Hope, Pa., where he and Chan had found a home, and Bellevue hospital where he was undergoing psychiatric treatment. He had dropped 20 pounds of unhealthy fat; he was like a new man, and New Hope seemed the right place for him to be living. The second time, a month ago, he was standing in a bar over Birdland, raggedly dressed. He said he had not been home to New Hope lately. The bloated fat was back. His eyes looked desperately sad. The final night, Charlie was playing at Birdland

for two nights only, with Bud Powell, Kenny Dorham, Art Blakey, and Charlie Mingus. One set was too much for anyone who had known and respected this man. He refused to take the stand, quarreled with Powell, stalked off after playing a few desultory bars, and a few minutes later was seen by a friend around the corner at Basin Street, with tears streaming down his face. "You'll kill yourself if you go on like this," said Mingus, who loved Charlie and was mortified at the spectacle of his imminent self-destruction. A week later, Charlie was dead.[62]

Fueling tabloid headlines, Charlie passed in the suite of the Baroness Pannonica de Koenigswarter in the Hotel Stanhope, located on Fifth Avenue across the street from the Metropolitan Museum of Art. An aristocratic maverick and woman of independent means, the Baroness, known as Nica to the jazz musicians she befriended, hailed from the English banking branch of the Rothschild family, longtime patrons of music. Raised in society, Nica married Baron Jules de Koeningswarter, a pilot and high-ranking official in the French diplomatic corps. During World War II, she fought alongside her husband in the French resistance, serving as an ambulance driver, decoder, and broadcaster. Becoming bored with her husband's postwar diplomatic post in Mexico City, Nica fled with her daughter to New York City in 1951. Having gotten the jazz bug as a teenager from her brother Victor, the third Lord Rothschild and Winston Churchill's diplomatic courier to the White House, she befriended Thelonious Monk, Charlie, and other modernists, making them welcome in her elegant suite at the Stanhope. Monk often stopped by, lingering in the lobby, sporting colorful, oddly matched outfits, much to the chagrin of the doormen charged with maintaining the staid decorum of the hotel. Charlie visited infrequently, helping himself to the well-stocked bar, playing records and games with Nica's teenage daughter.[63]

On Wednesday, March 9, 1955, Charlie stopped off at Nica's apartment after falling ill on the way to an engagement at George Wein's Storyville Club in Boston. She immediately noticed Charlie's grave condition and called the house physician, Dr. Richard Freymann. She recalled:

> The first thing that happened [that] was unusual was, when I offered him a drink, and he said no. I took a look at him, and I noticed he appeared quite ill. A few minutes later he began to vomit blood. I sent for my doctor, who came right away. He said that Bird could not go on any trip, and Bird, who felt

better momentarily, started to argue the point and said that he had a commitment to play this gig and that he had to go. We told him that he must go to the hospital. That, he said, was the last thing he was going to do. He said he hated hospitals, that he had had enough of them. I then said to the doctor, "Let him stay here." We agreed on that, and my daughter and I took shifts around the clock watching and waiting upon him and bringing ice water by the gallon, which he consumed. His thirst was incredible; it couldn't be quenched. Sometimes he would bring it up with some blood, and then he lay back and had to have more water. It went on like that for a day or two.[64]

Closely monitoring his patient, Dr. Freymann visited Nica's apartment three times a day.

Feeling better by Saturday, March 12, 1955, Charlie got up to watch the Tommy Dorsey program on TV. "We braced him up in an easy chair, with pillows and wrapped in blankets. He was enjoying what he saw of the program," Nica recounted.

> Bird was a fan of Dorsey's, and he didn't see anything strange in that. "He's a wonderful trombonist," he said. Then came the part of the show consisting of jugglers who were throwing bricks around that were stuck together. My daughter was asking how they did it, and Bird and I were being very mysterious about it. Suddenly in the act, they dropped the bricks, and we all laughed. Bird was laughing uproariously, but then he began to choke. He rose from his chair and choked, perhaps twice, and sat back in the chair. I was on the phone immediately, calling the doctor. "Don't worry, Mummy," my daughter said. "He's all right now." I went over and took his pulse. He had dropped back in the chair, with his head falling forward. He was unconscious. I could feel his pulse still there. Then his pulse stopped. I didn't want to believe it. I could feel my own pulse. I tried to believe my pulse was his. But I really knew that Bird was dead. At the moment of his going, there was a tremendous clap of thunder. I didn't think about it at the time, but I've thought about it often since; how strange it was.[65]

Just thirty-four years old, Charlie died from lobar pneumonia due to visceral congestion. Surveying Charlie's abused body for the police report, Dr. Freymann judged his age as fifty-three.

Nica, desperate to contact Chan before the newspapers and radio stations got wind of the story, kept Charlie's death to herself while making discreet inquiries as to Chan's whereabouts. She finally got in touch with Chan's mother on Monday, the day before news of Charlie's death broke. As Chan made plans for a simple funeral, Doris arrived from Chicago, marriage certificate in hand, and claimed the body. Working in concert with Addie, Charlie's mother, Doris arranged for a public funeral at the Abyssinian Baptist Church in Harlem, then final internment in Kansas City. Chan protested that Charlie did not want a "showbiz funeral" or to be buried in Kansas City, only to be overruled by Doris and Addie. Doris temporarily put aside her animosity and graciously seated Chan in the front row, while taking a seat in the back.

Chan found little comfort in her ringside seat to the spectacle:

All Harlem had turned out: pimps, pushers, whores in their finery mingled with fans, and the businessmen who had had a vested interest in Bird when he was alive and looked forward to bigger profits now that he was dead. Adam Clayton Powell being a senator in Washington was replaced by the Most Reverend Licorice, who conducted the service. The coffin was surrounded by huge floral displays and my little daisy bouquet looked lost and innocent in that exotic garden. An organist played "The Lost Chord." (Bird never lost a chord in his life!) Reverend Licorice pontificated on what a fine man Charlie Bird had been. It was surreal. After the interminable service, there was another long wait in an alcove where Mingus mumbled insanely in my ear that it wasn't Bird in the coffin. Later, I realized what he meant. Then the coffin was clumsily carried past me by a sweating Teddy Reig, a distraught Leonard Feather, and others whose faces I didn't recognize. As they walked down the steps, someone stumbled and the coffin almost fell. Lennie Tristano an honorary pallbearer, who was nearby, intuitively reached up and caught the coffin as it fell. It was placed in a hearse to be taken to Kansas City.[66]

Norman Granz quietly paid the funeral expenses and the cost of shipping the body home. The next morning, Doris and Addie accompanied Charlie's body to Kansas City.

Members of Local 627 carried Charlie to his final resting place atop a hill in Lincoln Cemetery, an African American cemetery located in an unincorporated area between Kansas City and Independence. Addie buried her son under a shade tree, so he would be cool during the summer. A simple granite headstone adorned by two small birds marked the spot. Sadly, the stone bore an incorrect date of death, March 23.[67] Back in New York, a more fitting epitaph appeared scrawled in crayon and chalk on fences, sidewalks, and buildings across Greenwich Village. Led by poet Ted Joans, the hipsters, writers, and poets who followed Charlie in life immortalized him in death with the simple declaration: BIRD LIVES.

Notes

Chapter 1. Kansas City Blues

1. Stanley Dance, *The World of Count Basie* (New York: Da Capo, 1985), 265.

2. Westbrook Pegler described the differences between the state of Kansas and Kansas City, Missouri, in his syndicated column published on February 21, 1938:

> Kansas City has been described as an overgrown trading post on the frontier, but that figure does justice to neither the facts nor the town. She is not a post at all, but a great city whose reputation has suffered from the inclusion in her name of the word "Kansas," a word signifying thin-lipped social bleakness, prohibition and an aversion to the pleasures of others. Kansas City is more like Paris. The stuff is there, the gambling joints and the brothels, including among the latter a restaurant conducted in imitation of that one in Paris, more haunted by American tourists than the Louvre, where the waitresses wear nothing on before and a little less than half behind. But, like the Parisians, the people of Kansas City obviously believe that such things must be and, also like the Parisians, are proud of their own indifference.

Subsequently, Kansas City, Missouri, became known as the "Paris of the Plains."

3. Mary Lou Williams, quoted by Max Jones in *Talkin' Jazz* (New York: Norton, 1988), 187.

4. See Frank Driggs and Chuck Haddix, *Kansas City Jazz: From Ragtime to Bebop—A History* (New York: Oxford University Press, 2005).

5. "Mrs. Nation Ordered Away," *Kansas City Star*, April 25, 1901.

6. Born Addie Brower Boxley, August 21, 1891.

7. See Llew Walker, "Bird Lives–Childhood," available at http://www.birdlives .co.uk/index.php/childhood.html (accessed February 20, 2013). The information is taken from the 1910 U.S. census.

8. See Walker, "Bird Lives–Childhood." The family is listed at 814 Freeman in the 1910 *Kansas City Kansas City Directory* and at 1613 North Ninth in the 1912 directory.

9. John Wesley Howard, John Parker's nephew, interview by Chuck Haddix, April 19, 2006, Kansas City, Missouri.

10. City of Kansas City, Kansas, Clerk's Office, Birth Record Registry, p. 72, Birth Record Book D, Index #18034.

11. Robert Reisner, *Bird: The Legend of Charlie Parker* (New York: Da Capo, 1977), 163.

12. Phone interview with John Parker's niece Juanita Howard Cherry, January 9, 2010.

13. Reisner, *Bird*, 159.

14. Addie is listed as a cook living at 852 Freeman Avenue; Charles is listed as a porter living at 844 Washington Boulevard in the 1925 *Kansas City, Kansas, Directory*.

15. Oliver Todd, interview by Chuck Haddix, July 17, 1997, Kansas City, Missouri.

16. In the 1930 census, the family is listed as living in a duplex at 109 West Thirty-Fourth Street, located two blocks north and one-half block east from the Wyandotte address. According to Brent Menger, who renovated the residence at 3527 Wyandotte, a long-time resident who lived next door recalled the block being converted into condos in 1930.

17. Arthur Saunders, phone interview by Chuck Haddix, June 28, 2005, Cleveland, Ohio.

18. Penn School folder, vertical file, Special Collections, Main Branch, Kansas City, Missouri Public Library.

19. Jeremiah Cameron, "Let's Consider: About Charlie Parker," *Kansas City Call*, December 11, 1998.

20. Saunders, phone interview, June 28, 2005.

21. Charlie Parker, interview by Marshall Stearns and John Maher, May 1950, New York.

22. Frank Douglas, interview by Chuck Haddix, January 4, 2006, Kansas City, Missouri.

23. According to Charlie's union record and his cousin Myra Brown, Addie moved up the street in the early 1940s to 1535 Olive Street to a two-story house, where she lived for the rest of her life.

24. Students attended first through seventh grades at Penn, Garrison, Sumner, or Crispus Attucks grade schools before enrolling in Lincoln High School as freshmen. There was no eighth grade in the Kansas City, Missouri, school district until World War II.

25. Sterling Bryant, interview by Chuck Haddix, Kansas City, November 19, 2008.

26. Thomas Miller, "We the Senior Class," *Lincolnite*, 1937.

27. "New Lincoln High School Realization of Many Years of Dreaming and Fighting," *Kansas City Call*, September 11, 1936.

28. Charlie Parker, interview by Marshall Stearns and John Maher, May 1950, New York.

29. Reisner, *Bird*, 129.

30. Charlie Parker, interview by John McLellan and Paul Desmond at radio station WHDH.

31. Reisner, *Bird*, 75.

32. Dance, *World of Count Basie*, 265–66.

33. Reisner, *Bird*, 129–30.

34. See Gary Giddins, *Celebrating Bird: The Triumph of Charlie Parker* (New York: Beech Tree, 1987), 34.

35. Giddins, *Celebrating Bird*, 34.

36. Giddins, *Celebrating Bird*, 36–37.

37. Robert Morris, "Kansas City Man on Bass," *Mississippi Rag*, August 1976, 2.

38. Mike Belt, "'Bird' Had a Lasting Effect on Those Who Knew Him," *Kansas City Kansas*, April 13, 1997.

39. Belt, "'Bird' Had a Lasting Effect."

40. Arthur Saunders, phone interview by Chuck Haddix, June 28, 2005, Cleveland, Ohio.

41. *Lincolnite*, June 1, 1935, vol. 7, no. 5, p. 11.

42. Advertisement for the Ten Chords of Rhythm, *Kansas City Call*, August 2, 1935.

43. Ernest Daniels, interview by Howard Litwak and Nathan Pearson, Kansas City, Missouri, April 6, 1977, *Kansas City Oral History Collection*, State Historical Society of Missouri Research Center–Kansas City.

44. "Young Orchestra Rapidly Increasing in Popularity," *Kansas City Call*, September 30, 1935.

45. "300 Members Are in Union of Musicians," *Kansas City Call*, September 14, 1928.

46. Interview with Myra Brown in Kansas City, Missouri, on August 17, 2005.

47. Reisner, *Bird*, 185.

48. Reisner, *Bird*, 185.

49. Count Basie, as told to Albert Murray, *Good Morning Blues* (New York: Random House, 1985), 162.

50. Reisner, *Bird*, 186.

51. Anita Dixon, "Charlie Parker, 'I Was His First, He Was My First, It Was All Special'" *Pitch Weekly* (Kansas City, Missouri), April 10, 1996.

52. According to Dixon, Charlie was fifteen and Rebecca eighteen when they married on July 25, 1936.

53. Dixon, "Charlie Parker."

Chapter 2. Buster's Tune

1. H. Dwight Weaver, *Lake of the Ozarks: The Early Years* (Chicago: Arcadia, 2000), 7–9.

2. Musicians refer to "woodshedding" as practicing for long hours.

3. See Miller County Museum & Historical Society, Progress Notes, December 28, 2009, available at http://www.millercountymuseum.org/archives/091228.html (accessed January 3, 2013).

4. Ernest Daniels, interview by Howard Litwak and Nathan Pearson, *Kansas City Oral History Collection*, State Historical Society of Missouri Research Center–Kansas City, 7–9.

5. Dixon, "Charlie Parker," 12–16.

6. H. Dwight Weaver, *Lake of the Ozarks: Vintage Vacation Paradise* (Chicago: Arcadia, 2002), 17–19.

7. Robert Morris, "Kansas City Man on Bass," *Mississippi Rag*, August 1976, 1.

8. Dixon, "Charlie Parker."

9. Dixon, "Charlie Parker."

10. "Charles Taibi Is Arrested in New U. S. Dope Case," *Kansas City Journal-Post*, May 23, 1936.

11. Undated interview with Harold M. "Bud" Calvert in the Robert (Old Uncle Bob) Mossman Collection, Marr Sound Archives, Miller Nichols Library, University of Missouri–Kansas City.

12. Dixon, "Charlie Parker."

13. Giddins, *Celebrating Bird*, 46.

14. Reisner, *Bird*, 82–83.

15. Dixon, "Charlie Parker."

16. Don Gazzaway, "Buster and Bird: Conversations with Buster Smith, Part III," *Jazz Review*, February, 1960, 13.

17. Mary Lee Hester, *Going to Kansas City* (Sherman, Tex.: Early Bird), 19.

18. Gazzaway, "Buster and Bird," 14.

19. Unedited interview with Jay McShann by John Anthony Brisbin for "I Always Thought Blues and Jazz Went Together," *Living Blues*, January/February, 2000, 16.

20. Chris Goddard interview with Buster Smith, Jazz Oral History Project Institute of Jazz Studies, January 13, 1981, 139–40.

21. Gazzaway, "Buster and Bird," 13.

22. "Basie Plays for 3,100 Dance Fans," *Kansas City Call*, April 15, 1938, 14.

23. Dave Dexter Jr., *The Jazz Story from the '90s to the '60s* (Englewood Cliffs, N.J.: Prentice-Hall, 1964), 146.

24. Correspondence from Sylvester E. "Snooky" Calloway Sr., Llew Walker collection.

25. See Buster Smith, interview by Howard Litwak and Nathan Pearson, April 14, 1977, in Dallas, Texas. *Kansas City Oral History Collection*, State Historical Society of Missouri Research Center–Kansas City.

26. McShann, interview by Brisbin, 18–19.

27. Dave E. Dexter Jr., "Kansas City," *Metronome*, May 1937, 40.

28. Haddix, interview with Jay McShann, June 26, 1997, Kansas City.

29. Haddix, interview with McShann.

30. Haddix, interview with McShann.

31. "McShann and Lee Click," *Kansas City Journal-Post*, November 19, 1938.

32. E. Leroy Brown Jr., "Names Make News," *Kansas City Call*, October 28, 1938, 17.

33. E. Leroy Brown Jr., "Names Make News," *Kansas City Call*, December 9, 1938, 8.

34. *Kansas City Call*, December 16, 1938, 9.

35. Bill Lane, "Harlan Leonard Recalls," *Los Angeles Sentinel*, April 9, 1970.

36. Reisner, *Bird*, 165.

Chapter 3. Hootie Blues

1. Billy Eckstine, "Bird Blew in His Socks!" *Melody Maker*, August 14, 1954, 3.

2. Don Gazzaway, "Buster and Bird," 13.

3. Ira Gitler, *Swing to Bop* (New York: Oxford University Press, 1985), 70.

4. According to Carl Woideck this quote, published in Nat Shapiro and Nat Hentoff, *Hear Me Talkin' To Ya* (New York: Rinehart, 1955), 354, was probably paraphrased from the article by Michael Levin and John S. Wilson, "No Bop Roots In Jazz: Parker," *Down Beat*, September 9, 1949, 1, 12.

5. Buster Smith, interview by Howard Litwak and Nathan Pearson, *Kansas City Oral History Collection*, Historical Society of Missouri–Kansas City.

6. Robert Reisner, *Bird,* 162.

7. McShann signed a management contract with Tumino's Consolidated Orchestras of America on January 1, 1940, effective on January 5. John Tumino Collection, Dr. Kenneth J. LaBudde Department of Special Collections, Miller Nichols Library, University of Missouri–Kansas City, box 1, folder 2, contract 25.

8. Haddix, interview with McShann, Kansas City, June 26, 1997.

9. "Crowd Attends Dance," *Kansas City Call*, March 29, 1940, 15.

10. Bernard "Step Buddy" Anderson, interview by Howard Litwak and Nathan Pearson, *Kansas City Oral History Collection*, State Historical Society of Missouri–Kansas City.

11. Haddix, interview with McShann, June 26, 1997.

12. Bob Locke, "Scab Bandsmen Laugh up Their Sleeves in K.C." *Down Beat*, July 15, 1940, 20.

13. Bernard Step-Buddy Anderson, "Sufferin' Kats," unpublished manuscript, Dr. Kenneth J. LaBudde Department of Special Collections, Miller Nichols Library, University of Missouri–Kansas City.

14. Dizzy Gillespie, with Al Fraser, *Dizzy: To Be or Not to Bop* (New York: Quartet, 1982), 117.

15. Gitler, *Swing to Bop*, 66.

16. Haddix, interview with McShann, June 26, 1997.

17. There has been some question about the order in which the songs were recorded. Set lists and a sign-in sheet in the Fred Higginson Collection list the personnel and the correct order. Fred Higginson Collection, Dr. Kenneth J. LaBudde, Department of Special Collections, Miller Nichols Library, University of Missouri–Kansas City.

18. See Frank Driggs and Chuck Haddix, *Kansas City Jazz: From Ragtime to Bebop—A History* (New York: Oxford University Press), 202.

19. Haddix, interview with McShann, July 3, 1997, Kansas City.

20. Haddix, interview with McShann, July 3, 1997.

21. See Driggs and Haddix, *Kansas City Jazz*, 205.

22. Haddix, interview with McShann, July 3, 1997.

23. Giddins, *Celebrating Bird*, 58.

24. "Kaycee Ork Waxes Eight Decca Sides," *Downbeat*, December 15, 1941, 14.

25. Haddix, interview with McShann, July 3, 1997.

26. Stanley Dance, *The World of Count Basie* (New York: Scribner's, 1980), 176.

27. Dance, *World of Count Basie*, 276.

28. Dance, *World of Count Basie*, 276–77.

29. Gitler, *Swing to Bop*, 71–72.

30. Advertisement for Minton's in the *Music Dial*, February 1944, inside cover page.

31. "Mary Lou Williams Continues Her Life Story: The Mad Monk," *Melody Maker*, May 22, 1954, 11.

32. Clyde E. B. Bernhardt, as told to Sheldon Harris, *I Remember: Eighty Years of Black Entertainment, Big Bands, and the Blues* (Philadelphia: University of Pennsylvania Press, 1986), 154.

33. Dance, *World of Count Basie*, 253.

34. Dance, *World of Count Basie*, 277.

35. See Driggs and Haddix, *Ragtime to Bebop*, 213.

36. Dance, *World of Count Basie*, 277.

37. Jay McShann, interview by John Anthony Brisbin, "I Always Thought Blues and Jazz Went Together," *Living Blues*, January/February 2000, 25. Jay McShann confided to the author on several occasions that Jackson took the solos for Parker on this session.

38. Bernhardt, *I Remember*, 154–55.

Chapter 4. Bebop

1. Dance, *World of Count Basie*, 247.

2. The deep forest referred to the band's theme song "Deep Forest."

3. Billy Eckstine, "Bird Blew in His Socks," *Melody Maker*, August 14, 1954, 2.

4. Eckstine, "Bird Blew in His Socks," 3.

5. "Musician of the Month," *Music Dial*, November 1943, 10.

6. Gitler, *Swing to Bop*, 148.

7. See Gary Giddins's liner notes to Charlie Parker, *Birth of Bebop* (Stash, 1986), 260.

8. Interview with Junior Williams by Ken Posten, Norman Saks Collection. Tran-

script: We had a job at Princeton . . . out in Jersey. . . . and we got there kind of early and we—Charlie, myself—we walking up to campus and Charlie happened to look up and say, "Hey look!" I say, "What is it?" And he said, "You know who that is?" I said, ""No." He said, "That's Einstein." He had a wool sweater, a big bulky wool sweater on. He had a black fez on. He was walking down the walk, you know. Charlie walked up to him and said "Is this Einstein?" He said, "Yeah." He said, "'I finally got to meet you." . . . He shook his hand. He got a twinkle in his eye, I never will forget that, and they start talking. Charlie was a very intelligent man. Very intelligent. He didn't go to no college but, boy, he grasps all that knowledge out on the road and they was talking about different things . . . So he took us to his house and we had tea and crumpets, talked, and Charlie was asking him about theory, different things, evolution, you know, and just things in general. But everything he brought up Charlie could talk to him about.

9. Reisner, *Bird*, 108–9.

10. Reisner, *Bird*, 25.

11. "Jazz Man Recalls KC's Golden Era," *Foolkiller* 3, no. 2 (Winter 1977): 7.

12. Reisner, *Bird*, 17.

13. Reisner, *Bird*, 71.

14. Gillespie, *Dizzy: To Be or Not to Bop*, 176–77.

15. Addie is listed as a widow at 1516 Olive Street in the 1941 city directory. She is not listed in 1942 directory. According to Myra Brown, Addie's niece, she moved to a farm in northern Kansas with Daniels. The second page of Parker's Local 627 union record for 1942–1944 gives the 1535 Olive address. The address is written in a different hand than the original entry.

16. Reisner, *Bird*, 67.

17. George Hoefer, "Buddy Anderson," *Down Beat*, December 19, 1963, 44.

18. Buddy Anderson interview by Frank Driggs, Marr Sound Archives, Miller Nichols Library, University of Missouri–Kansas City, 1980.

19. Leonard Feather, "Billy Eckstine," *Metronome*, January 1945, 12.

20. See Donald L. Maggin, *Dizzy: The Life and Times of John Birks Gillespie* (New York: HarperCollins, 2005), 158.

21. See Arnold Shaw, *52nd Street: The Street of Jazz* (New York: Da Capo, 1977).

22. Billy Eckstine, "Leading My Outfit," *Melody Maker*, August 28, 1954, 13.

23. Gillespie, *Dizzy: To Be or Not to Bop*, 188.

24. Reisner, *Bird*, 51.

25. Anita Dixon, "Charlie Parker 'I Was His First, He Was My First, It Was All Special,'" *Pitch Weekly* (Kansas City, Missouri), April 10, 1996.

26. Miles Davis with Quincy Troup, *Miles: The Autobiography* (New York: Simon and Schuster, 1990), 49.

27. Gillespie, *Dizzy: To Be or Not to Bop*, 190.

28. "Eckstine Spots Strong Trumpets," *Down Beat*, September 1, 1944, 1.

29. Michael Levin and Jon S. Wilson, "No Bop Roots in Jazz: Parker," *Down Beat*, September 9, 1949. 12.

30. Alyn Shipton, *Groovin' High: The Life of Dizzy Gillespie* (New York: Oxford University Press, 2001), 136.

31. Leonard Feather, "New York Roundup," *Metronome*, April 1945, 23.

32. Mike A. Bloom, "Trummy Young: Interview," *Cadence*, May 1981, 5.

33. Budd Johnson, interview by Gitler, *Swing to Bop*, 119.

34. John S. Wilson, "Armstrong Explains Stand against Bop," *Down Beat*, December 30, 1949, 3.

35. Gitler, *Swing to Bop*, 100.

36. "Diggin' the Discs with Don," *Down Beat*, August 1, 1945, 8.

37. "Igor Stravinsky's Re-bop Style," *Down Beat*, September 11, 1945, 3.

38. Gillespie, *Dizzy: To Be or Not to Bop*, 231–32.

39. Levin Wilson, "No Bop Roots in Jazz," 1.

40. Barry Ulanov, "Dizzy Dazzles for an Hour; Rest of Concert Drags," *Metronome*, June, 1945, 22.

41. See Chan Parker, *My Life in E-Flat* (Columbia, South Carolina: University of South Carolina Press), 15.

42. Parker, *My Life*, 21.

43. Parker, *My Life*, 22.

44. Leonard Feather, "Manhattan Kaleidoscope," *Metronome*, August, 1945, 10.

45. "52 St. Jumps as Top Jazz Names Return Home," *Down Beat*, November 1, 1945, 3.

46. "Alley Back in Business Again," *Down Beat*, December 1, 1945, 1.

47. "52nd Street Invades Toronto Studio," *Down Beat*, December 15, 1945, 2.

48. Sadik Hakim interview in Reisner, *Bird*, 103.

49. See James Patrick and Bob Porter liner notes to *The Complete Savoy Studio Sessions* (New York: Savoy Records 5500), 3.

50. Teddy Reig, interview by Bob Porter, in liner notes, *Complete Savoy*, 17.

51. See James Patrick and Bob Porter, liner notes, *Complete Savoy*, 7.

52. In the introduction, Gillespie alludes to Thelonius Monk's "Round Midnight."

53. There is some controversy about whether the pianist on "Meandering" is Gillespie or Thornton. In his liner notes to *Complete Savoy* Bob Porter reports Gillespie is at the keyboards, while Carl Woideck in *Charlie Parker: His Music and Life* claims Thornton accompanied Parker on the selection. After comparing the style to Thornton's solos earlier in the session, I concur with Porter.

Chapter 5. Relaxing at Camarillo

1. See Donald L. Maggin, *Dizzy: The Life and Times of John Birks Gillsespie* (New York: Harper, 2005), 182.

2. Maggin, *Dizzy*, 182.

3. See Ross Russell, *Bird Lives!* (New York: Charterhouse, 1973), 199–203.

4. Hal Holly, "Los Angeles Band Briefs," *Down Beat*, December 15, 1945, 6.

5. Ross Russell, "Bebop," *Le Jazz Hot*, France, Ross Russell Collection, Harry Ransom Humanities Research Center, University of Texas at Austin.

6. Ken Poston, liner notes for *Central Avenue Sounds: Jazz in Los Angeles (1921–1956)* (Rhino Records), 46.

7. See Ross Russell manuscript for "Chez Billy Berg," from *Yardbird in Lotus Land,* published in *Le Jazz Hot*, January 1970, Russell Collection, Ransom Center, 7–12.

8. "Chez Billy Berg," *Yardbird*, 12- 13.

9. "Los Angeles Band Briefs," *Down Beat*, January 1, 1946, 6.

10. Gillespie, *Dizzy: To Be or Not to Bop*, 248.

11. Gillespie, *Dizzy: To Be or Not to Bop*, 249.

12. Reisner, *Bird*, 196.

13. Ross Russell, *Dial Records*, Russell Collection, Ransom Center, 2.

14. Reisner, *Bird*, 196.

15. Oddly, Gillespie did not rank in the trumpet category but placed twelfth in the small combo category. Readers rated Parker fifth in the alto category. "Woody & TD Win, Ten New All-Stars," *Down Beat*, January 1, 1946, 19.

16. Barry Ulanov, "And Then I Wrote . . .," *Metronome*, March, 1946, 23.

17. Russell, *Bird Lives!*, 204–5.

18. Maggin, *Dizzy*, 185.

19. Gillespie, *Dizzy: To Be or Not to Bop*, 243.

20. Hal Holly, "Los Angeles Band Briefs," *Down Beat*, January 28, 1946, 6.

21. Reisner, *Bird*, 144.

22. Reisner, *Bird*, 206–7.

23. Ross Russell, Manuscript for "Yardbird in Lotus Land," Russell Collection, Ransom Center, 4.

24. Parker, *My Life*, 24—25.

25. Parker, *My Life*, 26.

26. Russell, *Bird Lives!*, 208–9.

27. Ross Russell, "Ornithology Date," Russell Collection, Ransom Center, 7.

28. See Woideck, *Charlie Parker: His Music and Life* (Ann Arbor: University of Michigan Press, 1996), 126.

29. See Woideck, *Charlie Parker: His Music and Life*, 127.

30. Roy Porter, *There and Back: The Roy Porter Story* (Baton Rouge: Louisiana State University Press, 1991), 57.

31. Carl Woideck, *The Charlie Parker Companion* (New York: Schirmer, 2000), 153.

32. Russell, *Bird Lives!*, 222.

33. Russell, *BirdLives!*, 223.

34. Ross Russell, letter to Edward Komara, Febuary 15, 1995, 4. Russell Collection, Ransom Center.

35. Elliott Grennard, "Sparrow's Last Jump: A Story," *Harper's*, May 1947, 426.

36. Woideck, *The Charlie Parker Companion*, 158.

37. Russell, *Bird Lives!*, 224–30

38. Carl Woideck, *Charlie Parker: His Music and Life*, 35.

39. Woideck, *Charlie Parker: His Music and Life*, 35–36.

40. Russell Collection, Harry Ransom Center.

41. See Russell, *Bird Lives!*, 232–33.

42. Letter from Thomas W. Hagerty, M.D. to Ross Russell, December 24, 1946. Russell Collection, Ransom Center.

43. Draft of letter to Mr. Shaeffer, Russell Collection, Ransom Center.

44. See Russell, *Bird Lives!*, 234.

45. Russell Collection, Harry Ransom Center.

46. (Chuck) Charles H. Copely Jr.; home address was 2524 Canyon Drive, Los Angeles, California.

47. See Lawrence O. Koch, *Yardbird Suite*, (Bowling Green, Ohio: Bowling Green State University Popular Press), 91–92.

48. See Koch, *Yardbird*, 135.

49. Russell, *Bird Lives!*, 240.

Chapter 6. Dewey Square

1. Maggin, *Dizzy*, 208–9.

2. Miles Davis with Quincy Troupe, *Miles: The Autobiography* (New York: Simon and Schuster, 1990), 100.

3. "The Bird," *Metronome*, June 1947, 27.

4. Olly Wilson, "Max Roach," *New Grove Dictionary of Jazz* (London: McMillan, 2002), 424.

5. Davis, *Miles*, 100.

6. Reisner, *Bird*, 223.

7. "Weird Wizard," *Down Beat*, September 10, 1947, 1.

8. In the liner notes to *The Complete Savoy Studio Sessions* (New York: Savoy), 13, Bob Porter concludes that Charlie and Lubinsky created the Savoy agreement supposedly from 1945 after Charlie's return to New York in April 1947.

9. Russell, *Bird*, 248.

10. Letter to Ross Russell from Alan J. Berlan, July 7, 1947, Ross Russell Collection, Harry Ransom Center, University of Texas at Austin.

11. Leonard Feather, "Yardbird Flies Home," *Metronome*, August 1947, 42–44.

12. Barry Ulanov, "Moldy Figs vs. Moderns!" *Metronome*, November 1947, 23.

13. Barry Ulanov, "Dizzy Heights," *Metronome*, November 1947, 50.

14. Koch, *Yardbird*, 110.

15. Michael Levin, "Diz, Bird and Ella Pack Carnegie: Despite Bad Acoustics, Gillespie Concert Offers Some Excellent Music," *Down Beat*, October 22, 1947, 1.

16. Ross Russell, letter to his mother, October 22, 1947, Russell Collection, Ransom Center.

17. Levin, "Diz, Bird and Ella," 3.

18. "Here's That Ban Again!" *Metronome*, November 1947, 9.

19. Ross Russell letter to Edward Komara, February 15, 1995, 1–2, Russell Collection, Ransom Center.

20. Ross Russell letter to Edward Komara, February 15, 1995, 4.

21. See "Charlie Parker: Rauscher's comments on royalty payments," Russell Collection, Ransom Center.

22. "Metronome's All Stars," *Metronome*, January 1948, 25.

23. "Influence of the Year: Charlie Parker," *Metronome*, January 1948, 22.

24. Charles Emge, "How Norman Granz' Flourishing Jazz Empire Started, Expanded," *Down Beat*, December 15, 1954, 4.

25. Davis, *Miles*, 124.

26. "Grantz's Philharmonic Artists Wow K.C. Fans," *Kansas City Call*, May 7, 1948.

27. Red Rodney letter to Ross Russell, March 8, 1969, Russell Collection, Ransom Center.

28. Leonard Feather, "The Street Is Dead: A Jazz Obituary," *Metronome*, April 1948, 16–17, 32–33.

29. Ross Russell letter to Lee Phillips, July 27, 1948, Russell Collection, Ransom Center.

30. Reisner, *Bird*, 170.

31. Norman Granz, Telephone interview by Nat Hentoff, from Geneva, for Verve Records, June 1994, 63–66.

32. Granz telephone interview by Hentoff, 63–66.

33. "Bird A Floperoo: Hawk Still Tops," *Down Beat*, December 15, 1948, 7.

34. "Bopper Granz Raises Mercury's Temperature," *Down Beat*, February 25, 1949, 1.

35. Davis, *Miles*, 123.

36. Ken Vail, *Bird's Diary: The Life of Charlie Parker 1945–1955* (Surrey: Castle, 1996), 47.

37. "Charlie Parker," *Metronome*, January 1949, 18.

38. Once allies, the two leading French jazz historians and producers, Hugues Panassié and Charles Delaunay, engaged in a bitter feud over the merits of bebop, splitting French jazz fans into two factions: the traditionalists and modernists.

39. Marian McPartland, "Crowds Jam Paris Jazz Festival," *Down Beat*, July 1, 1949, 3.

40. Reisner, *Bird*, 183.

41. Russell, Bird Lives!, 271.

42. Leonard Feather, *Inside Be-Bop* (New York: Robbins, 1949), 45.

43. Barry Ulanov, "Skip Bop and Jump," *Metronome*, December 1949, 37.

44. Reisner, *Bird*, 224.

45. Gitler, *Swing to Bop*, 226.

46. John S. Wilson, "Birdland Applies Imagination to Jazz," *Down Beat*, January 27, 1950, 3.

47. Advertisement for King in *Metronome*, January 1950, 26.

48. *"Charlie Charlie with Strings,"* *Metronome*, August 1950, 30.

49. Undated letter from Red Rodney to Ross Russell, Russell Collection, Ransom Center.

50. Reisner, *Bird*, 170.

51. Barry Ulanov, *Metronome*, August 1950, 19.

52. See Russell, *Bird Lives!*, 292–96.

53. See Russell, *Bird Lives!*, 296–99.

54. Parker, *My Life*, 38.

Chapter 7. Parker's Mood

1. Parker, *My Life*, 31.

2. Reisner, *Bird,* 46.

3. Reisner, *Bird*, 46–47.

4. Reisner, *Bird,* 47.

5. Parker, *My Life*, 36.

6. "Addict Drags NYC Clubs, Musicians Into Testimony: Frisco Dope Drive Nets 2," *Down Beat*, July 27, 1951, 3.

7. Rusty Tucker related the story to the author during many conversations. Bassist Oscar "Lucky" Oscar confirmed the event in an interview on January 9, 2008.

8. "Woody Herman, 'Yardbird' Perform in Best 'Show Must Go On' Tradition," *Kansas City Call*, July 27, 1951, 9.

9. Parker, *My Life*, 44–45.

10. Parker, *My Life*, 33.

11. Vail, *Bird's Diary*, 103.

12. Vail, *Bird's Diary*, 105.

13. Nat Henthoff, "Granz Wouldn't Let Me Record With Charlie, Says Roy Haynes," *Down Beat*, April 4, 1952, 7.

14. Review of "Autumn in New York" and "Temptation" in *Down Beat*, June 18, 1952, 11.

15. Letter from Red Rodney to Ross Russell, March 21, 1969, Ross Russell Collection, Harry Ransom Collection, University of Texas at Austin.

16. Reisner, *Bird*, 227.

17. James Gavin, *Deep in a Dream: The Long Night of Chet Baker* (New York: Knopf, 2002), 52.

18. Gavin, *Deep in a Dream*, 52.

19. Gavin, *Deep in a Dream*, 52.

20. Gavin, *Deep in a Dream*, 53.

21. Vail, *Bird's Diary*, 111.

22. Reisner, *Bird*, 192.

23. Vail, *Bird's Diary*, 112.

24. Vail, *Bird's Diary*, 115.

25. Reisner, *Bird*, 68.

26. Bee Flatt, "Running the Scale," *Kansas City Call*, July 25, 1952, 8.

27. Reisner, *Bird*, 11.

28. Parker, *My Life*, 33.

29. Brian Priestly, *Chasin' the Bird: The Life and Legacy of Charlie Parker* (New York: Oxford University Press, 2006), 92–93.

30. Mark Miller, *Cool Blues: Charlie Parker in Canada, 1953* (London, Ontario: Nightwood, 1990), 29.

31. Miller, *Cool Blues*, 34.

32. Steep Wade and Alfie Wade Jr. were not related.

33. Miller, *Cool Blues*, 44.

34. Miller, *Cool Blues*, 45–51.

35. Miller, *Cool Blues*, 53.

36. "Music USA," *Metronome*, March 1953, 6.

37. Priestly, *Chasin' the Bird*, 93.

38. Reisner, *Bird*, 12.

39. Miller, *Cool Blues*, 61.

40. Gillespie, *Dizzy: To Be or Not to Bop*, 374.

41. Miller, *Cool Blues*, 94.

42. Miller, *Cool Blues*, 95.

43. Woideck, *Charlie Parker Companion*, 119.

44. Parker, *My Life*, 43–44.

45. Parker, *My Life*, 43.

46. Vail, *Bird's Diary*, 138.

47. Vail, *Bird's Diary*, 138.

48. Reisner, *Bird*, 207.

49. Bob Rush, "Bill Perkins Interview," *Cadence*, November 1995, 13.

50. Vail, *Bird's Diary*, 152.

51. Vail, *Bird's Diary*, 152.

52. Vail, *Bird's Diary*, 152.

53. Parker, *My Life*, 46.

54. Reisner, *Bird*, 141.

55. The Charlie Parker Residence. *Interview with Kim Parker at 151 Avenue B, 2005*, available at http://www.charlieparkerresidence.net (accessed February 20, 2013).

56. Parker, *My Life*, 37.

57. Vail, *Bird's Diary*, 162.

58. See Russell, *Bird Lives!*, 330–32.

59. Parker, *My Life*, 49.

60. Reisner, *Bird*, 42.

61. Reisner, *Bird*, 39.

62. Leonard Feather, "Charlie Finally Finds Peace," *Down Beat*, April 20, 1955, 6.

63. See Russell, *Bird Lives!*, 314–15.

64. Reisner, *Bird*, 133.

65. Reisner, *Bird*, 133–34.

66. Parker, *My Life*, 53.

67. Over the years, the memorial marker for Charlie's grave has been replaced a number of times. Shortly after the mistake on the date of death was discovered on the original marker, it was replaced by a similar one with the correct date. When Addie died in 1967, bandleader Eddie Baker, the director of the newly formed Charlie Parker Foundation, raised money for matching memorial markers with bronze nameplates for Charlie and Addie. In 1992, the nameplates for both graves were stolen. The graves remained unmarked until March of 1994, when the Kansas City Jazz Commission replaced the markers for Charlie and Addie with a single 3' by 7' granite slab mounted in concrete. Charlie's side of the marker featured a dove taking wing above a saxophone. Unfortunately, because of miscommunication between the Jazz Commission and the monument company, the saxophone engraved on the marker is a tenor saxophone instead of an alto saxophone. The granite slab with the wrong saxophone still marks Charlie's grave.

Sources

I drew from a wide variety of secondary and primary sources in telling Charlie Parker's story. The pioneering research and musical analysis of numerous individuals who have previously researched and written about Charlie Parker, particularly Robert Reisner, Ross Russell, Carl Woideck, Gary Giddins, Brian Priestly, Lawrence O. Koch, Ken Vail, and Chan Parker formed the foundation for this new biography.

Llew Walker, a leading Parker scholar and host of the website *Bird Lives* generously shared his extensive research into Parker's family genealogy (http://www.birdlives.co.uk/index.php/childhood.html). That information, along with my interviews with relatives, census records, and city directories helped trace the journey of Charlie's family from the South to Kansas City and then their moves to and from various residences in Kansas City, Kansas, and Kansas City, Missouri, and to clear up previous misinformation about his family history.

Interviews with childhood friends Oliver Todd, Sterling Bryant, Arthur Saunders, and Jeremiah Cameron shed new light on Charlie's early life. A little-known interview with Charlie's first wife Rebecca Ruffin by Anita

Dixon published in a local publication *The Pitch* revealed new information on his first marriage and the circumstances surrounding how Charlie became an addict at the age of sixteen.

H. Dwight Weaver's research into the history of the Lake of the Ozarks and surrounding area provided new context to two watershed incidents in Charlie's life: the near-fatal automobile accident on Thanksgiving Day 1936 while on his way to play at Musser's Ozark Tavern and the following summer spent at Musser's, where he came of age musically.

Coverage of Charlie's career in local newspapers (the African American *Call*, and the *Kansas City Star* and *Journal-Post*), his musician's union record, the privately held Harlan Leonard collection, and interviews with bandleaders Jay McShann and Buster Smith along with bassist Gene Ramey clarified the chronology of his early professional career and musical development.

The Kenneth LaBudde Department of Special Collections in the Miller Nichols Library at the University of Missouri–Kansas City contains deep archival jazz resources used for this project, including the Dave Dexter, John Tumino, Buddy Anderson, Fred Higginson, and Jay McShann collections. Interviews in the Institute of Jazz Studies at Rutgers University Libraries and the Kansas City Oral History Collection in the State Historical Society of Missouri Research Center–Kansas City provided keen insight into Parker's development as a young man and musician.

Interviews with trombonist Trummy Young, vocalist Billy Eckstine, and other musicians published in *Melody Maker* and *Cadence* described how Charlie and Dizzy Gillespie worked together as members of the Earl Hines and Billy Eckstine bands.

Down Beat, *Metronome*, *Music Dial*, and other rare periodicals and interviews chronicle the ups and downs of Charlie's musical partnership with Gillespie, ranging from their work together on New York's famed Fifty-Second Street to their parting ways following a disastrous engagement at Billy Berg's nightclub in Los Angeles.

The Ross Russell Collection in the Harry Ransom Center at the University of Texas at Austin provided a fresh perspective on Charlie's time spent in California, the recording sessions for the Dial label, and his complicated relationship with Russell. An interview with Howard McGhee balances out Russell's sensationalized version of Charlie's time in California.

The Norman Saks Collection, the largest privately held collection of Charlie Parker–related material, and Chan Parker's biography *My Life in E-Flat*, published in 1999 by the University of South Carolina Press, helped tell the story of Charlie's personal and professional rise and decline during the last years of his life. Together these resources paint a lively, insightful portrait of Charlie "Bird" Parker, one of the most influential musicians of all time.

Index

Chuck Haddix is the director of the Marr Sound Archives of the University of Missouri–Kansas City Libraries. He is the coauthor of *Kansas City Jazz: From Ragtime to Bebop—A History* and the producer and host of KCUR-FM's "The Fish Fry," a popular radio program featuring the finest in blues, soul, rhythm & blues, jumpin' jive, and zydeco. He also teaches Kansas City jazz history at the Kansas City Art Institute.

MUSIC IN AMERICAN LIFE

The University of Illinois Press
is a founding member of the
Association of American University Presses.

Composed in 10.75/14.5 Marat Pro
with Trade Gothic display
by Jim Proefrock
at the University of Illinois Press
Manufactured by Sheridan Books, Inc.

University of Illinois Press
1325 South Oak Street
Champaign, IL 61820-6903
www.press.uillinois.edu